Presenting Archaeology to the Public

Digging for Truths

edited by
John H. Jameson, Jr.

technical editing by
Virginia Horak

ALTAMIRA
P R E S S

A Division of Sage Publications, Inc.
Walnut Creek ▪ *London* ▪ *New Delhi*

For information contact:

AltaMira Press
A Division of Sage Publications, Inc.
1630 North Main Street, Suite 367
Walnut Creek, California 94596 U.S.A.

Sage Publications Ltd.
6 Bonhill Street
London EC2A 4PU United Kingdom

Sage Publications India Pvt. Ltd.
M-32 Market
Greater Kailash 1
New Delhi 110 04S India

Printed in the United States of America

Library of Congress Cataloging-in-Publication Data

Jameson, John H.
   Presenting archaeology to the public: digging for truths
John H. Jameson, Jr.
     p. c.m
   Includes bibliographical references and index.
   ISBN 0-7619-8908-0. — ISBN 0-7619-8909-9 (pbk.)
     1. Excavations (Archaeology)—Interpretive programs—United States.
2. Historic sites—Interpretive programs—United States. 3. Archaeology and history—United States. 4. United States—Antiquities. I. title.
   E159.5.J36   1996
   930.1—dc20   96-45776
                                                                        CIP

97 98 99 10 9 8 7 6 5 4 3 2 1

Interior Design and Production by Labrecque Publishing Services
Cover Design by Denise M. Santoro
Editorial Management by Nicole Fountain

The subject matter and articles for this book were developed under the auspices of the Southeast Archaeological Center, National Park Service, U.S. Department of the Interior.

Presenting Archaeology
to the Public

Digging for Truths

■

Contents

Acknowledgments

I want to acknowledge two individuals who have played important roles in the creation of this book. John Ehrenhard, Chief, Southeast Archaeological Center, has lent this project unabated and vital support. John's enthusiasm for this volume and the Public Interpretation Initiative program reflects his unequivocal appreciation of the subject matter. Virginia Horak, Public Affairs Specialist, Southeast Archaeological Center, has put in long hours and made notable contributions with her technical editing.

I am grateful to the contributors for their patience and understanding during what has been an excruciatingly drawn out and lengthy process of bringing this volume to press. I want to thank Professor Brian Fagan of the Department of Anthropology, University of California, Santa Barbara, for his helpful suggestions and support. I am indebted to Professor Richard Wilk of the Department of Anthropology, Indiana University, for his interest and support and for his reference to AltaMira Press for publication.

Foreword

While it will always be true that archaeologists need to communicate effectively among themselves, it now is abundantly clear that unless they also communicate effectively with the general public . . . all else will be wasted effort. (McGimsey and Davis 1977:89)

Americans of all ages are inherently curious about archaeology. Archaeology, the study of cultural remains, will always attract widespread interest because the information generated by archaeological research is part of our humanity. Ironically, this interest has led to a frightening commercialization and even to frequent abuse of the human record. Our responsibilities as archaeologists and historians must encompass reaching out to the public and empowering it to understand and appreciate what archaeology can provide. We do this both by providing the opportunity and tools to learn about archaeology as well as by opening the doors for their involvement. We can make the past more accessible by helping our fellow Americans understand how and why the past is relevant to the present. In so doing, we are building a foundation of awareness and cultivating an appreciation of our nation's cultural heritage that will serve us all for generations to come.

How we involve the public in the rich fabric of the American experience is one of our great challenges as we enter the 21st century. With the cooperation of federal, state, and local organizations, we archaeologists are continually striving to improve the quantity and quality of archaeological site information available to the public. To best accomplish this, though, we must *first* educate ourselves.

Undoubtedly, the key to our success lies in the realization that each one of us can help define and mold the interpretive and educational programs that meet the public's view. As archaeologists, interpreters, educators, scientists, and historians, we must work together to focus the public eye on the value of archaeology.

While many innovative interpretive programs have been created, little has been written about them. Furthermore, unique problems arise when technical information is popularized. The contributing authors to *Presenting Archaeology to the Public* address broad concepts and strategies, present case studies, and suggest innovative solutions. We believe that their shared experiences will help stimulate discussion and will inspire dynamic, future programs in the public interpretation of archaeology.

Introduction

What This Book Is About

It is likely that the waning years of the 20th century will be identified in the history of archaeology as a time when the profession, as a whole, came to the realization that it could no longer afford to be detached from the mechanisms and programs that attempt to communicate archaeological information to the lay public. In the face of an increasing public interest and demand for information, archaeologists are collaborating with historians, museum curators, exhibit designers, and other cultural resource specialists to devise the best strategies for translating an explosion of archaeological information for the public. The 1980s and 1990s have seen a great proliferation of efforts to meet this demand, with varying degrees of success. While many innovative interpretive programs have been created, little has been written about them.

This book is part of the Public Interpretation Initiative (Jameson 1994a), a public outreach program initiated and coordinated since 1990 by the Southeast Archaeological Center's Technical Assistance and Partnerships Division (formerly the Interagency Archaeological Services Division). The Initiative programs are designed to foster an exchange of ideas between archaeologists and education professionals who are striving for a more holistic approach to the public interpretation of archaeological information. The program's activities have included the organization and coordination of academic symposia, workshops, and training sessions presented in a variety of national and international forums. The articles in this volume were generated by these sessions or from follow-up discussions. With the exception of some notable contributions from Stone and Molyneaux's *The Presented Past*, published in 1994 (Stone, this volume), comparatively little has been published on the subject of public interpretation.

The purpose of putting together this volume was to begin to fill this void in the literature by providing some philosophical background and examples of approaches and programs that have worked. Although the case studies described here are examples of successful strategies, some include warnings of pitfalls to avoid. While the models presented in this volume are worthy of replication, they also provide some useful guidelines against reinventing the wheel.

What Is Public Interpretation?

The articles in this book can be grouped under a developing specialty in archaeology that can be termed the "public interpretation" of archaeological information (Jameson 1994a). As used here, public interpretation includes a broad scope of endeavors ranging from formal education and curriculum development to less structured programs such as site tours and museum displays. The term also encompasses singular communicative devices such as the publication of popular histories, public awareness posters and brochures, and development of multimedia presentations including the fast emerging Internet sources and World Wide Web sites of modern cyberspace. It embraces outreach programs and other systematic attempts to provide educational and awareness services beyond conventional boundaries.

Public interpretation involves the development of communication strategies between the technical scientist-archaeologist and nonspecialists such as park interpreters, whose job is to deliver the "message" of archaeology to a variety of public audiences. The specialists and professionals who carry out these programs include archaeologists, historians, on-site interpreters, teachers, writers, artists, curators, exhibit designers, and other cultural resource specialists. They are often assisted by trained volunteers who help alleviate the inescapable shortages of staff power and resources needed to carry out successful programs. When resources allow, programs are most effective when these specialists form interdisciplinary teams for design and implementation (Honerkamp and Zierden, this volume).

Although closely tied philosophically, public interpretation differs in its scope from more technical discussions of interpretation of academics in that it has as its focus the translation and simultaneous communication of archaeological information and concepts to a wide array of audiences that comprise the general public. This is not to say that many research-oriented archaeologists do not engage in public interpretation of their data, as Stanley South and others aptly demonstrate in this volume. The differences between technical or academic versus public interpretation can be explained in terms of intended audience. When scholars such as Ian Hodder (1991c; Hodder et al. 1994) discuss the current approaches to archaeological interpretation, their primary intended audience is other archaeologists and social scientists. While their observations and conclusions are useful in debating the intellectual issues of the interpretation of observed phenomena in archaeology, rarely do they encompass the issues of effectively conveying archaeological information to public audiences. Nor do they include concerns about engaging, entertaining, and informing in an ethically sensitive manner—issues that are among the central themes of public interpretation (Jameson 1994a; 1995).

In today's increasingly multicultural and technological world, archaeologists working in tandem with professional interpreters and exhibit designers are challenged to make archaeologically generated insights more accessible to the public. They do this by empowering members of the public to participate in the critical evaluations of historical and archaeological interpretations that are presented to them and helping them to understand how and why the past is relevant to the present (Jameson 1994b; Davis and Hoffman, both in this volume).

The Importance of Educating the Public

It has been 30 years since the passage of the National Historic Preservation Act of 1966, the key legislation that began a surge of federally mandated archaeological and historical studies in the United States. Since passage of the Act, hundreds of thousands of professional reports have recorded millions of archaeological and historical sites containing hundreds of millions of cultural objects. Yet, in most areas, we are just beginning to sample and record the evidences of the rich archaeological and historical heritage left behind by our cultural forebears. The continuing flow of information and the evolution of field methodologies and standards have sharpened our ability to focus on the important aspects of this heritage. In fact, we often cite these success stories as the principal arguments and justification for continually building and adding to this already vast database. But, despite the promises and predictions of 30 years ago, what has the public, who has footed most of the bill in terms of tax dollars spent on these studies, appreciably gained?

In our enthusiasm to enforce the 1966 Act and a bevy of other protection laws, have we lost sight of the ultimate purpose and *raison d'être* of the compliance process, which is to provide public enjoyment and appreciation for the rich diversity of past human experiences? I believe that we need to reevaluate how we carry out the letter and spirit of these laws that recognize the reality, as expressed in the 1966 Act, that: "the spirit and direction of the nation are founded upon and reflected in its historic heritage"; that this heritage should be "preserved as a living part of our community life in order to give a sense of orientation to the American people"; and that federal agencies are required to take the lead in establishing programs for the protection of significant historic resources "for the inspiration and benefit of the people." (Jameson 1994b).

The spirit of these legal mandates requires us to ensure that archaeological information is provided to the public in an informative manner. While most people do not have the necessary knowledge or training to evaluate the results of archaeological research directly, they can and should be given this information in an accurate, "de-jargonized," and entertaining manner. When research is not adequately made meaningful to the nonspecialist, it is ultimately an empty endeavor.

As pointed out by Karen Lee Davis and others in this volume, we also need to foster a dialogue with the public that distinguishes between the goals and objectives of public interpretation and those of pure research. Just as archaeological methodology is guided by well-defined research goals, public interpretation must be guided by an understanding of what it focuses on, and to whom it is directed. The ultimate relevance of public interpretation and outreach programs lies in the ethical responsibility among professional archaeologists to make the past accessible and to empower people to participate in a critical evaluation of the pasts that are presented to them (see Davis, this volume). We achieve success when we recognize and practice this ethical imperative.

Public interpretation of archaeological research is essential if we are to provide increased access to and input about the past. While only a relatively small percentage of practicing archaeologists are involved in researching the past, there is no reason why the public cannot participate in this process through a critical evaluation of the interpretations that are presented to them. To do this we must provide the public with opportunities to participate as well as to develop evaluation skills. As we prepare for the 21st century, we must summon ourselves to reach out to the people and involve them in the rich diversity of their national and ethnic experience. The challenge is to bring the fascinating subject of archaeology into focus. To do that, we must learn and instruct ourselves in the most effective public interpretation and outreach methods (Jameson 1994a, 1994b; and in this volume, Davis, Hoffman, Yamin, and Honerkamp and Zierden).

Organization and Topical Focus of This Volume

We have organized this volume into four parts, ranging from more broad, philosophical discussions, to more specific case studies. Part I contains general concepts that should be relevant to all settings in the public interpretation of archaeology. While contributing additional philosophical backdrop, the subject matter in Part II is more focused and contains descriptions of proven strategies of broad application. The articles in Part III concentrate on programs and strategies applied to urban settings, and Part IV includes detailed descriptions of successful programs and how they were carried out.

In "Part I: Background," four authors discuss broad philosophies of how information about the past, generated through archaeology, can be presented to enable the public to enhance its knowledge of the past, and, consequentially, its quality of life.

Background: Archaeology and Education

In "Presenting the Past: A Framework for Discussion," Peter Stone of English Heritage introduces us to basic concepts in framing a discussion of effective public interpretation within formal and informal education venues. This article describes what he calls "the educational role of archaeology" as it has been applied around the world. One key conclusion is that archaeology is an excellent tool in training students to work more carefully and critically rather than memorizing information about a particular time period or culture, as is often the case in the formal curriculum of schools.

Students learn the value of unrecorded information not found in the traditional curriculum or textbooks, and discover how archaeology can fill important gaps and even provide corrections to historical records and accounts. By seeing history as nonstatic and constructed, and therefore open to reinterpretation and coexisting divergent interpretations, students learn that "true history" is redefined and rewritten as new information becomes available. Since archaeology nearly always produces new information, conclusions about "truths" in history are only temporary, subject to reinterpretation, and never complete. Stone also cites research showing that students who study the past through archaeology rather than the traditional document-based approach retain more and enjoy their studies more.

Background: Empowering the Public to Appreciate the Past

In the second and third articles in Part I, Parker Potter and Nancy Jo Chabot expand on another important concept mentioned by Peter Stone: that, in the realm of public interpretation, the interests and the prejudices of the messenger/interpreter have as much to do with the message as do the inherent qualities of the information. Archaeologists should strive to empower the public to be more in control of its own learning by giving it the intellectual tools that archaeologists and historians use to interpret sites. With these tools, people can participate in the creation of historical knowledge and in the definition of the historical context of both themselves and their culture. This knowledge produces a greater sense of well-being. Potter and Chabot concentrate their discussion on the makeup of an effective site tour, citing examples from Annapolis, Maryland, and Lochmere, New Hampshire, respectively. They frame their discussion around varying approaches to interpreting the "truths" about the past that exist among the visiting public. Each tour or presentation is seen as a unique event (an artifact, if you will) that depends on the identity and approach of the interpreter as well as the makeup of the audience. With this approach, each presentation can reveal multiple truths about the site that transcend mere description of what was found in the ground.

As are several other authors in this volume (for example, Davis, Honerkamp and Zierden, Hoffman, and Yamin; also the reactive comments by South), Potter and Chabot are influenced in their thinking by the philosophy of critical theory in archaeology, which argues that when the past is interpreted and becomes history it tends to become ideology (Leone et al. 1987). The consciousness or awareness of that process helps those who write about or explain (interpret) the past to realize the ideological notions that generate modern everyday life. Interpreters realize that the meanings they impose on the past are particular to their own cultural and social background. With this awareness, site interpreters can help their audiences appreciate that many, if not all, of their preconceived notions about time and space are actually part of their own, modern, historically based ideology (Hodder 1991c:174–180; 1994:164–168). Thus, audiences can appreciate that knowledge about the archaeologically revealed past is useful in giving meaning to the present (Potter, this volume).

Reacting to what he calls "the current antiscience fad of critical theory," Stanley South provides the last contribution to the background section of this book by discussing the value of generalized interpretations that are "sensitively done and based on empirical data." He warns archaeologists against going too far in accepting the conclusions of critical theorists, posits that there are no facts or truths in archaeology, and asserts that the past is not knowable with any integrity (Hodder 1991c:178). If the past has no integrity, then anyone's interpretation is as good as anyone else's. Thus, the interpretation would be open to anyone's political or ideological whims. South offers an analogy to some museum displays that pour too much on the visitor and leave them bored: "You can never literally re-create a complete account of past lifeways, but a generalized display based on empirical data, if done properly, can fire the imagination at every turn." In pointing out the achievements in archaeological interpretation of historical archaeologists in America, he shows how a generalized approach to interpretation provides a visual image that allows the visiting audience to imagine the past. It is interesting to note that all case studies and strategies described in this book by necessity employ elements of generalized interpretation as South defines it, but also, when available, supply details of the site and material culture that are corroborated by the archaeological evidence.

Strategies That Work

In "Part II: Strategies That Work," three authors describe proven strategies of broad application in the public interpretation and teaching of archaeology. These programs are exemplary and provide basic guidelines for success relevant to archaeological research facilities, government agencies, managed sites, and parks.

In explaining the successes of the Crow Canyon Archaeological Center in Colorado, Megg Heath emphasizes the importance of integrating the public into actual research. The maintenance of high-quality research allows the Center's staff archaeologists to emphasize the importance of systematic methods in research design, analysis, and record keeping. This also allows the staff to follow and transmit ethical standards.

Expanding on the theme of public participation, Teresa Hoffman describes the Arizona state government's efforts to make archaeology come alive for people. In a state where archaeology enjoys a high public profile, pioneering programs such as Arizona Archaeology Week and the more recently developed Archaeology Month have helped to raise public awareness and at the same time combat vandalism.

As background to her discussion of the special challenges at sites where fieldwork is no longer ongoing, Karen Davis articulates many of the key concepts of public interpretation in archaeology. With so much research funded by tax dollars or through the Cultural Resource Management (CRM) compliance process, archaeologists have a professional obligation to ensure that public interpretation of newly generated archaeological information is carried out; people support things they understand. Archaeologists should engage the general public in dialogues about why we should care about and preserve the past; this is essential, says Davis, to developing a supportive constituency. Archaeologists are socially responsible not only for preserving the past but also for making that past accessible. When active archaeological sites are not available, indirect approaches, such as exhibitions, tours of the property, and signing, are utilized.

Public Interpretation in Cities

Unique problems exist when public interpretation is practiced in large metropolitan areas. In "Part III: Interpreting Archaeology in Cities," the authors provide three examples of perseverance in the face of formidable political and logistical problems.

Karolyn Smardz describes the creation and development of her unprecedented and inspirational program that established archaeology as a formal element of the school curriculum in Toronto. In working with young students, the goal of Smardz and staff was to make archaeology accessible but also *fun*. The challenge was to foster successful, popular, and sustainable programs with a substantially international and multicultural audience.

In the second article of this section, Sherene Baugher and Diana Wall describe the evolution of three exhibits in New York City that, despite substantial legal and political issues as well as chronic problems of maintenance and design defects, were precedent-setting in the use of urban spaces for public interpretation. Building on their experiences with earlier projects, they were able to avoid certain political and logistical pitfalls that plagued previous efforts.

In an excellent example of public interpretation resulting from CRM-driven research, Nick Honerkamp and Martha Zierden recount the development of the Charleston Place project in South Carolina. Their conclusions emphasize the value of interdisciplinary cooperation in accomplishing both research and public interpretation goals. This project offers an excellent illustration of methods in presentation that allow the public to appreciate the value of archaeology in correcting and revising history.

Detailed Case Studies

The last section of this book, "Part IV: Interpreting Archaeology at Museums, Parks, and Sites," contains descriptions of on-site programs that have achieved success and, in some instances, that have even been the victims of this success (Whittlesey and Farrell), or that may have fallen short of their potential (Bograd and Singleton).

Describing the world-class interpretive center at Cahokia Mounds State Historic Site, Bill Iseminger recounts the history of public interpretation at the prehistoric Illinois site from 1925 to the present. The scheme of interpretation at Cahokia has changed as public awareness and site visitation increased. Cahokia has developed a program that attempts to engage and educate by targeting several categories of visitors that Iseminger terms "levels of public interest." These levels range from the professional interests of archaeologists and anthropologists to the personal and educational interests of tourists, students, and teachers. To avoid serving as "baby-sitters" for school groups, Cahokia adopted an educational program that makes efficient use of staff and well-orchestrated volunteer program. Before scheduling school group visits, teachers must attend an orientation workshop and receive a packet that includes pre- and post-visit activities. Native Americans participate in the Heritage America program and several other activities throughout the calendar year.

An exemplary case of collaboration between scientific and native communities is the program established at the Hatzic Rock Site, British Columbia. As authors David Pokotylo and Gregory Brass point out, the archeologists and indigenous peoples could have competed with each other for the authority to interpret the site, but instead they have come together in the spirit of compromise and collaboration in respecting each others' perspectives and philosophies. This cooperation and the resulting alternative perspectives for the interpretation of "truth history" at the Hatzic Rock Site show how the archaeological record can contribute to a diversity of uses and interpretations in contemporary society.

At Sabino Canyon, near metropolitan Tucson, Arizona, Stephanie Whittlesey and Mary Farrell confront a problem for public interpretation common to so-called "natural parks," where the significance of archaeology and cultural resources is overshadowed by the splendor of the park's natural environment. To combat this handicap, the approach at Sabino Canyon has been to "put people back into the landscape." They do this by showing that, for the prehistoric and indigenous peoples, the canyon was primarily a seasonal resource for food and water. Since prehistoric groups and the historic Hohokam spent only part of their time in the canyon, the interpretations have focused on providing a wider perspective by placing Sabino within the context of the local area and larger region. Thus, visitors can learn how people have adapted in various ways to the unique conditions of the Sonoran Desert.

Barbara Heath supplies another superior example of archaeology's filling important information gaps in the historical record. In this case, it is the life and environment of one of the most important "founding fathers" of the United States, Thomas Jefferson. At Poplar Forest, Jefferson's Bedford County plantation and retreat, archaeological information is being gathered that will shed new light on the material world and standards of living of Jefferson, his slaves, and his free workers. Public interpretation of this information is carried out through a variety of media ranging from temporary exhibits, guided tours, and lectures to written communications, including brochures and articles. At Monticello, the Thomas Jefferson Memorial

Foundation uses all of these interpretive media, plus permanent exhibits, restored buildings, gardens, and modern reproductions of archaeologically recovered objects that are produced for sale in the museum shops.

An alternative perspective is offered in the article by Mark Bograd and Theresa Singleton, who see archaeology as a tool to help fill the information and interpretation voids of social history: "The mission of social history," they write, "is to render significant what has been thought incidental; to make central the important contribution that the common person has made to America's past. The ultimate goal of social history and good interpretation, is not simply to add voices to mainstream history, but rather mainstream those voices into history." If history museums espouse to be representations of America, they "have an obligation to present a history that includes all of us." Sites such as Monticello and Mount Vernon are seen as "interpretive islands of black history surrounded by a sea of interpretation that neglects the contributions of women, minorities, and the poor." At Colonial Williamsburg, where the line between the interpretation of history and the commercialization of history can be blurred, the interpretation of slavery is obscured. "There is always the fear," the authors write, "that, if we depict and discuss slavery or present a mussed-up version of history, we may offend visitors, who may then not want to return to visit. Underlying this fear is a presumption that the public does not want to be challenged they come simply for entertainment or to have their preconceived beliefs affirmed." The reader will note that this discussion has direct parallels to the points made by Peter Stone (this volume) that the archaeological approach can provide a "reinterpreted" and more complete historical record of society's disenfranchised that allows individuals to better understand and appreciate their historical role.

Rebecca Yamin gives us a case in point to discussions by Potter and Chabot (this volume) and others, following the example of Mark Leone and colleagues, that "people do make their own history and can change it by their actions in the present" (Tilley 1989:114). The experience of visitors to the Morven House excavations, through the public interpretation programs, was that they were able to momentarily drop their romantic vision of how things *should* have been and begin to appreciate and accept the changes that had taken place through time. Politics and public symbolism intervened, however, when orders came that the site was to be restored to a single idealized moment in time: the late 18th century setting of the home of Richard Stockton, signer of the Declaration of Independence. In this case, despite the generally positive reaction of the visiting public, the local media, reacting to political hype, venomously attacked the project for its destruction of the pristine 18th century setting and for its attention to other historic periods. One question can be asked from this experience: "Is the dismantling of public symbols an appropriate role for archaeology?"

Meggett Lavin describes the transformation of public interpretation at Drayton Hall plantation in the aftermath of Hurricane Hugo in 1989. Prior to that year, site tours focused on the architectural significance of the 1790s main house, the state of preservation, and the unprecedented decision to leave the house unrestored and unfurnished. Interpreters were often tempted by the abundance of undocumented stories and local legends to expand on the "great planter, great wealth" story line, inspired by the dramatic and aesthetic surroundings. Eventually, however, the documentary, oral history, and archaeological research projects focused on the "truth" of everyday living, information that has created a new and much more interesting story line rooted in reality. Archaeology's most critical contribution to Drayton Hall has been to provide a model for examining the site as a whole and broadening interpretive thinking beyond the "great family, great wealth" approach. The focus of present-day interpretive programs is to help visitors understand how the architecture of the building, in combination with archaeology and history, documents changes in everyday life over the past three centuries. An education program for school children is framed by the question, "How do we know what we know?" Elements of this program include: Diaries in the Dirt, a program that puts students in the role of archaeologist trying to piece together the time line of events using oral history accounts, architectural clues, documents, artifacts, and photographs of actual excavations; and Plantation Excavation, where the students participate in a three-hour model excavation.

Doug Scott of the National Park Service describes another example of "a blessing in disguise" in relation to a natural disaster that has prompted new opportunities for archaeological research and public interpretation. Following a grasslands wildfire in 1983, the superintendent of Little Bighorn Battlefield National Monument recognized the opportunity to investigate the newly exposed battlefield for archaeological evidence. Since the site of the Battle of Little Bighorn is one of the most notorious and debated battlegrounds in America, and a popular unit of the National Park System, there was certain to be widespread public and press attention focused on the project. As Scott points out, with the strong public interest, the on-site interpretive program quickly evolved from a one-person operation to a highly coordinated team effort involving daily briefings by the archaeologists, press releases, daily updates furnished to staff interpreters, and small group tours. These presentations served to inform the public about the process of archaeology. The approach taken, which met with great success, involved comparing the archaeological investigation to a crime scene investigation.

In the final article, David Kirkpatrick describes another example of a project that had to cope with a subject where the "truth" is often lost in legend and myth. For over one hundred years, Billy the Kid and the Lincoln County War (1876–79), New Mexico Territory, have fascinated historians and the public and have provided material for western novels and movies. Archaeological excavations at the McSween House, site both of a famous five-day battle between rival factions and of Billy the Kid's daring escape amid gunfire, provided an opportunity to develop a unique public education and interpretation program. The program focused on revising the public's perception of archaeology and archaeologists, the reality versus the myth of Billy the Kid and the Lincoln County War. Site tours, museum displays, active excavations, and a well-organized volunteer program all provided opportunities for better interpretation that resulted in increased public awareness about the role of archaeology in enhancing everyday life.

▪ *Part One* ▪

Background

Chapter One

Presenting the Past:
A Framework for Discussion

Introduction

Although this article was originally written as the introduction for *The Presented Past* (Stone and Molyneaux 1994), a book I coedited for publication in Great Britain, the framework described herein is certainly appropriate in the context of this book. Basic to the discussion is the understanding that there is a confluence of four approaches to the interpretation and presentation of the past: academic or theoretical archaeology; indigenous views of the past; school history; and the past as presented to the general public in museums and "historic sites." All four approaches have their own priorities and agendas but, although they frequently draw on different sets of data, they have as their common thread the interpretation of past human activity. I and many of my colleagues believe that the presentation of the past in school curricula and in museum and site interpretations will benefit from a greater understanding of how the past is interpreted by archaeologists and/or indigenous peoples.

Within, at least British, academic archaeology during the past 20 or so years there has been an increase in the number of archaeologists who have argued for the extension of teaching about archaeology to an audience wider than their own students. The reasons have varied at different times and from person to person, and have included the desire to extend the understanding of the development and progress of the human species (e.g., Alcock 1975:2); the belief that the study of archaeology can be used as a tool to extend the "judgement and critical power" of students of all ages (e.g., Evans 1975:6); and as a preparation for the study of archaeology at university (e.g., Dimbleby 1977:9–10).

This interest in more extensive teaching about archaeology can also be seen as part of the much wider debate that has discussed the role and value of the past as an element of public "heritage" (see, e.g., Cleere 1984, 1989; Gathercole and Lowenthal

Originally published in 1994 as "Introduction: a framework for discussion" in *The Presented Past*, edited by P. G. Stone and B. L. Molyneaux. Routledge: London and New York.

1990; Hewison 1987; Layton 1989, 1990; Lowenthal 1985; Ucko 1994; and Wright 1985). While many (most?) museums and historic sites seem to be concerned with the presentation of a frequently static, well-understood past that reflects the achievements of a specific period—and frequently a particular section of society—as part of a national inheritance (Hewison 1987), modern archaeology is more concerned with questioning the validity of any interpretations or presentations of the past (see, e.g., Hodder 1986; Shanks and Tilley 1987), arguing, for example, that "interpretation owes as much to the interests and prejudices of the interpreter as to the inherent properties of the data" (Renfrew 1982:2).

At the same time, the study of the past in schools is predominantly the study of the past as documented by written records and, as such, is universally referred to in curricula as "history." This emphasis on the documentary past not only excludes much of prehistory from school curricula but has also tended to exclude the interpretation of the past through archaeological study and through indigenous (and usually oral) views of the past as well (Stone and MacKenzie 1990). Given this school view of "the past," the contemporary archaeological suggestion that the past is "constructed"—and is therefore open to constant reinterpretation and coexisting different interpretations—is one that does not easily equate with the way that history is taught in school curricula (Stone and MacKenzie 1990).

There have been various attempts to link together some or all of these four aspects of teaching about the past. The projects described in *The Presented Past* (Stone and Molyneaux 1994) have particular local or specific aims and objectives—for example, the introduction of "archaeofiction" in classrooms in France (Masson and Guillot 1994) or the introduction of indigenous values into local education policy in Canada (Jamieson 1994)—but they all also share a common belief that an extension of the way(s) in which the past is studied and understood by students and/or members of the general public would be a "good thing" and, if it is achieved, will enhance contemporary, and future, society as a whole. This is a belief that is frequently left largely unsubstantiated by its adherents—partly, at least, because it is almost impossible to quantify. There is, for example, no empirical evidence to prove that a greater understanding, on the part of the general public, of what can be gained from the archaeological study of a given site will ensure any greater level of protection for that site, or for any other site. However, the association between greater understanding and better protection has been accepted by many as a worthy aim to pursue (Cleere 1989:8–9; Gregory 1986; Seeden 1994), and there is certainly no evidence to refute the suggested association. Equally, the argument that students have better judgment and critical awareness because they have studied the past through archaeology, as opposed to the more usual document-based study of the past, has, to my knowledge, never been systematically tested until the recent work of Dahiya (1994) in India. Dahiya's work certainly suggests that those students who studied the past through an archaeological rather than a document-based approach did learn and retain more information and, at the same time, appeared to enjoy the work more. Dahiya's work introduces a specifically educational element to the debate: from an educational point of view the success of one methodological approach over another (effectively "hands-on" as opposed to didactic) is just as important as the fact that one group of children now has more information about the past than another, as the successful methodology may be transferable to other subjects. Until recently archaeologists have, perfectly legitimately, taught about the past in order to increase the amount of information assimilated and understood by their students about a particular period or culture. More recently, as archaeologists have seen their subject used—and abused—for political and social advantage (Layton 1989, 1990; Ucko 1994), many of them have accepted a wider role for archaeology. This wider role is also based on the acceptance that archaeology has an educational role in that it is a subject that requires students to work critically and carefully, without accepting any single "true" version of the past.

This educational role of archaeology—illustrated in one instance by the methodological work of Dahiya—has yet to be accepted by those in control of teaching about the past. Also ignored is the educational role of indigenous views of the past (see, e.g., Blancke and Slow Turtle 1994; Jamieson 1994) and any educational benefit of teaching specifically about prehistory (Stone 1992; also see Corbishley and Stone 1994).

Formal Curricula

The acceptance by archaeologists of the educational importance of the wider teaching of the past—much of which has been defined as "the excluded past" (MacKenzie and Stone 1990)—has its roots in a relatively few practical initiatives that go back little further than the mid-1970s (see, e.g., Corbishley and Stone 1994; McManamon 1994; Podgorny 1994; Richardson 1988; Stone and MacKenzie 1990). Unfortunately, there has been little or no comparable acceptance of the value of teaching about the excluded past within the world of formal education (Corbishley and Stone 1994; Stone and MacKenzie 1990). Extolling the virtues of an "excluded past" as an essential part of a curriculum is not the same as making it part of that curriculum. Authors contributing to *The Presented Past* (Stone and Molyneaux 1994) bear continued witness to the gulf between the need for inclusion expressed by archaeologists, other academics, and indigenous and minority groups, and the general failure to accept this need by those with power within the educational establishment (see, e.g., chapters by López and Reyes; Mbunwe-Samba, Niba and Akenji; McManamon; Wandibba; and Witz and Hamilton). Even where part of the excluded past is recognized—for example, the existence of the past of a particular indigenous group—other significant minority groups may be overlooked, as in Colombia (Wade 1994), or dealt with unsympathetically, as in Argentina (Podgorny 1994).

It is an important point that, if the "excluded past" is to be accepted within the curricula of formal education, its value must be couched in educational terms, as defined above. Zimmerman, Dasovich, Engstrom, and Bradley (1994) (also see Davis 1989) suggest that most archaeologists want to teach archaeological skills and ideas in the classroom, whereas educationalists look for the means to stimulate the educational, rather than archaeological, development of children. Zimmerman and his colleagues caution that continued attempts to teach archaeology in schools, without reference to the priorities of educationalists, will merely confirm the view of the latter that archaeology has no role within school curricula.

The excluded past is not always simply ignored as irrelevant, however (MacKenzie and Stone 1990:3–4). It may be kept out of the curriculum because education authority finance is controlled by those who, for political reasons, explicitly oppose its presence, as Jamieson (1994) describes in his attempts to introduce indigenous culture in a school curriculum in northern Canada. Occasionally, a pragmatic need is identified that results in the exclusion of specific archaeological information where its inclusion would destroy a consensus fundamental to the acceptance of using any archaeological information in the curriculum. Devine (1994) describes such an occurrence from her work in Alberta, Canada, where the good working relationship between educators, archaeologists, and Native people was threatened by a disagreement over the interpretation of some specific information. The problem was avoided by the omission of certain parts of the archaeological interpretation, which itself raised the question of control and ownership of the interpretation of the past (also see Ucko 1994). In other instances, the study of archaeology and prehistory may be the victim of attitudes about their economic potential and so is denied resources. This problem is especially clear in Third World countries, as development programs ignore the teaching of the "excluded past" under the belief that it has little or no immediate economic value (e.g., Kiyaga-Mulindwa and Segobye 1994; Mbunwe-Samba, Niba, and Akenji 1994). (See Addyman 1991, Collett 1992, and Ucko 1994 for a debate of the economic and social value of the archaeological heritage with specific regard to Zimbabwe.) Other developing countries regard it as a vocational subject and therefore do not include it in employment planning (Wandibba 1994).

Despite these practical problems the work that archaeologists and others are now putting into producing new educational materials and courses is not only encouraging but also critical to the future of heritage education. However, convincing the educational establishment that these efforts are not merely attempts to ensure the existence of archaeological jobs is not easy, and requires cooperation among government departments, educational authorities, and teachers (see, e.g., Devine 1994; Jamieson 1994). The nurturing of such an acceptance also requires those fighting for the extension of the study of the past to develop a theoretical and educational basis for their arguments. It is, and has always been, insufficient to argue that the "excluded past" should be taught "because it is important"—such bland statements have almost certainly contributed to the exclusion of the prehistoric, archaeological, and indigenous pasts from school curricula around the world. In *The Presented Past* (Stone and Molyneaux 1994) some of the authors outline the history (if any) of such arguments; others set out methodological arguments for teaching about the past with the help of archaeological information. A few actually begin to address why and how the way the past is taught should be extended.

Informal Learning

The cooperation between archaeologists and those involved in the planning and organization of formal curricula is, however, only one aspect of teaching about the past. Although success in this area may go some way toward guaranteeing that future societies will be more aware of the reasons for the preservation, study, and interpretation of the historic environment, there is a pressing need to educate contemporary society if the fragile database is not to be lost before any such enlightened future societies take on responsibility for its preservation. A number of authors in *The Presented Past* (Stone and Molyneaux 1994) refer to the continuing destruction of the historic environment and the associated illicit trade in antiquities.

The issues and events referred to in *The Presented Past* emphasize that education concerning the protection and preservation of the material past must consist of more than merely claiming that it has intrinsic value. Archaeologists need to know and, equally important, must be able to explain why such tangible evidence is vital if they are to stop the theft of artifacts and the careless or intentional destruction of sites. If archaeologists do not explain why the physical heritage is important, they cannot blame those who, having no archaeological training or education, consciously or unconsciously destroy or sell parts of that heritage (see, e.g., with relation to damage caused by metal detectors in the United Kingdom, Gregory 1986). Such explanations will vary from archaeologist to archaeologist and from situation to situation, but will always include the statement that archaeological evidence (as well as indigenous views of the past) can and will be used as a means of interpreting the past, in addition to documentary sources.

This use of archaeological evidence can enrich all individuals'—or a society's—understanding of the past and, used in this way, can be regarded as beneficial. However, if access to the evidence of archaeology is not available to all, through its inclusion in formal and informal education programs, then society runs the risk of the interpretation of archaeological evidence being biased—as it was, for example, in Germany in the 1920s and 1930s (also see MacKenzie and Stone 1990; Podgorny 1994). If such a message is put across well enough and is convincing enough, then there may be some justification in the belief that contemporary society will protect the historic environment for future generations. Time is of the essence here, as the failure to include archaeological interpretation in curricula can be argued to have contributed to the lack of understanding on the part of the general public, with regard to the archaeological-cum-educational-cum-political importance of sites. This can lead to a situation, such as that found in Colombia where so-called (by the archaeological community) "looters" see nothing wrong in digging into burial sites—even attempting to legitimize their activities by applying to form their own trade union (Ereira 1990:21). Similarly, in Lebanon, the public appear to be content to sit back and watch the wholesale destruction of archaeological sites (Seeden 1994). It follows that archaeologists, and others who control the data of the past or who regard themselves as having a custodial role with regard to the historic environment, must use every means available to them—including film, television, radio, newspapers, and popular publications—to reach the general public (see, e.g., Bender and Wilkinson 1992; Borman 1994; Frost 1983; Groneman 1992; Hoare 1983; Momin and Pratap 1994; Seeden 1994). There are, of course, dangers associated with this approach: media communications is an industry in its own right and responds first to business imperatives, rather than cultural or academic ones, thus creating a constant risk of distortion or sensationalizing archaeological material (Momin and Pratap 1994; Witz and Hamilton 1994). Indeed, as Seeden points out (1994), publicity can actually increase the likelihood of the destruction of archaeological sites by attracting people to them in search of "buried treasure." However, the potential benefits in informing society at large must surely outweigh such concerns (Andah 1990a, 1990b; Burger 1990:148–149; Ekechukwu 1990:125; McManamon 1994). It is essential that those already involved in this work begin to cooperate and share their successes and failures if the present rate of destruction is to be stemmed. In addition, those archaeologists who take on this responsibility must not be penalized in their careers, as they seem to be in some parts of the world, including the United States of America, by an out-of-date peer assessment process that sees such work as less important than other aspects of an archaeological career (Bender and Wilkinson 1992). Nor must archaeologists continue to ignore the value and importance of teaching about communication within archaeology undergraduate courses. A number of universities offering archaeology degrees now have optional courses in heritage management, and some of these include a lecture on heritage education. Such courses, together with the study of archaeological tourism, should be included as necessary components of all archaeology degree programs throughout the world, and should incorporate both academic and practical training (see Ekechukwu 1990).

Museum Display

The traditional method of communicating with the general public has been through museum display. However, despite huge advances in the methods and technology of display, museums still reach only a tiny proportion of the population (Hooper-Greenhill 1991a). Many argue that museums are generally regarded as places for specialists or particular (usually elite) groups within society (e.g., Nzewunwa 1994; Wandibba 1994). This point is supported by Andah (1990b) in his assertion that African museums were created for the colonial population *about* the indigenous population. Andah's argument is all the more depressing when he suggests that little has changed in museum displays since the independence of African states—a point supported by Mazel and Ritchie (1994) in their discussion of Botswana and Zimbabwe and also discussed by Ucko (1994) in his analysis of the present plans for the development of the National Museums and Monuments of Zimbabwe. Further north in Africa, it is interesting (even shocking?) to note that less than 5 percent of the visitors to the Cairo museum are Egyptians (Boylan 1991:10). Andah (1990b) argues strongly that museum and cultural tourism must be aimed first and foremost at the local population, since anything else simply maintains the colonial dependency of, in this case, Africa on the western world. Ekechukwu (1990) develops the point by emphasizing that local tourism is an essential element of the creation of a national identity, and the creation of a national museum for the national population has been identified as one of the four most vital symbols of independent nationhood perceived by newly independent governments (Boylan 1991:9). Andah (1990b:152) looks forward to a time when "The museum can begin to be transformed from a reservoir of folklore for tourists thirsting for exotics, to a living image of the past, a source of culture, a crossroad for ethnic culture, a symbol of national unity." And, in much the same way as Ucko (1994) supports the ideal of culture houses in Zimbabwe, he sees such museum centers as being designed to:

> Serve the function of the market place in the African past—namely an open air school; a forum for healthy debate, formal and informal on any problems of life—an institution available to all with its greenery, its gardens, local flora and fauna, aquariums and ponds, special exhibition halls (featuring both permanent and temporary exhibitions), recreational (theatre) areas, hair dressing salons, restaurants serving local dishes, craftsmen at work, craft and technology experimentation units, etc. (Andah 1990b:152)

The important point is that this is not a museum in the conventional western sense but rather it is an attempt to create an institution that emerges from traditional African society and custom.

Western museum structures and contents may, as Devine argues (1994), actually alienate Native peoples by presenting stereotypes of their culture—and so make such peoples museum pieces themselves (see also Hall 1991). This often unconscious stereotyping has not only adversely affected the relationship between two groups (archaeologists and Native peoples) who could be working together in the presentation of the past, but has also helped to reinforce a negative image of Native peoples among the rest of society. The insensitivity to the beliefs of Native peoples in the museum environment is testified to by Momin and Pratap (1994), who describe a scene in which some "ethnic groups visiting museums bow down and leave religious offerings in front of images of gods and goddesses, and are understandably upset that their sacred objects are regarded by those in authority as museum artifacts" (also see Andah 1990b:149; Carmichael et al. 1994). It seems obvious that Native peoples and other minority or oppressed groups should be consulted on the display and interpretation of objects related to their pasts. Indeed, such consultation should also extend to the content of formal education syllabi referring to Native cultures (see Devine 1994; Jamieson 1994; Riley 1992). Unfortunately, this creative—and appropriate—approach to curriculum development does not appear to be commonplace (see Andah 1990b; Momin and Pratap 1994; Ucko 1994).

The International Code of Professional Ethics, adopted by the International Council of Museums (ICOM) in 1986, "insists that the development of the educational and community role of the museum must be seen as a fundamental ethical responsibility" (Boylan 1991:10). In order to meet this ideal—in effect to be successful in attracting people to visit museums and heritage sites and to help them to leave happy, fulfilled, and somewhat the wiser—museum staff need to agree on the function of their institutions and their presentational role (Lowenthal 1993). They need to ask "not only 'Who are we serving?' but, more important, 'Who are we not serving?'" (Hall 1991:14; also see Hooper-Greenhill 1991b).

Hall (1991:11) lists a set of fundamental questions asked of southern African museums at the start of such a review. They have relevance everywhere.

Why do museums educate?
Who are our audiences?
How should we educate?
When and how often should we present programmes?
Where should we present programmes?
By whom should the programme be carried out?
What are the main subjects we ought to teach?

Others offer similar tentative checklists to be discussed when setting up new exhibitions. Borman (1994) argues that for too long European museums have been concentrating on how archaeologists know about the past rather than what information they have about it. He accepts that archaeological remains tend to be fragmentary records of a past culture removed from their original context that will never present a "true" picture of what life was like in the past, but he argues that even such relatively mysterious objects can be used as an "entrance" to the past, where visitors, having been given an introduction to the evidence by an exhibition, can be challenged to make their own personal conclusions about what life may have been like. In this way visitors may begin to relate to museum displays in a way that was impossible when one "correct" story was disseminated through a didactic exhibition.

These developments are a very long way from the opinion expressed in 1968 by an English professor of history (and quoted in Olofsson 1979) when he argued:

> Let me say at once that I hate the idea of museums being used primarily as teaching aids of any sort. Their first job is to house valuable objects safely and display them attractively. The second responsibility is to those who are already educated, to the student, the collector, the informed amateur. A third responsibility to put above anything specifically educational is, in the case of certain museums, a loyalty to their own personalities.

Olofsson rejects this opinion, and the chapters in her book reflect the recently more common view of museums as educational tools. However, just as there is at present a lack of communication between archaeologists and educationalists over the teaching of the past, so too Olofsson identified "insufficient contacts" between museum staff and "the school system, the main recipient of their services" as being the major obstacle to the developed use of museums in education (1979:11).

While some of this lack of communication has now been resolved, at least in western museums—especially through the hard work of many museum-based education officers (see, e.g., Hooper-Greenhill 1989)—there are still many practical obstacles and problems to overcome before the two worlds work in harmony. For example, in the Cameroon, Mbunwe-Samba, Niba, and Akenji (1994) note that most secondary-level history teachers never take their students to museums nor, in fact, have many of the teachers actually been to the museums themselves. Similarly, a recent survey in India shows only 1 percent of history teachers using museums as part of their normal teaching (Raina 1992; also see Dahiya 1994). In a recent study in England only two out of ten museums had any liaison with the local education authorities (HMI 1990). Only when such links are made between curriculum planners and museums can the "abysmal gap" (Delgado Cerón and Mz-Recaman 1994) between museums and formal curricula be closed. And if this gap is not closed, museums are "in danger of becoming irrelevant, expensive luxuries" (Hall 1991:13).

We seem to be now faced with a three- (sometimes four-) way failure of communication (archaeologist [indigenous expert]/educator/museum curator) that must be solved before museums will be able to take a major role in the teaching of the past within formal education.

Archaeologists and, where they exist, museum education staff, who work on the fringes of formal education, have helped to develop teaching programs that extend the database that children can use to study the past. A number of contributors to *The Presented Past* (Stone and Molyneaux 1994) describe attempts to develop museums as active rather than passive partners in teaching children about the past (see, e.g., chapters by Dahiya; Delgado Cerón and Mz-Recaman; Giraldo; Mbunwe-Samba, Niba, and Akenji; Nzewunwa). The unifying factor in all of their projects is the use of authentic historic artifacts as stimuli for creative work that encourages children to begin to understand the reasons why archaeologists and others value the past rather than simply to learn dates and "facts" and visit "treasures" behind glass cases.

Previous studies of the advantages of teaching within such a creative "hands-on" experimental framework have in the main failed to make a direct comparison between their success and a more didactic approach (Olofsson 1979). Dahiya (1994) confronts this failure head-on and provides powerful testimony by doing so. Unfortunately, she faces enormous practical problems in convincing teachers in India to move toward a more "hands-on" approach to teaching about the past, as over 86 percent of Indian history teachers rely almost entirely on a "lecture/narration method" of teaching (Raina 1992:24). According to Raina, the purpose of teaching about the past in Indian schools seems to be to pass exams and "it is a myth to think of teaching history to 'either develop the skills of a historian' or to develop a proper attitude and interest in the subject" (1992:26).

Such developments in how museums communicate and display their historic collections require the retraining of museum staff (Reeve 1989) and the introduction of, at least, discussion of the role of museums within undergraduate archaeology, history, and education courses. On a more practical level, in Zimbabwe, for example, a Certificate in Heritage Education and Interpretation has been developed specifically in order to train the Education Service of the National Museums and Monuments Commission (Stone 1994). While this course has been initially conceived as part of an internal staff development program, other countries have expressed interest in using it as a basis for similar courses. In Kenya, annual seminars organized by the National Museum aim to reduce the gulf between museum educators and their counterparts within formal education (Karanja personal communication; also see Uzzell 1989 for a number of case studies of the training of interpreters). Such retraining must become commonplace before museums can take on their leading role in the extension of the database used in the teaching of the past.

The Role of Native People in Curriculum Development and Museum Display

As part of this extension of teaching about the past, both archaeologists and educationalists must accept that there are indigenous specialists in the past who are outside the western academic and pedagogical traditions, but who nevertheless should have a central role to play in the development of teaching about their own pasts (see Ahler, Belgarde, Blancke and Slow Turtle, Devine, and Jamieson in Stone and Molyneaux 1994). Archaeologists have consistently offended the sensibilities of Native peoples by excavating burial sites and removing sacred objects and other significant cultural materials as a matter of routine, as have museums and academic institutions by studying and displaying such objects for educational and entertainment value (see Hubert 1989, 1991). Although such insensitivity is declining (at least in some areas), encouraged by legislation that often compels archaeologists and museums, among other things, to consult with Native groups and their specialists (McManamon 1994), archaeologists and museum curators still have considerable problems in interpreting and displaying the results of archaeological research to Native people—especially where, so often, the different interpretations conflict with one another (also see Carmichael et al. 1994). However, if these professionals cannot work with and appreciate the beliefs and feelings of those that they often most directly affect, then what hope is there of changing the common charge that archaeology is simply a self-indulgent pastime?

Similarly, the idea of a common curriculum across countries that contain culturally diverse groups has led to educational systems that are often insensitive to the different intellectual and social traditions of the students they are trying to reach (Belgarde

1994). This is not a particularly new observation and was, for example, at the heart of Jomo Kenyatta's dislike of European education:

> We have therefore to ask ourselves whether a system of [indigenous pre-Colonial] education, which proves so successful in realising its particular objectives, may not have some valuable suggestion to offer or advice to give to the European whose assumed task it is in these days to provide Western education for the African. (1938:120)

The failure of western-style education to even take note of indigenous methods of education has resulted, in many instances, in the alienation of the majority of Native students (see Belgarde, Blancke and Slow Turtle, and Devine in Stone and Molyneaux 1994). Several authors in *The Presented Past* (Stone and Molyneaux 1994) advocated new approaches to curriculum that make use of the educational insights of traditional Native teachers, rather than simply relying on western-oriented and educated curriculum theorists (e.g., see chapters by Ahler; Devine; and Jamieson). Others went even further, arguing for an integration of "universal" and Native approaches (Blancke and Slow Turtle 1994) or placing Native students in tertiary education in their own schools (Belgarde 1994; also see Burger 1990:147).

Of fundamental importance here is that most "indigenous" systems of education have a strong foundation in the traditional beliefs of their particular group. By imposing western-style curricula on indigenous peoples, educationalists have—often as a conscious decision—removed them from their own cultural heritage (see, e.g., Barlow 1990; Kehoe 1990; Watson 1990).

The Future

There are eight specific ways in which those committed to the teaching of the past, which includes the evidence of archaeology and the viewpoints of indigenous groups, can help to bring about such an extension of school history and public presentation and interpretation. Wherever possible they should:

- Develop professional courses in collaboration with education authorities in the presentation of archaeological evidence and indigenous viewpoints
- Stress the importance of communicating about their work in archaeology undergraduate programs
- Educate student and practicing teachers about the "excluded past"
- Publish their research in language accessible to teachers and students
- Develop contacts with the media—through television, radio, newspapers, and popular publications
- Develop stronger links between traditional museum display and good educational practice

- Train museum staff in the educational value of their displays and collections
- Accept that those involved in education have their own agendas and priorities as to the role of the past in teaching

These eight steps are not a panacea that will, overnight, change the way the past is interpreted, taught, and presented. However, they do combine to form the first steps of a program that should begin to change the way the past is taught.

Chapter Two

The Archaeological Site
as an Interpretive Environment

Introduction

My initial intention in writing the paper on which this article is based was to focus on methodological issues; I wanted to explore the differences between archaeological sites and the other interpretive environments in which archaeological materials are presented to the public. However, before dealing with the technical side of on-site archaeological interpretation, I need to lay a bit of groundwork.

How, What, and Why

While most of this article concerns how to do archaeological interpretation, "how" is only part of the story. People who study interpretation typically spend a great deal of time discussing—both in print and at conferences—the "hows" while saying relatively little about "what" we teach and "why" we teach it. This is an oversight, one I nearly fell into in writing this piece, despite the fact that on several occasions I have criticized other interpreters in a variety of disciplines for focusing on "how" at the expense of "what" and "why" (Potter 1989b:1–2, 1990:608–610; Potter and Leone 1986:97–100). My initial notes for this article are a long list of reasons why archaeological sites are wonderful places to do historical interpretation. In fact, this list was nearly as long as my arm before I stepped back to ask myself from what perspective I was judging the interpretive value of archaeological sites. To keep from making the same mistake I have accused others of, here is the "what" and the "why" behind all the "hows" I'll get to later on.

This article is based primarily on my experience with "Archaeology in Public in Annapolis," in Annapolis, Maryland, which is, among other things, an experiment

Adapted from a paper presented at the annual meeting of the Middle Atlantic Association of Museums, Princeton, New Jersey, October 1990, in a session devoted to "selling" several varieties of archaeological interpretation to museum professionals.

in the application of Frankfurt School critical theory to historical archaeology (Leone, Potter, and Shackel 1987; Potter 1989a, 1994). In Annapolis, what we teach is the archaeological evidence for the roots of modern everyday life (and modern ideology) in a capitalist economy. Another part of what we teach is the various ways in which versions of the past that serve the narrow interests of dominant social groups are often passed off as objective and universal, even though they sometimes serve to impede the interests of the people to whom they are directed.

Why we teach at all, and why we present the material we do, is to show people that many aspects of contemporary social and economic life that are taken for granted are neither natural nor inevitable but are, instead, open to question, challenge, and even change. To use the highly charged theory language of the Frankfurt School (Geuss 1981; Held 1980), "Archaeology in Public in Annapolis," as a critical archaeology, aims to inspire enlightenment, which may lead to emancipatory social action. At the very least, we hope to help our visitors become more informed consumers of historical knowledge and less dependent on so-called experts. We want them to ask of any historical interpretation, "What is this particular story about the past trying to get me to do, right here and now?"

These are the "whats" and the "whys" behind "Archaeology in Public in Annapolis." These "whats" and "whys" may not be the same ones that lie behind any other archaeological interpretation program, and that's fine. I mention them here only because whether I acknowledge them or not, my content and my reasons for teaching with archaeology clearly shape my understanding of how to teach it on an archaeological site. Furthermore, whenever archaeological interpreters fail to be explicit about their own "whats" and "whys," they run the risk of having their interpretations appropriated and used to support agendas that are different from or even opposed to the initial reasons for presenting a given interpretation. This misappropriation cannot always be avoided, but it can be guarded against through careful self-reflection.

Understanding the Audience

My second piece of groundwork is more straightforward, while, at the same time, less certain. Specifically, this piece of groundwork is a confession I made to the audience in Princeton to whom I delivered the initial version of this article. To that audience I said: "I don't know who you are. Usually when I give a paper like this I give it to a room full of archaeologists—students and professionals, academics, contractors, and public servants like me. But I don't know who you are, and that made this paper rather difficult to write. When I talk about archaeological interpretation to a group of archaeologists, I can make quite a few assumptions. I can count on common knowledge and shared objectives. For better or for worse, I can't do that here. Some of you may be archaeologists, but I'll bet that most of you are not. Either way, *all* of you have some conception of archaeology and some idea of what you think archaeology can do for you and your museum. Given that, my job in this paper is to sell you archaeology." I continued by saying: "Stop for a minute and think about what I just said. I told you that I don't know who you are, but I've gone ahead and made a guess. And now I'm going to talk to you for another 15 minutes based on that guess. I'm taking the time to make this point because many of us do to our visitors what I'm about to do to you. It is dangerously easy to present an interpretation without giving careful consideration to what our audiences want and need, and without giving careful consideration to the social agendas embedded within our own interpretations. 'Archaeology in Public in Annapolis,' to which I often refer for examples, does not completely solve this problem. However, this interpretive program does incorporate the key element of self-reflection; and self-reflection is the single most important technique for helping interpreters interact meaningfully and productively with their audiences" (see Potter 1991a, 1991b).

Taking the Museum "Out" to Archaeology

With this background in mind, I return to my theme by relating archaeological sites to our society's most traditional interpretive environment—the museum. At the meeting for which I originally wrote this article, my fellow presenters and I talked about a "more perfect union" between archaeology and museums. Such a union can take a variety of forms. Some museum workers see archaeology principally as a tool for stocking their shelves. Others go one step further and bring the discipline of archaeology and not just archaeological finds into the museum. These are both valid approaches, but I would like to turn them around. Rather than bringing archaeology (or its finds) into the museum, I want to bring the museum out to archaeology, out to the field. Instead of seeing archaeology as a generator of museum specimens or as a topic for museum exhibits, I believe archaeology can be a museum experience in and of itself (see also Leone 1983, 1989a, 1989b; Potter 1984; Potter and Leone 1987). A focus on the process rather than the products of archaeology can transform archaeology from a tool for filling museums into a vehicle for discussing how museums fill themselves up. Archaeology is just one of many disciplines that contribute objects and ideas to museums, but by knowing even one of these disciplines, one of these ways by which things get into museums, visitors can interpret much more critically that which they see on display. Museum visitors should be allowed to understand the wide variety of factors and forces that bring objects from "out there" into display cases. This is at least an intellectual need if not a basic right of museum-goers. When used to achieve this end, archaeological interpretation can provide a commentary on both past and present. Such dual commentaries are a key element of "Archaeology in Public in Annapolis."

To better see how "Archaeology in Public in Annapolis" enacts these commentaries, it is important to understand some of the reasons why archaeological sites are a stimulating and productive environment for historical interpretation.

Archaeological Sites as an Interpretive Environment

Perhaps the most frequently cited reason for doing on-site archaeological interpretation is that "people love archaeology." However, this "reason" is really a red herring. Saying that people "love" this or that kind of interpretation tells us nothing about what people actually get out of it. And if we don't know what our visitors get out of what we do, we have no way of judging how well we have met our interpretive aims. The observation that people love archaeology is, on its own, a good reason to undertake archaeological interpretation if and when our only goal is entertainment. One premise of "Archaeology in Public in Annapolis" is that the costs of doing competent archaeological interpretation demand that we aim for a higher goal than simple entertainment. For projects and institutions that attempt to empower visitors by giving them access to some of the intellectual tools we use to create historical knowledge, on-site archaeological interpretation is well worth considering.

The strongest argument in favor of on-site interpretation is based on epistemology. When a visitor takes a tour of a working archaeological site given by a crew member, epistemology is right out front. An important part of any such tour is an explanation of the tools and techniques used by archaeologists, which teaches visitors how we know what we know, which, in turn, accomplishes two things. Information about our techniques helps visitors decide whether or not they agree with our conclusions. Furthermore, it allows them the opportunity to use our intellectual tools for themselves, if they choose to do so.

Second, not only does on-site interpretation give visitors access to epistemology, it also gives visitors access to people using the epistemology. When people visit an "Archaeology in Public in Annapolis" open site, for example, they can speak directly with working archaeologists. In this way, historical interpretation becomes a real dialogue rather than a monologue filled with nothing but established "answers" delivered by everybody's worst nightmare of a fifth-grade teacher. Such dialogue is difficult to initiate and is infrequently achieved in more traditional interpretive settings. Furthermore, this dialogue is not just a tool visitors can use to get more or more specific information. Rather, we have found in Annapolis that our site visitors often bring us important data or provide perspectives and insights that we had missed. So while visitors don't leave our sites with conclusions carved in stone, they have unquestionably seen and participated in the creation of historical knowledge.

A third significant advantage of on-site interpretation concerns the nature of what the interpreters are asked to present to the public. Most historical interpreters and tour guides are asked to present third- or fourth-hand information (Potter 1989a:277–278).

Quite honestly, I don't envy people who have to interpret this way. In contrast, "Archaeology in Public in Annapolis" interpreters present information with which they are both familiar and involved. This direct involvement with content makes it much easier for guides to answer visitors' questions in a satisfying and substantive way. In other words, "Archaeology in Public in Annapolis" interpreters know a good bit more about archaeology than they are able to fit into a 20-minute tour.

Yet a fourth advantage of archaeological sites as an interpretive environment is that they don't require visitors (or interpreters) to "imagine away" the 20th century. How many historical walking tours are there where guides encourage visitors to try to "see" some particular streetscape or vista without the cars, the electric wires, or the Pizza Hut? Rather than asking visitors to expend their mental energy blocking out part of what they see, "Archaeology in Public in Annapolis" interpreters are encouraged to focus on the very things that more traditional interpreters consider distractions. Interpretive value can be found in virtually anything that catches our visitors' attention. Sometimes the attention-getter is an exotic piece of archaeological equipment or a strange-looking technique. Given our commitment to discussing techniques and method, these potential distractions are well worth weaving into the day's interpretation. Another source of "distraction" is the world just beyond the site. Because "Archaeology in Public in Annapolis" is committed to linking past and present, off-site distractions can help us demonstrate that contemporary social context influences the creation of any version of the past, including the archaeological one(s) we are producing. In short, on-site interpretation with a focus on method relieves us of the obligation to give visitors some kind of "time machine." Rather, "Archaeology in Public in Annapolis" visitors are themselves, in a very real sense, the time machines we hope to create.

"Archaeology in Public in Annapolis"

My reasons for believing that archaeological sites lend themselves to thought-provoking historical interpretation have been conditioned by my interest in interpretation that empowers the visitor. And this interest has been greatly influenced by my experiences with the "Archaeology in Public in Annapolis" interpretive program.

Every summer I was in Annapolis from 1982 through 1987, "Archaeology in Public in Annapolis" opened one or more archaeological sites to the public. The standard open site is interpreted through three media: a set of one to ten interpretive placards, a short brochure for use on- or off-site, and a 20-minute site tour given by a working archaeologist. These site tours are designed to take place in the middle of a two-hour visitor experience that begins with a 20-minute audio/visual program (see Potter and Leone 1992 for a discussion of the audio/visual program *Annapolis: Reflections of the Age of Reason*) and ends with a self-guided, city-wide walking tour based on the 24-page guidebook *Archaeological Annapolis* (Leone and Potter 1984).

The audio/visual has been made and the guidebook has gone to a second printing, but all three elements of the program have not yet been presented to the public as a unit. As for the tour program, by the time I left the project in 1987, nearly 50 student and professional archaeologists had given "Archaeology in Public in Annapolis" tours to upwards of 40,000 visitors at eight different sites. All tours are followed by an open-ended question-and-answer period. Each tour has been evaluated through a one-page questionnaire distributed to a 10 percent sample of our visitors (Hoepfner, Leone, and Potter 1987:13–14; Potter 1989a:370–404). The program sounds simple enough, but, as one might imagine, this marriage of research and interpretation requires constant attention.

A Handful of Pointers

For those interested in attempting a program similar to "Archaeology in Public in Annapolis," it is important to realize that this is a tremendously rewarding mode of interpretation but, at the same time, a demanding one. For this reason, I conclude with a few pointers from the Annapolis program that may be of use to other archaeological interpreters.

First, we don't do "show" digging. All our sites are bona fide archaeological sites excavated in accordance with a valid, scholarly research design. The "reality" of our sites enhances the visitor experience, but that is not why we insist on doing only "real" archaeology. Rather, if our work itself is an important part of the content of our interpretation, there would be absolutely no educational value in digging a fake site or a site with no research significance. The interpretation of such an excavation would have an inescapable subtext, namely that archaeology is a game or a diversion rather than a discipline (Hume and Potter 1991:5). Beyond this, the excavation of a site that does not need to be excavated for research or preservation purposes violates every conceivable code of archaeological ethics. So, the sites we interpret are in all respects "real" archaeological sites.

This does not mean, however, that the logistics of interpretation do not enter into site selection and excavation strategy. We have executed our project's citywide research design so as to dig and interpret sites in the tourist areas during the tourist seasons. This is only sensible, but it never entails digging a site that we wouldn't have excavated otherwise. Furthermore, public interpretation requires considerable coordination between the excavation crew chief and the lead interpreter. The site must be excavated intelligently from an archaeological perspective; at the same time, visitors need paths to walk and places to stand. Good solutions require creative planning, but in our experience these issues are never insurmountable.

Here is my most important piece of advice. After choosing a particular interpretive medium to use on site, it is essential to seek professional advice and instruction in the use of that medium. Popping up out of a test pit to talk to a handful of visitors sounds like the simplest, most natural thing in the world. It may be natural, but it's not simple. In Annapolis we have relied on the expertise of Philip Arnoult, Director of the Theatre Project in Baltimore, Maryland. The following story is just one example of the value of a media consultant.

In 1982, before we hired Arnoult, we spent six weeks trying to attract visitors to the Reynolds Tavern site, but visitors were not breaking down the gate to get in. Arnoult immediately showed us at least part of the reason why. Hanging right in the middle of our gate, big as life, was a black and orange "No Trespassing" sign. Arnoult took it down. We would have removed it, but we never even "saw" it. My point is that to mount a successful program of on-site archaeological interpretation, media expertise is essential.

Arnoult's major role with "Archaeology in Public in Annapolis" is twofold: he deals with both the site and the people on the site. We rely on Arnoult to transform an archaeological site into an interpretive space. While we worry about stratigraphy and back dirt, Arnoult designs not only ways to attract visitors to and guide them through the site, but also strategies for using what is available on the site to help us deliver our interpretive message—all without compromising the archaeological integrity.

As for people, Arnoult directs the training of site interpreters. Rather than teaching them to play a role, Arnoult works with interpreters to find ways for them to present themselves as themselves. The tour for each site has a basic outline that interpreters are supposed to follow, but guides are encouraged to use their own words and phrases. Furthermore, Arnoult sees each tour presentation as a unique event or meeting and teaches guides to pay attention to the here-and-now of each particular tour. This means that very few "Archaeology in Public in Annapolis" tours sound like a little train rattling down a bumpy track, eager to get back to the station in one piece.

Shortly after he began consulting for "Archaeology in Public in Annapolis," Arnoult stated firmly that he didn't "do" content. That he said so, up front and of his own volition, is praiseworthy and noteworthy. Beware of any media expert who does not or will not take the same pledge. Arnoult would sometimes comment on what pieces of content "played well"—by which he meant they engaged the visitor—but he never suggested using a piece of content *only* because it played well, nor did he ever suggest inventing a piece of content because it *would* play well. "Archaeology in Public in Annapolis" always benefited from Arnoult's refusal to allow the medium to dominate the message.

Another of Arnoult's key early insights is that site visitors are as interested in archaeologists as they are in archaeology and artifacts. Arnoult observed that when visitors asked questions of student archaeologists working at open but uninterpreted sites, many of those questions centered on such topics as: the amount of training it takes to become an archaeologist, the kind of career that archaeology makes, and the different places that various crew members had worked before digging in Annapolis.

Based on these observations, Arnoult set out to create an interpreter training program that taught archaeologists to present *themselves as themselves* to the public.

Arnoult's goal was not to turn each guide into an interchangeable version of every other guide or the tour's authors. Rather, he used various selection from his considerable bag of theatrical tricks to help guides enhance their ability to speak with the public about what they were doing and the project they were a part of. Furthermore, because "Archaeology in Public in Annapolis" interpreters were not trying to be clones of the tour's authors, they were freer than many interpreters to respond to a question by saying "I don't know" and to seek answers from artifact bags, excavation notes, or other crew members—right in front of inquiring visitors. Only a small portion of what Arnoult has done for "Archaeology in Public in Annapolis," these examples nevertheless demonstrate the value of seeking out media expertise.

My next suggestion is something else I learned from Arnoult—a story from my own experience that illustrates the dilemma some interpreters face as a result of interpretive displacement. In 1983, Mark Leone and I coauthored the Victualling Warehouse site tour, which was part of the "Archaeology in Public in Annapolis" interpretive program. The tour was designed to link the archaeology of an 18th century commercial site with the commercial renaissance that began taking hold in Annapolis in the 1960s and 1970s—or rather, to explore the unexamined linkages that already existed. One archaeologist/guide, however, didn't quite "buy" the tour's central interpretation; while she didn't reject it outright, she wasn't sure she agreed with it either. This was a problem, and an important one. The previous year, "Archaeology in Public in Annapolis" had adopted a somewhat unusual interpretive stance under Arnoult's guidance. Contrary to what most would expect from a theatrical impresario, Arnoult insisted on creating an interpretive format that encouraged guides to deliver tours that explicitly acknowledged the circumstances of their delivery. These circumstances—any one of which could potentially end up in the content of a tour—included the size and composition of the audience, the weather, the current condition of the site, and even the relative experience level of the particular guide delivering a particular tour. The goal was to present individual, unique, and contingent tours with the same basic message, rather than canned performances delivered by rote from an inviolable script. Arnoult wanted not only the archaeological message on display, but also the attitude and authority of the person delivering it.

To the dilemma posed by the guide's reaction to the tour, there were three possible solutions, two conventional ones and the one proposed by Arnoult and embraced by "Archaeology in Public in Annapolis." Conventional solution No. 1 would have been to thank the guide very much and then dismiss her from the interpreter training program until she converted to the party line. Conventional solution No. 2 would have been to force the guide to deliver the part of the tour she wasn't sure about while feigning confidence, with refusal to do so bringing on solution No. 1. The problem with this second solution, as Arnoult so clearly recognized, is that most archaeological interpreters couldn't do it. Those who could, would end up being actors rather than archaeologists. And by turning archaeologists into actors, Arnoult reasoned, "Archaeology in Public in Annapolis" would be sacrificing the single most interesting component of any archaeological site—the archaeologists themselves. Artifacts can be seen in museums any old time, and theaters are full of actors, but where else can one go to see a living, breathing, working archaeologist?

The next step was turning this realization into a solution to the problem at hand. Following his commitment to authenticity and to respecting the moment, Arnoult decided not to paper over the guide's concern but, rather, make something of it. He advised her to deliver her tour as she normally would. At the point where she began to be unsure about the interpretation, she was to say, for instance, "I'm not too sure about this next part. My bosses have written it, and I don't know if I agree or not. One way or the other, it's a pretty interesting idea. I'll go ahead and present it to you so you can make up your own minds."

This solution is noteworthy in two respects. First, Arnoult's suggestion, as enacted by the guide, made an *artifact* out of the tour she was delivering, and artifacts don't just exist, they are made by people. Rather than attempt to stand in for the authors of the tour, she delivered both the tour and a commentary on the tour. She was not an empty vessel, worth listening to only when she was filled with the information she was presenting; she was an active participant in the process, with an appropriate degree of control over the material and the message she was delivering. The tour was an artifact open for discussion among its authors, the guide, and the audience. Arnoult's solution allowed the guide to deliver a much less "displaced" interpretation than the one she would have delivered otherwise. Armed with the freedom to put on display her interpretation of her bosses' interpretation, within mutually agreed-on limits, she became something of an author and something more than just a reader.

This transformation of the tour from 15 minutes of historical and archaeological truth into a social artifact led to the second value of Arnoult's solution. Specifically, by commenting on the tour she was delivering, the guide became a model of sorts for her visitors, showing them that they *too* had a variety of choices for reacting to the tour. They could accept the interpretation, reject it, argue with it, or respond in any number of other ways to various parts of it. And this model for visitor response was provided in the context of a program of archaeological interpretation that attempted explicitly to link past and present by showing how contemporary social, economic, and political interests influence the production of history.

Providing visitors with a model—or a set of models—for relating to historical information is especially important, considering the lack of such models in most popular historical and archaeological interpretation. A substantial portion of the archaeological interpretation available today is based on the premise that if the facts about the past are true enough, they are important. Under such circumstances, interpretation becomes simply a matter of presenting data to passive audiences. The basic job of such an audience is to appreciate the skills of the scholars who provide the data without intruding on their authority, questioning their point of view, or inquiring about their interests. Furthermore, interpretations like this assume that people care about the past, without ever acknowledging that "caring about the past" is an issue worthy of examination in its own right. Who cares about which parts of the past in a given community? Who doesn't? Of what use is the past to whom in a particular setting? Who wins and who loses in a present based on this or that version of the past? These issues can be explored more productively through an interpretation that shows visitors that they *can* be—and that shows them *how* to be—something other than simple consumers of historical information.

So Philip Arnoult's relatively simple move of encouraging a guide to share her response to an interpretation demonstrated that there can be a range of appropriate responses. With Arnoult's guidance, she made an artifact of the tour and gave her audience a model for relating to it—hinting, at least, at a broad range of possibilities.

My final suggestion comes from my more recent work in New Hampshire. Because Annapolis is a living city, almost every "Archaeology in Public in Annapolis" site has been relatively small. One can easily see the whole site from a single spot, and tours are about 20 minutes long. Up in New Hampshire, I helped with the interpretation of a large prehistoric site located in an isolated rural area (see Chapter 3, *Locating Truths on Archaeological Sites,* in this volume for more on the interpretation of this site). Visitors worked hard to get there and tended to stay for an hour or more. We interpreted that site with a series of six stations and a combination of open pits and display boards. Our key technique was staging the stations progressively so that visitors recognized concepts from the early stations as they moved to the later ones. We found that by the end of their tours, many were able to start telling us what we were about to tell them. They recognized things at Station 3 because they had begun learning about them at Station 1. This knowledge-building represents good educational technique, but, just as important, visitors who picked up what we were teaching about archaeological techniques will undoubtedly be more in control of their own learning the next time they visit an archaeological site.

Conclusion

On-site archaeological interpretation is a complex undertaking that demands just as much technical expertise as the archaeological excavations themselves. However, the benefits far outweigh the complexity, which only make the rewards that much greater.

Chapter Three

Locating Truths on Archaeological Sites

Authors' Prelude

In the spirit of fostering a postmodern archaeological discourse, we are adopting a somewhat unconventional convention—we are presenting the product of our coauthorship as a pair of solos in two movements, rather than as a duet sung in unison. There are three reasons for this.

First, since our examples are drawn directly from separate personal experiences, we would like to preserve our independence and individuality. We do not always speak with one voice and are uncomfortable with literary conventions that would suggest we do.

Second, we are interested in exploring alternatives to traditional modes of academic discourse, particularly those that homogenize or genericize authorship. To this end, we hope to (re)capture something of the quality of a joint interview we once gave a newspaper reporter. Working together, we pushed each other to provide more information than we would have otherwise, and we also found ourselves expressing fresh insights we would not have gained had we been interviewed separately. In addition, the resulting article contained useful juxtapositions based on dual points of view.

Finally, the main point of this article is our suggestion that the most important truths to be found on archaeological sites are the products of dialogues among participants in and witnesses to the practice of archaeology, and clearly dialogues require multiple voices.

Thus, we hope to present a rich and harmonious symphony of form and content, of medium and message.

Philosophical Overture

PBP/NJC: The primary inspiration for this article is the idea of "truth" in archaeology. At first, we were put off (perhaps even appalled) by the suggestion that the end result of archaeological digging is a "truth" somehow located at the bottom of a test pit (or in a screen or on a laboratory drying rack). But then we came to understand the subtlety of the idea, which hinges on dual meaning, not unlike the use of the term "history" to denote both what historians *do* and what they study. Following this logic, truth about the past may be what archaeologists find (but we don't think so), or, alternatively, truths about our society's creation and use of the past may be byproducts of archaeological work when such work is conducted in a social context that has been studied and taken into account. This second way of thinking takes truth to be a social process rather than a scientific product; it is also the assumption behind and the focus of this article. Thus, we will not deal with the truths to be found in excavation units, but rather with the truths articulated and enacted by all the people (including us) who sit, stand, and kneel around the edges of those excavation units.

Since the advent of the "New Archaeology" in the 1960s, archaeologists have known that the sites we study are not full of answers—at least not until people approach those sites with a set of questions. And any set of questions is based on a deeper set of assumptions or truths, whether the inquirer is an archaeologist or a member of the public. While a vast majority of archaeological literature presents answers based on the analysis of material culture, or deals with the process of finding answers, we are more interested in the genesis of questions. In this article we will discuss archaeological interpretation in Annapolis, Maryland, and Lochmere, New Hampshire, from the standpoint of the various truths (and approaches to truth) that exist among the people for whom we presume to interpret the past. A part of our concern with the social context of our work stems from the realization that the people who make up the audience for our interpretations are not blank slates; they frequently come to our sites with strongly held ideas about history, archaeology, and the past. We need to respect these ideas, especially if we claim to be the anthropologists Gordon Willey and Philip Phillips told us to become back in 1958 (Willey and Phillips 1958).

First Movement:
Archaeological Interpretation on Main Street

PBP: To demonstrate what we mean when we suggest that it is necessary to look beyond archaeological data in the search for truth on archaeological sites, I would like to focus on one particular episode in my experience—the creation of the 1986 "Archaeology in Public in Annapolis" tour for the Main Street site (see Leone, Potter, and Shackel 1987, Potter 1989a, and Potter 1994 for more detailed discussions of this site tour). The Main Street tour was the eighth "Archaeology in Public in Annapolis" site tour, and, at the time Mark Leone and I started working on it, several of our post-processual colleagues were telling us that our previous tours weren't quite as strong as the radical theory we were using. While we weren't out to silence our critics with the Main Street tour, we *were* conscious of our self-imposed obligation to link past and present as forcefully as we could in that tour.

Against this theoretical backdrop, I went to work in the fall of 1985 to write a tour for an 18th century domestic site (the remains of the Thomas Hyde house) scheduled for intensive excavation the following summer. As I began my work, test excavations were showing intact 18th century deposits, including structural features, as well as all the creamware and other ceramics one would ever need to illustrate an interpretation focusing on standardization, segmentation, and the Georgian Order (Deetz 1988; Leone 1988). In addition, preliminary documentary research had hinted at the possibility that George Washington, on one or more of his many trips to Annapolis, had visited a coffee house that once stood on the site or just next door.

Given our knowledge of the site's research potential, coupled with our project's citywide focus on the history of capitalism, we could have easily written a "creamware tour" that discussed the ways in which we archaeologists can use ceramics to study patterns of labor and patterns of domestic consumption. Such a tour would have put on display our attempt to extract a particular truth (or set of truths) from one well-understood class of artifacts. But such a tour would have said relatively little to contemporary visitors about the "truths" of their contemporary lives.

While trying to write a tour that incorporated our particular approach to 18th and 19th century ceramics and discussed the Georgian Order and perhaps George Washington, I was simultaneously reading a shelf full of Annapolis histories (Norris 1925; Riley 1887; Stevens 1937) and participating, as a local voter, in the 1985 Annapolis city elections. The election campaign was particularly interesting because it provided an occasion for a public discussion that went well beyond the candidates for mayor and city council and dealt rather explicitly with the very identity of the city. Rather than seeing the history books and the election campaign as extraneous, I paid close attention to them, treating them as data every bit as important as the minimum vessel counts being generated in the archaeology lab.

One of the key issues in the election campaign was Annapolis's status as a "tourist town." In the mid-1980s, the city expressed considerable ambivalence over this source of income, recognizing the economic benefit but seeking to minimize the impact by trying to direct visitor behavior. As I was writing the Main Street tour, this truth was just as important as the fact that Thomas Hyde used and discarded a good bit of creamware. From the monographs, I learned that Annapolis historians have told a fairly consistent and useful set of stories about George Washington's 18th century visits to the city. For almost as long as Annapolis has been worrying about visitor behavior, Annapolis historians have portrayed Washington in a way that makes him look just like the "quality tourist" that the 1985 mayoral candidates pledged to attract to the city. By focusing on social and domestic aspects of Washington's visits (rather than politics or business), the "Father of Our Country" has been made into a model for contemporary visitor behavior.

The link back to the archaeological record is not George Washington's well-documented appreciation for fashionable ceramics (Detweiler 1982), but rather our assertion that the concepts of standardization and segmentation behind the 18th century manufacture and use of creamware were also behind the 19th century invention of leisure time, vacations, and tourism. All of this went into our interpretation of the Main Street site, which became a tour about tourism given to tourists. The point of the tour was to encourage visitors to use our interpretation of the archaeological record to better understand their roles as tourists and to help them see the ways in which versions of history have been used by Annapolitans to gently guide them in those roles. We did not want to create a tourist revolt, though we did want visitors to at least consider the possibility that most stories about the past are trying, in one way or another, to get people in the present to do one thing or another.

The Main Street tour was based on the premise that there are issues of legitimate concern to archaeologists that lie beyond the archaeological record. Furthermore, these issues are uncovered by using the methods and techniques of ethnography to study the contemporary social context of excavation and interpretation (Potter n.d.) and by searching for truth among living people as hard as we search for archaeological data. I don't mean to suggest that the Main Street tour was entirely successful, but it does represent one way to use the contemporary social context as a source of issues that may be addressed archaeologically. The tour may have had its mistakes and rough spots, but there is little question that in 1986, people in Annapolis, both residents and visitors, recognized tourism as something that needed to be talked about. It is this truth to which we directed the excavation and the interpretation of the Main Street site.

Intermezzo

PBP/NJC: The George Washington tour at the Main Street site achieved some of its goals; it may have tied past to present better than any of the "Archaeology in Public in Annapolis" site tours that came before it. At the same time, it is not unreasonable to ask of most "Archaeology in Public in Annapolis" site tours: Where is the real dialogue? And where are the native voices? This is especially important, given the project's use of a social theory that has enlightenment, emancipation, and empowerment as its goals. In Annapolis we used critical theory (Geuss 1981; Held 1980) and basic anthropological techniques to satisfy ourselves that we had figured out what Annapolis residents and visitors needed to know. We have been accused, with some justification, of presuming as "experts" to know better than Annapolitans themselves what matters most about the city's past.

The following examples outline three possible archaeological site tours, targeted for a particular site in the Lakes Region of New Hampshire. These tours are much more a proposal for future interpretation than a report on past work. They presume to know somewhat less about public needs for history than the Main Street tour, while they offer more opportunities for alternative modes of historical discourse. Rather than presenting a single (overly?) authoritative voice, these examples, taken together, explore the possibilities of creating a multivoiced interpretive environment, which acknowledges that there are multiple ways of knowing and appreciating the past, multiple truths to which we should be attuned.

Second Movement:
Archaeological Interpretation in the Lakes Region

NJC: Remaining connected with the present while presenting the past is a concept I first explored as a student participating in "Archaeology in Public in Annapolis." But now as I research prehistoric sites, my question is: How does one try to connect the Native American past to visitors who are not Native American Indians? The Annapolis philosophy applies here as well—one can do the ethnography of contemporary visitors to prehistoric site and the society in which they live. In turn, observations on the context of Native American Indian representations in popular non-Indian culture and history can become the basis for an archaeological site tour.

Popular culture images in New Hampshire are found in newspaper articles, advertisements, school mascots, and so on. Popular history images are found in state and local historical markers, town histories, and other repositories. During the summer of 1990, two of the major New Hampshire daily newspapers ran articles regarding Native Americans every three or four days, on average. Subjects ranged from murders to obituaries to museum exhibition announcements. A prominent subject that summer was the Mohawk warrior clan in southern Ontario; a disagreement over jurisdiction over tribal land had turned violent, as had a disagreement over legal gambling. Advertisements in the yellow pages included images of both Indians and tepees for services that seemingly had nothing to do with those symbols. Sporting mascots included Indian representations, which had been brought to public consciousness that summer because of a dispute between Dartmouth College—which had changed its Indian mascot upon protests from its Indian students years before—and the *Dartmouth Review,* which was again using the derogatory symbol. High school athletic teams in New Hampshire include "warriors," "chiefs," and "Indians," along with "cougars," "lions," and other symbols of unrelenting fierceness and wildness. This matches quite well with images of Native American Indians in New Hampshire's popular history. Often Indians are represented as vicious killers of settlers, and in most of those rare instances in which they are not portrayed as killers, they are portrayed as being killed *by* settlers. A typical reference to Native Americans in New Hampshire may be found in the text of a state highway historical marker in New Hampton that mentions "a band of marauding Indians and their captives" (Potter 1989b:16).

People might suggest that such images can be dismissed as the product of an earlier era, and that, as in the case of Dartmouth, those stereotypes have changed. However, during the summer of 1990, an Indian image was co-opted as part of a successful reelection campaign. Besides the usual bumper stickers and buttons, campaign paraphernalia included a paper headband with Indian Thunderbird symbols that was held together in the back by a tall green feather. The front of the band had the public official's name printed on it. The conclusion that the candidate-officeholder may have wanted voters to draw once they saw his name on an Indian headband was that he could be fierce like a warrior, which is not the characterization that most commentators then were applying to his previous term in office.

The artifacts found at 27-BK-16—a large, well-preserved, multicomponent prehistoric site in Lochmere, New Hampshire (Hoornbeek 1978; Hume 1982)—contradict the stereotyped image of Indians found in popular culture and in popular history. At the site in Lochmere we have found no evidence of viciousness or ruthlessness, nor evidence of violent deaths. What we did find were the materials people used to fish, hunt, cook, hold rituals, dance, keep warm, and, in general, to live.

An archaeologist could present a tour based on these findings (and contradictions), and such a tour would have three parts. The archaeologist/guide would start by introducing herself or himself and stating the reasons for the project. Next would come a discussion of archaeological techniques and method. And third, the archaeological interpretation would relate the pursuit of the past to modern reality by explaining the "archaeology of stereotypes," focusing on the differences between popular perceptions and what the archaeological record actually shows. This is not a complicated formula, but it does link excavated evidence about Native American life with "evidence" about Indians that is already available to non-Indian site visitors. The tour links what visitors could learn about Native Americans to what they may think they know on their own, without archaeology or anthropology.

The tour I have just outlined, in conjunction with the two additional tours yet to be discussed, may be used to present the same site from alternative perspectives. The purpose of this approach to interpretation is twofold. First, instead of telling visitors what Native American life in the past was like, we would reveal the various processes by which we come up with stories of the past. The goal of these interpretations would be to show that there are many different definitions of "data" and a variety of possible conclusions that may be drawn from those data. Furthermore, these three tours would stress that different versions of the past have different implications in the present. If one interpretation supports a stereotype, an alternative interpretation may be neutral or may contradict the same stereotype. (As archaeologists, interpreters, and people, we are allowed and indeed obligated to have opinions about both the content and the implications of our interpretations.) Second, the interpretive program proposed here should give equal voice to completely nonarchaeological approaches to understanding the cultural landscape. There are many voices that could be heard, an archaeological perspective being just one of them. Two other voices, at least, should probably be heard on prehistoric archaeological sites in New Hampshire.

One is that of an Abanaki Indian (rather than the voice of "the" Abanaki Indian). Common questions that archaeologists hear from Indians are, "Why do you need to dig? If you want to know about our past, why don't you *ask* us?" An Abanaki voice may complement the archaeology or it may contradict the archaeology, but it will present another way of seeing, thinking about, and experiencing this "archaeological" landscape.

I first imagined an interpretation in an Abanaki voice taking place as storytelling, conducted inside a small round structure—a replication of a contact-period Abanaki dwelling. But almost any attempt at "replication" would be based on European drawings, which made me consider some ethical issues. Is it truly an alternative perspective if the setting is based on European and/or archaeological evidence? Are there alternatives to models derived from European documentation or archaeological evidence? Where does the idea of replication come from anyway? Is this a Eurocentric, "architecture-centric" idea that doesn't necessarily have very much to do with Abanaki life and ways of thinking about the past? And then, who would build such a structure—an Abanaki, any Indian, an archaeologist? Finally, why reconstruct the setting of Abanaki storytelling when the participating visitors are not Abanaki and probably do not have the necessary Abanaki understanding to make that place meaningful? Ultimately I realized that the biggest issue in this interpretation was not selecting the best setting but, rather, figuring out how to select the setting. The location and the setting for this kind of interpretation will have to be the products of a cross-cultural negotiation that may well change from season to season, from interpreter to interpreter.

The Abanaki storyteller will tell not only about people who lived on the site and in the area, but also about the process by which she or he was taught to understand the past, about the importance of oral history and of listening to the stories told by elders, and about how these teachings may be used to understand the landscape at Lochmere.

Of course, archaeologists and Native American Indians are not the only groups of people interested in land, landscapes, and, for want of a better term, "placeness." My third tour for 27-BK-16 would draw on yet a third voice, another way to appreciate a place—geomancy, including both divination and the art of placemaking.

In one way, my interest in geomancy flows from my archaeological understanding of prehistoric Native American use of 27-BK-16. Archaeological evidence suggests that the site was not a meeting place for large groups of people; rather, the site has come by its archaeological "richness" through numerous visits by small groups of people over the course of seven thousand years. For what we can only presume to be a variety of reasons, people kept coming back to this place.

And people today are still drawn to the place. For example, Little Hawk, a Native woman, once said to me at 27-BK-16, "Every time I'm up here the hairs on the back of my neck stand straight out. Can't you feel the people here?" While I can't "feel the people" in the way Little Hawk does, I do feel myself drawn to the site, for reasons

I can't quite explain. Finally, I am amazed by the degree to which other people are drawn to the site. The site is in the woods, down a dirt road, difficult to find, and generally unmarked, yet surprisingly many people—several a day, alone or with their families—stopped by to visit when I was up there working. These various phenomena are hardly conclusive, but to me they do suggest the possibility that there may be more to 27-BK-16 than meets the eye (or the trowel).

New England is home to a fair number of people who practice various forms of geomancy, including dowsing. My third tour for 27-BK-16 would be led by a geomancer, and would focus on the use of dowsing and/or other similar techniques for exploring the "placeness" of the site. The geomancy tour would seek to identify "earth energies" or other phenomena that have drawn people to the site and would discuss this particular way of knowing a place. Just like the anthropological tour on stereotypes and the Native American tour, this tour would present not solely the "truth" about the site, but, rather, the truths that structure a way of experiencing the site.

To my way of thinking, the ideal interpretation of 27-BK-16 would be an open house arrangement that accommodates simultaneous interpretations from each of the three perspectives I have just discussed. The openness of the open house is key. Specialists in each of these three points of view would need to respect the integrity of the others; I do not envision a debate, or a competition that pits one interpretation against the others or that forces a visitor to choose among the three. Rather, I would want visitors to be able to teach themselves how to learn by interacting with three interpreters who are open to learning from one another.

Finale

NJC/PBP: The approaches to archaeological interpretation we have discussed here are not without their problems. In general, interpretive schemes that add voices and open up dialogues are not as simple or straightforward as more traditional interpretations, nor do such interpretations remove the problem of the authoritarian voice; instead of one there are several, but many are still left out. We would like to close with one problem and one potential benefit.

We decided to present the open house idea for 27-BK-16 in this article only after some hesitation. We hesitated because we have already bumped into some of the political ramifications of a multivoiced approach to interpretation. In an earlier paper on 27-BK-16, presented on behalf of the Division of Historical Resources to a statewide teachers' workshop, Nancy included a section on geomancy. However, at the recommendation of New Hampshire State Archaeologist, Gary Hume, she removed the section before she delivered the paper. Hume was concerned about seeming to slight the Native American community by giving geomancy a voice equal to archaeological and Native American voices in the interpretation of the site. This concern is not hard to understand, given the struggles Native Americans have gone through to wrest from the archaeological establishment some small bit of authority over the disposition of the remains of their own cultural ancestors. Hume's point was that whoever presents an interpretation gains a certain degree of control over the subject matter of that interpretation. In the current social climate, Hume was reluctant to endorse even the slightest suggestion that archaeologists and local Native Americans—the two groups with the largest political stake in the preservation of the site—have no more claim to 27-BK-16 than any other potential user group. The point of our multivoiced interpretive scheme is to create an environment for ongoing respectful discussion, which we see as a necessary precursor to determining the appropriate way to preserve and interpret the site (also see Leone and Potter 1992 on the topic of dialogue). Discussing Nancy's teachers' workshop paper demonstrates a point on which we agree with Gary Hume, namely, that the presentation of any version of the past has a variety of consequences in the present, consequences that will change as contemporary circumstances change.

However thorny the problems associated with our approach, it also has benefits. For example, many of the nonarchaeological things we have discussed here can have dramatic effects on the archaeological record, and our access to it. Time spent studying things other than arrowheads and potsherds can help us better understand the world in which we do our work. It is not hard to imagine that the recent discussions between archaeologists and Native Americans over reburial and repatriation would have been less acrimonious if more archaeologists had paid more attention to Native American ways of thinking about the past over the last 20 or 40 or 60 years, rather than "leaving well enough alone" until Native Americans had developed a powerful enough voice to force the issue.

In conclusion, it has been our intention to slightly recast the issue of truth on archaeological sites. Instead of seeing an archaeological site as some kind of "cache" of truths about the past just waiting to be liberated from the ground, we prefer to see on-site archaeological interpretation as an important way of using sites as an environment in which a relatively wide range of truths about the past may be identified, developed, discussed, and negotiated. Initiating dialogues can of course be a far less tidy undertaking than simply providing the fact about a particular piece of the past— but, on balance, we are willing to give up having the final word in exchange for the benefits of being able to hear all kinds of interesting voices other than our own.

Chapter Four

Generalized Versus Literal Interpretation

Background of a Half-Century "Heritage Boom"

In interpreting the past for the public's education and enjoyment, a compromise between the general, the literal, and the practical must often be found. I have for decades been an advocate of generalized interpretation when it is sensitively done and based on empirical data. There is, however, an unsettling trend in archaeology for interpretation to take place without supporting data.

In browsing through Renfrew and Bahn's *Archaeology* (1991), I was drawn to their discussion of critical theory. I learned that "philosophers of this school stress that there is no such thing as an objective fact. Facts only have meaning in relation to a view of the world, and in relation to theory." I also discovered that critical archaeologists "call into question most of the procedures of reasoning by which archaeology has hitherto operated" (1991:430). Supporters of critical theory assume that folk knowledge has more relevant interpretive power than scientifically recovered data. Some would even have us discard the scientific method in favor of interpretive stories contrived to satisfy the preconceptions and political views of laypersons. In truth, archaeologists are often faced with the dilemma of either satisfying the political will of those involved in historic site development or refocusing that will so that interpretations are more consistent with the archaeologically revealed data.

The critical archaeologists with their "poverty of research methods and wealth of rhetoric" (Fagan 1990) seemingly disregard what archaeologists are accomplishing in the real world. It is strange to hear authors such as Hodder (1991a) imply that a "heritage boom" is a new development. As early as 1965, J. C. Harrington, the "dean" of historical archaeology in America, pointed to a "heritage boom" when he wrote about "the increasing interest throughout the country in the preservation and interpretation of historic sites and structures." In 1970, I spoke of "a continuing florescence" of interest among historical societies and commissions in the use of archaeology for the preservation and interpretation of historic sites (South 1971).

I was further surprised when Hodder, in "Interpretive Archaeology and Its Role," discussed the increasing need for interpretive archaeology that is meaningful to both the local sponsors and the public and observed that interpretation from archaeological data "forces us to unlock the abstract ivory-tower theory and show what it means in practice, in relation to the data" (1991a). For the past 50 years, historical archaeologists in America have been doing just this—effectively interpreting historic sites to the public based on archaeological data derived through scientific method. It is ironic that most of Hodder's references are to theoretical "ivory-tower" sources. They do not include a single American historical archaeologist. For example, there is no reference to the reports of J. C. Harrington written between 1940 and the 1960s; or to John Cotter and J. Paul Hudson's "New Discoveries at Jamestown" (1957); or to the more recent interpretations of Noël Hume (1969; 1982) and South (1964, 1971, 1977). So while Hodder urges archaeologists not to remain indoors (1991a:16), I urge Hodder and his colleagues to step outdoors where historical archaeologists have been for decades. I strongly recommend that they begin by touring America's national and state parks and historic sites to see what has been going on outside.

I agree with Hodder that "interpretation is translation. It involves the archaeologist acting as interpreter between past and present, between different perspectives of the past, and between the specific and the general" (1991a:15). This is what the archaeologists cited above have been doing, as have others at such sites as Town Creek Indian Mound and Brunswick Town in North Carolina; Camden, Ninety-Six, and Charles Towne Landing in South Carolina; Moundville in Alabama; Etowah and Ocmulgee in Georgia; and Jamestown in Virginia, to mention only a few.

As I continued to read Hodder, it became obvious that the younger generation of archaeologists, particularly those who ascribe to the school of critical theory, might benefit from the experiences of archaeologists who have long been outdoors gathering data from the earth with which to address interpretive ideas about the past—ideas dictated by the archaeological record, not impressed onto it so as to grind today's public political axes. These archaeologists have long shared ideas with laypersons who need well-founded information from scientifically derived empirical data as a brake against their own, and the archaeologist's, political zeal. If the current antiscience fad of critical theory prevails, if one person's interpretation of the past is as good as any other's, we may again see a rash of explanations of archaeological data in terms of behavior of extraterrestrials brought to earth in flying saucers (Renfrew and Bahn 1991:430).

Theory alone is not meaty enough to touch the hearts and minds of the people. The "heritage boom" that Hodder recently discovered is caused by people's love for interpretations anchored in reality. Stories not based on facts leave them cold, as demonstrated by poor visitation to reconstructed "of the period" houses. In contrast, as we know from our Santa Elena experience (South 1992), people will sit for hours on bleachers beside an archaeological dig, as if it were a sporting event, totally enthralled as the archaeologist interprets the data being revealed before their eyes.

Fortunately, there are still archaeologists who insist on taking their chances cling-ing to the lifeboat of archaeological science as the foundation for interpretive archae-ology, who adamantly refuse to be rescued by the flashy *Titanic* of critical archaeology as it races toward the future.

The Role of Generalized Interpretation

In light of the current trend toward critical theory, where does the skillful use of generalized interpretation based on empirical data fit in? To what degree should we be compromising our science to political expediency, if at all? How do we resolve conflict when our archaeologically based interpretations run contrary to the vision of others involved in the interpretive process?

A generalized interpretive level can help site-visitors better understand the past, especially when a literal interpretation is impossible for reasons of cost, availability of materials, or other factors. Archaeologists, however, not only must operate within the framework of archaeological science but also must demonstrate imagination and courage when judging the level of generality most appropriate to the archaeological and documented record.

As trained professionals, archaeologists must avoid involvement in the creative schemes of self-serving individuals and groups. They must act as informed modera-tors in virtually every instance of archaeological site interpretation. Sometimes the power of the archaeological record competently interpreted prevails against argu-ments mustered from tradition, history, and political interest—and sometimes it does not. In this touchy area, where science comes face to face with ideas strongly held in the minds of laypersons, politicians, and exhibit curators, the archaeologist must become a diplomat. The following examples demonstrate how this can be done and has been done over the years.

Generalized Interpretation at Archaeological Sites

Fort San Marcos

Through the years, a generalized approach has been adopted for a number of interpretive field exhibits on historic sites, including Ninety-Six and Camden, South Carolina; Fort Fisher, North Carolina; and Fort San Felipe at the 16th century Spanish colonial capital of Santa Elena on Parris Island, South Carolina.

Perhaps the earliest interpretive use of a fort ditch with accompanying parapet as a generalized exhibit for public education was carried out at the Spanish Fort San Marcos at Santa Elena. The fort, dating from 1577 to 1587, was excavated and interpreted by Major George H. Osterhout, Jr., in 1923. A major problem, however, was that the fort was misidentified as Charlesfort, a French fort dating to 1562.

Politically speaking, this is understandable. World War I had recently ended and France was an American ally. The climate was right for a French fort to be interpreted. This is an example of a politically motivated interpretation in the absence of archaeological science.

Without the empirical facts recovered in recent years through scientific archaeology on the site, the monument erected to honor the French fort of Jean Ribault would still be the primary interpretation of the site. However, once research countered the politically correct interpretation of the 1920s, the interpretive story began to include the Spaniards who actually constructed the fort.

Meanwhile, the monument to honor the French, authorized by an act of the U.S. Congress and erected in 1925, still stands in the center of the Spanish Fort San Marcos site. This is appropriately symbolic since the Spaniards and French were in constant conflict during the period of the fort. The stone monument is also an excellent example of the efforts made in the 1920s to mark America's historic sites. Interpretive errors such as this become, after decades, long burned into the consciousness of visitors. These relics become symbols of another era. While subject to new interpretation in light of new empirical data, they are nevertheless significant by virtue of the interpretive era they represent.

The Roanoke Island Fort

In 1950, J. C. Harrington reconstructed the sconce built by colonists in the late 16th century at Ralph Lane's "new Fort in Virginia" on Roanoke Island, North Carolina. Prior to Harrington's work, an imaginative palisaded fort with a blockhouse had been erected on the site based on what was considered politically correct at the time. For decades viewers took away with them the image of a palisaded fort. Harrington's generalized interpretation of the ditch and parapet in the original location, based on the archaeology and anchored in empirical data, has given us an interpretive image far closer to the reality of the past.

Harrington later wrote, "Upon completion of excavations in which a structure is involved, one of an archaeologist's obligations is to provide an interpretation of what the original structure looked like" (1962:24). If we take Harrington literally, we would often be hard put when it comes to details. He showed us, however, that we can provide an "impression" of what the structure looked like, or perhaps an exhibit that will provide a "feeling" for it in its general form, while remaining true to the empirical data. Recently, additional work has been carried out, casting newer light on the "new Fort in Virginia" (Noël Hume 1994).

Town Creek Indian Mound

Some 40 years ago at Town Creek Indian Mound State Historic Site in North Carolina, Joffre L. Coe supervised the rebuilding of the palisade around the Native

American Mississippian period temple mound. He used Juniper posts imported from the coastal region because they were available at no cost. His concern was not so much to literally match the pine wood from the postholes with reconstructed pine posts but, rather, to create a general impression of a palisaded compound around the temple mound, the smallest at the site. The palisade posts were set one foot away from the original posthole pattern to preserve the original features in the ground.

Using Coe's empirical data, I reconstructed a temple on the Town Creek Temple Mound. I used concrete and mud for the walls and put an aluminum roof beneath the thatched roof, neither of which are noticed by the visitor. This deviation from the literal was for practical purposes, so that the reconstruction would last longer. The original thatch, put on in 1958, is still in use. Only minor replacement of thatch bundles have been necessary in the past 36 years. In what was the first rebuilding of a Mississippian temple based on archaeological data, our goal in 1958 was to present a generalized temple based on the best synthesis of data from archaeology and ethnography we could come up with.

Bethabara

As an interpretive exhibit, I recommended palisades in the original archaeologically revealed fort ditch at the French and Indian War period town of Bethabara in North Carolina. Some argued that instead of a palisade of wooden posts, a low brick wall over the palisade ditch would be an appropriate way to symbolize a palisade wall of wooden posts! A wooden row of palisade posts in the ditch, they argued, would give a false impression since the appearance and literal height of the posts were not known. Fortunately, I won that controversy. Today visitors to the site get a general impression of a fortified 18th century settlement.

The cellar holes of the houses in the town are left open for visitor viewing, similar to the interpretation at the site of Jamestown in Virginia. The palisade posts themselves have been placed in the original archaeologically excavated palisade ditch. Some time after we completed the reconstruction, a 200-year-old drawing of the settlement was discovered in an archives in Germany. The artist, who drew the town from the hill above, depicted the palisade as I had rebuilt it.

Charles Towne

My experiences at the Charles Towne site saw generalized interpretation carried out to different degrees. The site, situated across the river from present-day Charleston, is the location of the original 1670 settlement by the English in South Carolina. Before I became involved in the site's archaeology in 1968, the plans of some imaginative souls were underway to put a group of fiberglass-front buildings, similar to a movie set, on the site. A model had even been constructed showing where it would be located on Albemarle Point, the site of the original settlement. About $10,000 had already been spent on preparation of the model, so pressure to continue this interpretation was powerful.

I came to the site to carry out scientific archaeology, to recover data relating to the original settlement that might be of value in interpreting the site to the public. I was faced with an interpretive stance determined not by empirical data, but by the wishes of the local citizens interested in constructing their imagined version of the Charles Towne settlement. Today, archaeologists advocating interpretations based on the will of the people might feel that I should have accepted the fiberglass-front plan.

When my archaeology revealed a fortification ditch built by the Charles Towne settlers in the place where the planned fiberglass-front, craft-oriented houses were to be built, I was immediately embroiled in a controversy. The fiberglass supporters were vocal in urging that I backfill the ditch so the "interpretive town" could be built over it. The fact that the ditch was dug by the colonists as a protective measure against possible Spanish attack was of no interest or concern to them. They believed science was interfering with their freedom to interpret the site in whatever manner they felt appropriate. Without the archaeology there would have been no way to discourage "Charles Towne Reconstructed." Fortunately, a state senator, who had worked with archaeologists Philip Phillips, James A. Ford, and James B. Griffin on a survey of the Mississippi Valley, took up our political battle, and an interpretation based on evidence won, rather than an unfounded interpretation based on preconception.

When I proposed a parapet embankment and open ditch interpretation to mark the location of the fortification ditch at Charles Towne, I immediately received the suggestion that I rebuild the gun platforms and install fiberglass artillery pieces to reconstruct the fort as literally as possible, like forts "of the period." I was told that guides, dressed in "authentic" versions of 17th century costume, would tell stories "interpreting" the fiberglass features to the visitors. In lieu of this, I suggested using dioramas, drawings, paintings, and other literal interpretive devices inside a museum to explain the details of the generalized presentation the visitor was seeing outside. This battle was only partly won because the recommended exhibits were never built. At least visitors to the site do not have to endure being subjected to fiberglass guns.

The sides of the fortification ditch at Charles Towne were almost vertical. To literally interpret them and expect them to stay vertical through years of rains would have been difficult. I suggested a ditch with sloping sides and an embankment that would not rapidly wash into the ditch but would resemble, after several years of settling, the fortification as it may have looked some years after the colonists abandoned it. This interpretation would provide a general impression of the fort without having to provide the sodded ditch walls, the faggots, the careful contouring of the original ramparts, parapet and embrasures, woodwork, fascines, and other myriad details for a literal interpretation. Although we compromised the original vertical walls, our decision was appropriate for a presentation of the ditch and parapet, not as they appeared when the colonists were using it, but as they may have appeared after the fort had been abandoned, suffered erosion, and then stabilized.

The palisade ditch was situated a few feet from, and parallel to, the fortification ditch. We used chemically treated palisades along a portion of the open ditch and parapet embankment to give the general feeling of the original fortification wall, not to literally copy it. Documents from similar fortifications of the period helped us determine the eight-foot height. This is one more example of a generalized statement using posts, ditch, and embankment.

Halifax State Historic Site

In interpretive reconstructions, we have seen that compromises must often be made between the general and the literal, and that practicality and cost play important roles. This is as true for architectural reconstructions as it is for archaeological sites. At Historic Halifax State Historic Site in North Carolina, architects have erected the Montford Interpretive Structure to house archaeological exhibits and protect the excavated ruins where Joseph Montford's house once stood. While the general exterior appearance and spatial mass of the structure suggest an 18th century house of the historic Halifax period, certain features meet modern needs. For example, the chimneys are air-conditioner cooling towers and the siding is modern. From a distance, the building appears in keeping with other surviving structures. Up close it is obviously not a reconstruction.

This type of interpretive exhibit is admirable in that it falls neatly into the generalized, interpretive twilight zone I have urged here. In the absence of original fabric, literal reconstructions of houses leave so much to be desired that I would argue against going to the inevitable exorbitant expense, just as I would argue against erecting a Quonset hut over the archaeological ruin of the Montford house.

Sensitive, well-thought-out decision making is important to successfully translate archaeological findings into interpretive exhibits. In most cases, where archaeological data is involved, a generalized interpretation is usually as accurate and effective as a literal one, while cheaper to execute.

Museums and Interpretation Through the Years

Just as archaeological sites should be treated with a sensitivity to the past, so too should archaeological museum exhibits. Those of us who visited the Smithsonian in the 1930s remember the old cases filled with numerous artifacts, the ethnographic masks and spears on the walls, the metates, and the regal buffalo head surveying the scene from above. All are gone now, victims of numerous faceliftings and changes in interpretive focus through a parade of curators and exhibit designers.

A few years ago I visited a county museum where lack of funding had preserved such a room in all its 1920s–1930s cluttered splendor. It came complete with cases holding collections of everything from shrunken heads and arrowheads to a little dried-up "mermaid," once the pride of the museum. The curator caught me spending my time there and apologized for the room. I, who was fascinated with the variety and multicultural, multidisciplinary, multifunctional conglomeration of things no longer found in the more modern, remodeled, and revised sections of the museum, quickly told her she should leave it untouched. I suggested she preserve it as "The Early Museum Era Room," for instance. I pointed out that somewhere in America a creative museum curator might be poring over archival photographs of old exhibits, desperately trying to put together a relic room—such as she had in all its pristine, untouched authenticity—so as to produce a "correct, period museum room" for the enjoyment of visitors who haven't experienced such a fascinating wonder. Since my visit, this room has had a modernizing face-lift, successfully destroying it as an example of the antiquarian room that mixed natural history with science and history.

I would like to think that some curators somewhere would have the presence of mind to hold such a room suspended in time, to share with visitors the feeling and magical charm of the museums of the past that many of us grew up loving. Such rooms are now as rare as the items they were devoted to preserving. In the name of education, thematic story line, and simplicity, we have destroyed a facet of our museum heritage, even though these rooms, if any can still be found, can be excellent examples for the melding of general and literal aspects of interpretation.

Modern museums specialize and focus the attention on a theme, such as birds, for instance. There you will see more than you could possibly want to know, from their evolutionary development to the variation in species of color, size, function, subsistence, and mating habits, complete with a diorama literally re-creating the environment in which they live. This "everything you could possibly want to know" encyclopedic approach can be seen in all types of displays, from those on spearpoints and arrowheads, transformed as a visual treatise on the evolution of tools, culture, and man, to a wing devoted to the snake, from the Garden of Eden to your backyard, as a symbol of fear through the ages. By the time you walk through such a scientific knowledge bank, your mind is boggled and your feet are tired and you long for blessed relief from the exhausting educational particulars bombarding you from all sides. In short, you are bored!

Curators pride themselves on such definitive displays, combining erudition with objects. The antiquated generalized approach is abhorrent today in the face of literal exhibits that explore every nuance of each subject. What ever happened to the generalized room with a stuffed owl sitting on a case of Indian relics on which a rattlesnake was coiled? You had to have a short attention span in that kind of museum room because the display was a general one that fired the imagination at every turn. Children, particularly, enjoyed such exhibits, running from one thing to another, "Look! Momma! An owl! Ooh! A snake! Look at that rattle! Wow! Indian arrowheads!" Too general? Not educational? I think not. What do many people do in front of the television to fight boredom? They change channels, sometimes watching three slow-paced programs at a time. The generalized museum room "changed channels" so often there was no time to become bored.

I am not saying we should do away with dissertation exhibits so endemic in today's museums. I am simply saying that the generalized approach in historic site development from archaeological data allows the visitor to fill in the details with imagination, and follow up later with reading, just as the generalized museum room stimulated the imagination in a wonderful way and led to reading to discover more, making the viewer a participant rather than a passive observer.

Conclusion

In America, examples of interpretive archaeology are legion. A tour of interpreted sites will reveal many examples of what to do, and what not to do. Sometimes the latter can even, if used creatively, become an effective tool by contrasting past interpretation methods with those currently in fashion.

Although recognized late by those who have remained too long inside, the "heritage boom" has been underway in America for half a century. Archaeologists have long been outdoors, translating their scientific findings into meaningful educational exhibits that utilize both generalized and literal interpretations. Whether full-scale on the landscape or on a smaller scope, as in museums, these exhibits are changing forever the images visitors carry away with them. Through work being done by the National Park Service and many state agencies, interpretive archaeology is alive and well in America.

■ *Part Two* ■

Strategies That Work

Chapter Five

Successfully Integrating
the Public into Research:
Crow Canyon Archaeological Center

The demand for learning experiences using our natural resources has spilled over to both prehistoric and historic archaeology. The thrill of discovery inherent in archaeology makes it a tempting target for interpreters looking for ways to interest the public in historic resources. For economically depressed areas, archaeology can be a needed shot in the arm to draw in tourism dollars. Archaeologists, anthropologists, and historians offer local areas a unique opportunity to capture their pasts through tourism and oral history projects that benefit both residents and scientists alike. Crow Canyon Archaeological Center near Cortez, Colorado is so successful because it integrates the public into actual research. The keys to Crow Canyon's success lie in the involvement of archaeologists in the program, the experiential quality of the programs, and high-quality research. Research of that quality allows archaeologists to follow and transmit ethical imperatives to the public and academic community alike.

Attractiveness to Educators

With its air of mystery and excitement, archaeology fascinates teachers and their students as few other subjects can. Besides its natural attraction, teachers recognize its potential as a learning tool. Archaeology is interdisciplinary; there are few subjects that cannot somehow be related to it, from the obvious—history, geography, and anthropology—to the less evident—geology, physics, chemistry, biology, language arts, math, art, music, foods, nutrition, and physical education. Although anthropology and archaeology are rarely found in school curriculum guides, creative teachers, either alone or as members of teams, are discovering that the study of an archaeology-related subject can knit an entire array of topics into a cohesive unit. At a time when demands are put on educators to offer more realistic curricula, such a unit is just what teachers are looking for. They are also finding archaeology to be an excellent focal point for organizing curricular materials to meet *America 2000* goals, especially in science and math.

Given the goal of historians and archaeologists to increase appreciation for cultural and historic preservation, it would seem an excellent time for them to join forces with public school teachers. Today, however, educators are being bombarded with demands from legislators who want higher test scores and more kids graduating from high school for less money. "Threats" are coming not only from state houses, but from also from citizens who are tired of high property taxes. Teachers may be so distracted by constricting budgets and greater demands for higher scores that they may not be open to adding a new subject or revising their curricula to include archaeology. In fact, schools are being forced to drop programs rather than add new ones. This is not the best time for archaeologists to interest themselves in becoming more involved in schools. However, archaeologists shouldn't give up; they simply must find more creative ways to enter the educational system.

Attractiveness to Local Communities

While archaeologists are discovering their common bond with educators, they are also finding themselves in the limelight as archaeology becomes increasingly attractive to local communities. As interest increases in the human experience through time, the world is discovering its past. According to John Naisbitt and Patricia Aburdene in *Megatrends 2000:*

> Since 1965 American museum attendance has increased from 200 million to 500 million annually. *From the United States and Europe to the Pacific Rim, wherever the affluent information economy has spread, the need to reexamine the meaning of life through the arts has followed.* Much of humanity is freer to ponder, to explore what it means to be human. *It is spiritual quest, but its economic implications are staggering* (1990:62–63). [Emphasis added]

It is precisely this urge to discover more about humanity that makes archaeology appealing. Archaeologists and historians can help local communities record their recent history through oral history projects. They can offer communities an economic boost through tourism dollars generated at archaeological and historic sites. In areas such as southwestern Colorado, archaeological tourism has been recognized for its potential only within the last few years. This recognition is critical for the preservation of sites, so it is important that archaeological organizations become visibly active in the local economic scene.

Crow Canyon: Integrating the Public into Research

Crow Canyon Archaeological Center is located in extreme southwestern Colorado, 4 miles by road from the small town of Cortez and 14 miles from the entrance of Mesa Verde National Park. Established in 1983, this profit organization is dedicated to experiential education and archaeological research into the Anasazi culture. Over the years, Crow Canyon has had a significant impact on education and the local economy.

Educational Impacts

In 1991, over 4,000 people, ages 10 to adult, participated in Crow Canyon programs lasting from one day to several weeks. Crow Canyon sponsors traveling seminars throughout the Southwest with distinguished scholars as teachers. Its campus-based programs include cultural explorations and workshops, excavation and environmental archaeology programs for students ages 12 and above, and nonexcavation archaeology programs for elementary students. Participants are housed in comfortable hogans or dormitory-style rooms. All meals are provided on campus.

The core curriculum begins with "Inquiries into the Past," in which students are given an inquiry-based, hands-on introduction to southwestern archaeology and the Anasazi culture. Next, through excavation in a simulated site, the concept of a research design and the importance of context are stressed. All students attend a lab session to learn basic laboratory techniques. They also try their hands at Anasazi living and learn about the interrelationship of the Anasazi with the prehistoric environment. The week culminates with a visit to Mesa Verde National Park, where a series of stops at exhibits and at the museum reinforces the week's learning.

Adults follow the core curriculum, but spend from one-and-a-half to two-and-a-half days in excavation and one day in the lab. The introduction day includes "Inquiries into the Past," a detailed site tour introducing the research project, and an evening program introducing archaeological research. Some participants have virtually no background in the subject, but are able to contribute under careful supervision of their work. Adults are very satisfied with the program, as substantiated by the 40 percent return rate. This success is attributed primarily to the quality of the research. Adults interested in avocational archaeology appreciate the opportunity to contribute to actual research alongside archaeologists who act as teachers as well as scientists. In response to requests, Crow Canyon is creating a more in-depth excavation program for alumni who wish to make a greater contribution and learn more advanced archaeology techniques.

Economic Impacts

The impact of the Crow Canyon Archaeological Center on the local economy is as significant as it is on education. A member of three different chambers of commerce, Crow Canyon had a 1991 operating budget of $2.8 million, of which an estimated $2.2 million was spent locally. The expenditures included payroll, supplies bought from local vendors, transportation, automobile rentals, local restaurant patronage, and numerous institutional services. With a permanent staff of 50, and 23 part-time employees, Crow Canyon is one of the larger employers in Montezuma County, whose population numbers roughly 18,000—in an area twice the size of Rhode Island.

The economy of the county is primarily agricultural. No comprehensive data on tourism have been compiled despite efforts in recent years to promote the area. Statistics published by the Cortez Development Council show that in 1985 Mesa Verde National Park visitation was 656,271; in 1990 it decreased to 611,375. However, during the same period, the number of visitors at the more remote Hovenweep National Monument increased from 14,977 to 28,147. The Bureau of Land Management's Anasazi Heritage Center Museum opened in 1988, serving 21,378 visitors; in 1990, 37,702 passed through its doors. The numbers are remarkable considering that the nearest interstate access is two-and-a-half hours away.

Retail sales have also reflected the impact of tourism; restaurant sales rose from $8.8 million in 1985 to $12.1 million in 1990, and lodging sales from $4.8 million to $6.3 million during those same years. It appears that more people may be staying in the area to visit attractions other than Mesa Verde, and that archaeology in general is making a contribution to the local economy.

For economically depressed areas in general, archaeology can be a needed shot in the arm by drawing in tourism dollars. Archaeologists, anthropologists, and historians offer local areas a unique opportunity to both capture and share their pasts. With careful planning, this can be to the benefit of residents, scientists, and tourists alike.

Crow Canyon's Keys to Success

The following components are the basis of the Crow Canyon Archaeological Center's highly successful programs:

- The involvement of archaeologists in all stages of the program
- The experiential nature of the programs, which integrate the public into the actual research
- The quality of research
- The ability of archaeologists to follow and transmit ethical imperatives, such as the need to preserve and protect our cultural resources

Involvement of Archaeologists

At Crow Canyon there are separate research and education departments; however, the members of both departments work as teachers and archaeologists. Three members of the education staff hold bachelor's degrees in anthropology. Most of the education staff are certified teachers. Since the program is experientially based, it allows all the staff to act as educators and scientists while working closely with participants.

The inclusion of trained teachers in the program has allowed Crow Canyon to design a curriculum soundly based in educational theory. By including archaeologists, the curriculum is well grounded in anthropological and archaeological theory. The dual nature of the program gives it its strength and appeal to teachers, students, and adults. The strands are interwoven into a uniquely successful product.

Experiential Education

At Crow Canyon, education rather than interpretation is emphasized. Why? Because interpretation is oriented to the interpreter for the learner, education to what the learner does for himself or herself. Making this distinction is crucial not only to the program, but also to the mission of persuading the public to help preserve and protect our cultural and historic heritage. Crow Canyon educators are unique for two reasons. First, even in short programs, they spend more time with the public than do most interpreters. Second, they diverge from the traditional forms of social studies education that focus on lecture, reading, and memorization. They focus on experiential education.

Richard J. Kraft says "that experiential education includes all those environments in which the learner is actively involved in his or her own learning, and is not just a passive recipient of the knowledge of the teacher" (Kraft and Sakofs n.d.:15). Experiential education provides situations in which the learner can try to do the things that are being taught (Figure 5.1). As much as possible, Crow Canyon's educators avoid lecture formats. Research indicates that even if people become active listeners, they will likely forget 90 percent of what they hear within 24 hours, remembering only 10 percent if they are very interested in the subject (Stahl 1986). The educators at Crow Canyon expect people to use their own intuition and previous knowledge to learn from the materials presented. They constantly teach, yet rarely assume the guise of lecturers; rather they act as resource persons for participants.

Learning at Crow Canyon is an intensive immersion into a past or present culture. Participants may spend eight or more hours daily studying a topic. Because they are active learners, they must use many senses besides the auditory or visual. The additional senses of touch, taste, and movement reinforce learning. Participants are much more likely to retain in long-term memory what they have learned through multiple senses than through a single sense.

The setting also contributes significantly to the learning experience. Away from their normal surroundings, participants are immersed in the environment they are studying. The concerns and interests of their everyday world slip away as they are given ample time to direct their thinking to the topic at hand. Thus, they learn cognitively, through mechanical memory, and with their psychomotor system as well.

Students and adults learn how to do archaeology with simulated or actual sites, usually over an extended period. They learn the techniques to use. They learn how to process and catalog artifacts for permanent curation at the Bureau of Land Management Anasazi Heritage Center. But what are participants really learning? How to dig sites on their own land? Educators have agonized over the dilemma created by a possible misuse of such information. This dilemma make the final two keys to success all the more important.

Quality Research

The Sand Canyon Project focuses on the late Anasazi culture and the abandonment of the Four Corners region by A.D. 1300. The focal point is Sand Canyon Pueblo, a large site containing 300 to 400 rooms, 100 kivas, 14 or 15 towers, and several examples of community architecture: a great kiva, a multistory D-shaped building, a central plaza, one water impoundment area, and a low enclosing wall one-third of a mile long. Dendrochronological construction dates are estimated to be from A.D. 1248 to 1274, indicating that the site was used right up to the abandonment of the region. The Pueblo and many of the smaller testing sites are on Bureau of Land Management property. Begun in 1983, the project has consisted of sampling selected architectural units at the site itself, surveying portions of the surrounding area, and testing selected smaller sites. Several Ph.D. dissertations and master's theses have come from the project thus far. An interim report was published in 1992, and, excavation ended, preparation of final reports have begun.

Avocational historians and archaeologists and professional teachers are attracted to high-quality research programs. They want to contribute in a meaningful way to something significant. This can be financially—Crow Canyon currently generates 80 percent of its revenues from tuition, most of the rest from individual donations. It can also be through hard work digging in a hot desert site or cataloging artifacts in the laboratory in the middle of winter. Participants know that the Sand Canyon Project is long-term, producing doctoral dissertations and master's theses. They know the project is presented at major professional meetings, such as the Society for American Archaeology meetings. They are pleased to show their friends at home the results of their work as described, perhaps, in a Crow Canyon publication or newsletter, or an article in a prominent periodical or newspaper. They take pride not only in their work, but the way they spent their vacations.

Figure 5.1. Students at Crow Canyon Archaeological Center in Cortez, Colorado, assist in an excavation at Sand Canyon Pueblo.

Ethical Imperatives

As archaeologists and historians, our missions are value loaded; we believe we must preserve and protect our heritage, be it cultural or historic. We know we must reach out to the public in a nonoffensive, appealing way. Yet in the very act of reaching out, we sometimes find that the hands reaching back have their own agendas. For example, there is the teacher who knows that his or her students will be turned on to the thrill of discovery, so plans to dig up a site with little or no thought to the value of the information that erstwhile student archaeologists may destroy in the absence of careful professional guidance. There is the developer who has caught on that archaeology is appealing, so plans to develop a vast area just for the treasure-seeking, wealthy public. There is the participant who comes to your institution for a week and then travels to a spot thousands of miles away and introduces himself or herself as a professional archaeologist, using your institution's name. There is the incredibly sincere "new-ager" who discovers a site, and then sings, hums, or tones to it and buries crystals within it.

Do we give up in disappointment and disgust? The staff at Crow Canyon accept that they can't convert everyone to their own ethical and professional standards, but this doesn't stop them from trying. They are extremely open with their values; they cannot win people over if they are not firm in their own convictions. Rather than shunning those who don't at first agree with their programs, they continue the dialogue in a nonthreatening manner. They excavate only what is necessary, leaving the rest for the future. They commit funding to the publication and transmission of their findings. They include ethical discussions in all programs and live what they believe.

Conclusion

Historic archaeologists and interpreters can learn from the success of the Crow Canyon Archaeological Center. By involving archaeologists, by reaching out to children and adults through experiential learning and volunteerism, by maintaining high-quality research, and by promoting high ethical standards, interpreters can model their own successful programs—and perhaps touch those who will best help us preserve and protect our past for years to come.

Chapter Six

The Role of Public Participation:
Arizona's Public Archaeology Program

Introduction

Over the past decade, Arizona archaeologists have made a conscious effort to get people involved in archaeology, to make the past come alive for them. By giving people access to the past, we foster appreciation of, respect for, and increased activism on behalf of our irreplaceable heritage. Public participation is a valuable component in protecting, promoting, and interpreting cultural resources in Arizona; it is also one of the keys to our successful public archaeology programs (Rogge and Montgomery 1989).

We have a long history of taking positive and innovative approaches to interpreting and protecting cultural resources. Instead of coercing people by beating into their heads that vandalism is against the law—the "big stick" approach—we've taken the "carrot" approach. Not only do we provide the public with opportunities to learn about the past, we also explain how cultural resources are relevant to them and how the resources can enhance their lives.

It is this thread of public participation that ties together Arizona's Public Archaeology Program, whose major components include the annual celebration of Arizona Archaeology Month, the Site Steward Program, outreach to schools, and heritage tourism. The broadreaching success of this initiative was recognized at the state and national levels in 1986 when the Arizona State Historic Preservation Office (SHPO) was presented the "Take Pride in America" award in the state government category for its coordination of the archaeology program.

The following is a brief review of the development of public archaeology in Arizona that describes how the role of public participation in our interpretive programs has helped us move forward in both protecting and promoting our valuable cultural heritage.

Public Archaeology Takes Root: The Homolovi Ruins

Originally, Arizona's public archaeology programs derived from the concern of archaeologists and citizens over increased levels of vandalism and looting. In 1980, then Governor Bruce Babbitt of Arizona responded to this threat by inviting archaeologists and citizens to participate in the Governor's Archaeology Advisory Group. The Archaeology Group laid the groundwork for the development of public archaeology programs in the state. It promoted an action plan for protection of archaeological resources that focused on the Homolovi Ruins near Winslow in northeastern Arizona. This group of six Hopi ancestral sites had suffered some of the worst vandalism in the state. The Archaeology Group's efforts culminated in the establishment of Homolovi Ruins State Park by the state legislature in 1986.

The Archaeology Group formed a Management Board and Planning Committee—composed of private citizens who owned land on which some of the sites were located, as well as local and regional public officials and Hopi tribal members—to protect the unique resources at the state park. Development of a trail at the site of Homolovi II, funded by the State Land Department and the Jobs Bill through the SHPO, opened up the site for interpretation to the public and helped increase appreciation of and respect for the resources in the area. Development of the state park also stopped major vandalism at the sites, primarily by heightening public awareness of their importance to the Hopi tribe and their significance in the history and prehistory of the region.

The success of these first attempts at outreach can be attributed to a focus not only on deterring vandalism but also on creating a potential economic benefit for the local community and the Hopi tribe, while at the same time involving a variety of interest groups in the process from the beginning. What makes Homolovi Ruins State Park so distinctive is the thread of continuity between past and present Hopi culture and tradition, which is expressed in the interpretive programs at the park.

Through a cooperative agreement with the University of Arizona and the Arizona State Museum, an ongoing research program of excavation and survey is being carried out at the park. This program permits Earthwatch volunteers, local citizens, and even park visitors to participate in archaeology. The research and public participation program has been a turning point in the state in terms of site preservation and protection attitudes; it clearly shows the benefits of providing the public with opportunities to learn about archaeology and participate init.

This strong emphasis on involvement was also seen in other projects sponsored by the Governor's Archaeology Advisory Group. For instance, the nationally popular 1982 *Thief of Time* poster promoted a positive approach to antivandalism that focused on sharing archaeology with the public, rather than keeping it from them.

Interpreting the Past with Arizona Archaeology Month

Recognizing that public understanding of cultural resources is a key issue in combatting vandalism, the Archaeology Group initiated Arizona Archaeology Week in 1983. Held every spring, Archaeology Week is a program of events specifically oriented toward informing the public about archaeology and involving them in archaeological activities (Hoffman 1988; Hoffman and Lerner 1988, 1989). Coordinated by the SHPO, the program has expanded to involve over 60 federal, state, municipal, and private organizations. Responding to this growth, the SHPO initiated a month-long celebration (Archaeology Month) that has continued since 1993. The major interpretive and promotional components of Archaeology Month include theme development, poster production, and statewide events.

Theme Development

Every year since Archaeology Week 1986, a theme has been selected to provide a focus for the events and activities, to create a link between these, and to help the public see an overall continuity in the Archaeology Week/Month celebration. Each year's theme is publicized in the array of promotional materials, including the poster, that are prepared by sponsors across the state.

Year	Theme	Focus
1996	What Is the Future of the Past?	Statewide efforts in preserving archaeological resources
1995	Preserving 12,000 Years of Heritage	Recognizing the depth of our cultural heritage
1994	Explore the Past!	The adventure of discovering the reminders of the past
1993	Arizona's Heritage: Sharing the Responsibility	Each of our roles in protecting our heritage
1992	Partners in Preservation	The many partners in protecting cultural resources
1991	Discover Arizona's Past-Times!	The recreation/tourism potential of Arizona's archaeological resources
1990	Time Travel Arizona!	The recreation/tourism potential of Arizona's archaeological resources
1989	Tour the Past!	The recreation/tourism potential of Arizona's archaeological resources
1988	Volunteers in Archaeology: Preserving Our Heritage	The role of volunteers in cultural protection and preservation
1987	Take Pride in the Past: 100 Years of Arizona Archaeology	The centennial of the Hemenway Expedition, which launched organized archaeological research in Arizona
1986	The Past Made Public	Making the past available to the public

Poster Production

One of the most important components of Archaeology Month is the annual poster design competition that encourages artists, photographers, and archaeologists alike to lend their talents to promoting awareness and appreciation of Arizona's unique cultural resources. The winning poster is distributed statewide to advertise the program and the Archaeology Month theme. In past years, both adults' and children's poster art contests have been sponsored through the SHPO in cooperation with the Arizona Archaeological Council (AAC) and other organizations.

In 1991, the first photography competition was sponsored by the SHPO, AAC, Salt River Project (a local utility), and the Mesa Southwest Museum. That year over 70 entries were received, and the winning design resulted in a striking poster. The top 23 photographs were incorporated into a traveling exhibit promoting Archaeology Week. The five award-winning photographs (First and Second Places and three Honorable Mentions) became part of smaller traveling exhibits that have been featured in public libraries. Photography competitions have been used in subsequent years to generate the poster design, although in 1993 a drawing was commissioned for the poster artwork. Given the popularity of the photography posters, it is likely the photo contests will continue.

Statewide Events

For the past several years, over 100 events have been offered during Archaeology Month. The activities are designed so that professional and avocational archaeologists can interact with interested citizens and share information on our state's colorful prehistoric and historic past. The broad range of activities include archaeological site tours; open houses; tours of archaeological laboratories; public lecture series; audiovisual programs, exhibits, and activities presented by archaeologists in local schools and libraries, and for Chambers of Commerce and other community organizations; free admission days at museums and parks; archaeology "how-to" workshops for children and adults; and Archaeology Fairs. In 1994, events were offered in at least 30 communities statewide. The SHPO produces a statewide calendar of events in coordination with their cosponsors, which include federal and state agencies, avocational and professional archaeological organizations, museums, and private consultants.

For the past eight years, an Archaeology Fair or open house has been held at or near a site or sites. This allows archaeologists to explain what they do by example, interpret the resources, and directly interact with the public. Also, organizations that are involved in archaeology can assemble exhibits and demonstrate prehistoric crafts and archaeological techniques. Major emphasis is placed on hands-on activities for children. Replicating petroglyph rubbings, making "shell" jewelry with dyed macaroni, spinning cotton, grinding corn with a mano and metate, and making split-twig figurines proved to be quite popular with the adults as well as the children.

One of the main attractions of the Archaeology Fair is a Visitors' Dig where attendees of all ages work alongside archaeologists and learn about excavation techniques and archaeology first-hand. Several thousand people attend this weekend event every March. The Fair has been one of the most popular events of Arizona Archaeology Month. It clearly indicates public interest in interpretation through active participation.

Perhaps the greatest mark of our success is that other states have begun to see the benefits of public archaeology programs. Today similar annual celebrations have been initiated in many states across the country (Greengrass 1993).

Arizona's Site Steward Program: Volunteers Protecting Our Past

Also proving valuable in achieving our goals is the Arizona Site Steward Program. Begun in 1986, it is an initiative of the Arizona Archaeology Advisory Commission, which replaced the ad hoc Governor's Archaeology Advisory Group. The Steward Program is a statewide, cooperative response to the need to curb destruction, gather information on site condition, and provide positive opportunities for public involvement (Hoffman 1991). An organization of volunteers, the Steward Program has broad support through its sponsors, which include the U.S. Forest Service, Southwest Region; the National Park Service; the U.S. Bureau of Land Management; the Arizona State Land Department; Arizona State Parks, SHPO; the Hopi tribe; the cowboys of Horseshoe Ranch; the nuns of Santa Rita Abbey; the city of Phoenix; and the Maricopa and Pima county Parks and Recreation Departments.

The chief purpose of the Steward Program is to prevent destruction of prehistoric and historic archaeological sites through site monitoring. By the beginning of 1996, more than 500 stewards had been trained and certified, over 36,000 hours of steward service had been logged, and at least 600 archaeological sites and areas were being protected by monitoring efforts. The program has grown largely by word-of-mouth, and a measure of its success is the 1990 Governor's Award for Historic Preservation that recognized the outstanding contributions of the many volunteer stewards throughout the state. *Arizona Watch,* a quarterly newsletter, was initiated in 1990 by the SHPO to keep stewards, land managers, and the general public informed about the program's activities and progress. A logo was also adopted to provide further identity and cohesion.

For the past several years, the SHPO has placed considerable emphasis on providing stewards with diversified training opportunities, including surveying, oral history, rock art recording, stabilization techniques, and other skills. In 1991 the SHPO initiated the annual Steward Conference, which draws together program participants from all over the state for two days. One of the primary goals of the conference is to bring together stewards from different regions with different perspectives, and to provide opportunities for land managers to meet with them and other land managers. The conference also presents good opportunities to recognize the accomplishments of individual stewards with special awards and the overall accomplishments of the statewide program.

The annual conference also provides a forum for training stewards and enhancing their skills. For instance, in 1992, the focus was on effective documentation, both written and photographic, as a means to assist law enforcement agents with Archaeological Resources Protection Act (ARPA) vandalism cases. During a field exercise at a nearby site a "pothunting in progress" was staged, and stewards were challenged to use their new observation skills. The next day a mock trial of the pothunters was held at a real courtroom, and an Assistant Attorney General questioned stewards on the stand, pointing out how their notes and observations could help win or lose the case.

There are a number of advantages to the program. Not only do the stewards learn about the archaeological sites that they monitor and protect, but also they are in the field talking to people about these sites. As volunteers, they have a lot of credibility in convincing people about the importance of the resources. As Stumpf notes, "Without question, the Site Steward Program is winning more friends for archaeology, a benefit that is not just good for science [but] is also good for recreation and tourism and, ultimately, local economies" (1990:29).

Heritage Tourism and Community-Based Interpretation

There is no doubt that people are very interested in archaeology. The economic potential of this interest should not be overlooked. Knopf and Parker note that:

> Tourism builds social community. . . . Communities acquire solidarity through the actions they take to attract and create tourists. The benefits arise through the teambuilding that accompanies promotion of festivals, the organization of special event weeks, and the mounting of local tourism campaigns. Indeed, an inevitable consequence of escalated tourist promotion is the heightened sense of community togetherness. (1990:2)

More tangible economic benefits can be measured by tourists purchasing local goods and services. Community-based attractions, events, or activities can also provide data on the attitudes and spending habits of visitors, thus enabling the community to target its financial resources to the appropriate tourist markets (Arizona Department of Commerce 1989:2).

Tourism based on heritage resources is a growing field. Responsible interpretation and development of archaeological sites can capitalize on people's interest in cultural heritage and, in so doing, not only boost tourism but, at the same time, preserve resource integrity and promote an ethic of stewardship. It can also help secure the future of unprotected resources.

In Arizona, there are two good examples of heritage tourism and archaeological park development, Besh-Ba-Gowah and Casa Malpais. Their success is closely tied to participation by community members and visitors.

Besh-Ba-Gowah: Place of Metal

The Besh-Ba-Gowah Archaeological Park is situated in a small city park on the outskirts of Globe, an eastern Arizona mining community of around 7,000 people. The site represents a large, complex prehistoric puebloan community. The 450-room masonry pueblo was inhabited by the prehistoric Salado culture, which occupied the Tonto Basin of central Arizona between A.D. 1225 and 1450. The name Besh-Ba-Gowah derives from an Apache phrase meaning "Place of Metal."

The site was originally excavated in the 1930s, with archaeologists from Arizona State University (ASU) renewing investigations there in the 1980s. This captured the attention of city officials. With the collapse of the local copper mining industry—the major economic enterprise in the Globe area since the late 1800s—they were looking to tourism to stimulate the economy. The renewed interest led to the designation of Besh-Ba-Gowah as a city park. With the assistance of archaeologists, the SHPO, and others, the city has since preserved and partially reconstructed the ruins as a tourist destination. Today, the site exhibits the remnants of more than 200 rooms and an on-site museum (Hohmann 1989).

ASU worked closely with city and county officials to devise a plan that would fund not only the ongoing research and a public interpretation program, but a jobs training and economic project as well. Over the past few years, the project has resulted in a reconstructed site, a museum, interpretive trails, an ethnobotanical garden, and special interpretive programs that include public participation. The museum also offers many special programs, including museum studies, teacher education, and Southwest archaeology courses. The SHPO has supported the park with several Historic Preservation Fund (HPF) grants for the development of trails, signage, brochures, National Register of Historic Places nominations, and a Master Management Plan (Hohmann 1990).

The park was officially opened during Archaeology Week in March 1988 and has averaged about 1,700 visitors a month. The economic impact of tourist dollars is beginning to be felt. Local interest and support has been extremely high throughout this unique project, and Globe citizens take pride in the visible progress.

Casa Malpais: House of the Badlands

Globe's success with Besh-Ba-Gowah captured the attention of another Arizona rural community. The town of Springerville in northeastern Arizona is also receiving the SHPO's support to explore the protection, preservation, and recreation potential of the 14-acre Casa Malpais National Historic Landmark. Lying within the Springerville town limits, Casa Malpais is a 13th century Indian ruin that is noted for its unusual location, large ceremonial kiva, and subsurface chambers. Situated on terraces of a fallen basalt cliff along the upper Little Colorado River, Casa Malpais was initially recorded in 1948 (Danson 1957; Danson and Molde 1950). Several others have studied or recorded the site since then (Martin, Rinaldo, and Longacre 1961). Casa Malpais, Spanish for "House of the Badlands," apparently reflects the early Spanish settlers' characterization of the lands to the north of Springerville. The site borders the edge of the "badlands" (Hohmann 1991:22).

The development of Casa Malpais into a viable visitor destination was initiated by the Springerville Economic Development Commission and has received broad local and state support. The project's theme is "Respect for Our Past." A 1990 Survey and Planning grant from the SHPO helped finance a "Management, Protection, and Interpretation Plan" for the town (Hohmann 1991). The plan identified the tourism potential of Casa Malpais as an Archaeological Recreation Area. A 1991 Acquisition and Development grant from the SHPO provided funds for protective barrier installation around the park perimeter, stabilization of eroding and vandalized features, and initial trail development. The town hopes to expand the current site to 20 acres with a rest area accessible by a one- to two-mile loop trail.

By the spring of 1991, the town had made significant progress in reaching its goals. A contract was signed with an archaeological consultant, and a Casa Malpais Advisory Committee was established to provide input into the site development. The Casa Malpais Museum opened in downtown Springerville in March 1991. It showcases materials from the site and the surrounding area. In the museum's laboratory, visitors can view the reconstruction of ceramics and other artifacts. Guided tours of the site originate from the museum, which is staffed by local volunteers. The impressive community support can be seen in the establishment of the Mogollon chapter of the Arizona Archaeological Society (AAS) in Springerville. The AAS is a well-respected avocational archaeology group that has 17 chapters statewide and a comprehensive certification program. Many of the Mogollon chapter members volunteer at the museum and the site. They are also actively involved in the certification courses being offered through AAS.

The park officially opened in 1993, and the town has hired a full-time project director and archaeologist. In addition, the nonprofit Malpais Foundation was created in 1993 to oversee park development and raise funds. The foundation replaces the original advisory committee. The prospects for the development of Casa Malpais as a tourist destination are substantial, given the progress that has been made within such a short time.

Bringing Archaeological Interpretation into the Classroom

In addition to heritage tourism, Arizona archaeologists are also targeting schools in their interpretive efforts. Over the past nine years the AAC Schools Committee has worked directly with teachers, exploring numerous ways to integrate archaeology into existing curricula.

The AAC is a nonprofit voluntary association dedicated to maintaining and promoting the goals of professional archaeology in the state of Arizona. The Schools Committee includes as its members professional and avocational archaeologists, educators, museum professionals, and interested citizens. This dedicated group has created a successful program of workshops that benefit teachers, students, and archaeologists alike.

In the spring of 1987, the first pilot workshop was offered free of charge to approximately 30 teachers from the Phoenix area for in-service credit. Since then, the Committee has offered one or more workshops annually across the state. The group has also developed a comprehensive teachers' guide and student workbook (Rogge 1991; Rogge and Bell 1989). The core of the workshops is the hands-on activity sessions. Teachers work through each of the six lesson plan, copies of which are provided as part of the workshop packets. These basic lesson plans are designed to meet existing requirements for social studies, mathematics, science, biology, writing, and art. They include the following:

- "Culture Universals" and "Cultural History Mystery" challenge students to examine artifacts from various cultures and discuss how these artifacts reflect or represent the individual cultures. The lessons emphasize that culture, or the way people live and think about their world, is determined to a certain extent by where people live and what geographical and other natural conditions they must cope with. Artifacts—objects that are made or modified by people—reflect a culture's social and political institutions, language and number systems, beliefs, values, technology, economics, and livelihood.

- "Trowel It" and "Garbage Can Archaeology" encourage data gathering and basic skills as well as critical/creative thinking skills. "Trowel It" enables students to use the tools of the archaeologist and dig in replicated sites created in sandboxes by their teachers. The students uncover a set of artifacts and decide what stories they tell and what the culture was like based on the artifacts the people made. "Garbage Can Archaeology" is a related activity. By using two or more wastebaskets from different locations at school (library, classroom, and the like) and by looking at the types of materials and the order in which they were discarded, students learn how archaeologists use trash to interpret peoples' activities and behaviors.

- "Dating" offers background on two techniques commonly used to date archaeological sites in the Southwest. These are tree-ring dating (dendrochronology) and archaeomagnetism. Students learn the concepts of relative and absolute time in archaeological interpretation, along with tree growth and patterns in nature, cause and effect, and magnetism and compasses.

- "Simulating Prehistoric Pottery" promotes an appreciation for the process of pottery manufacture, particularly as it was practiced in prehistoric times, while providing an outlet for student artistic creativity.

Recent efforts of the Committee have focused on developing a teacher's handbook, "Discovering Arizona Archaeology," as a component of the Bureau of Land Management's Project Archaeology workshops.

While the concept of teacher workshops is not new, the unique success of the Schools Committee lies in the fact that its members volunteer their time and talents to plan and implement these archaeological workshops, which are based on active participation and interpretation. Their compensation comes from the knowledge that they are helping instill in the state's children a sense of stewardship for their cultural heritage. This is absolutely essential if Arizona's and America's dwindling cultural resources are to survive with integrity, to be appreciated by future generations.

Looking Toward the Future

One issue we must deal with in reaching our interpretation objectives is public perceptions, or misperceptions, regarding cultural resources and archaeologists. Some call this the "Indiana Jones syndrome." Although Harrison Ford's title character as an exotic archaeologist in a series of movies has indeed raised public consciousness about archaeology, the image strays considerably from reality. Not all archaeologists are male, swashbuckling, treasure-hunting, adventurers who pursue spectacular and valuable artifacts that must be wrested from the hands of villains, and who always "get the girl." Our image needs to be balanced.

Too often, however, we ourselves contribute to misperceptions by focusing our interpretations on the spectacular ruins and unusual artifacts that capture the imagination. It is imperative that we interpret a broad range of resource types, the large and small and in-between. We must include resources that represent not only the prehistoric Native American heritages, but also the many ethnic groups that contributed to the development and growth of this country. Too often we focus only on one site so that our audience doesn't see the broader picture of land use in the past; they don't realize that the sites were integrated communities whose influences reached far and wide. So too, we should address unexcavated sites. If part of our mission is to preserve cultural resources, it's important that people understand the value of a resource bank that saves information in reserve for future generations.

We have learned from our experiences in Arizona that, as archaeology continues to evolve as a discipline, it is essential that public access to our nation's cultural heritage be a part of our interpretive programs. We should be reaching a broader spectrum of the public, adults and children alike. Our programs should encourage public participation and stimulate feedback. People generally do not respond favorably to negative messages couched in legal terms, so our interpretations must incorporate positive anti-looting messages that foster pride in our heritage.

In Arizona, an increase in citizen activism and advocacy for archaeological resources has been noted over the past few years. For example, one private developer in north central Arizona owned property containing a significant Sinagua pueblo and associated burials. He had leased the land to a pothunter prior to construction of a housing development. Over 200 citizens, including members of local Native American tribes, turned out in protest and blocked the path of the bulldozer. This display of public outrage received state and national attention and subsequently convinced the landowner to reconsider his approach and establish a dialogue with the interested parties. As a result of this citizen activism, the Archaeological Conservancy purchased the Sugarloaf Ruin in 1993 and is now protecting the site through stabilization and public education. This demonstration of public concern also drew the attention of state legislators, leading to the passage of burial protection bills that had previously languished. Increased public participation and responsible interpretive programs can be constituency-building. In our interpretive programs, we should strive to generate this kind of grassroots support and awareness. Public advocacy might be the best way for archaeology to survive economic swings and the whims of government and elected officials.

Finally, because respect for our heritage resources is not a focus of our school curriculums, and because we live in such a mobile society, it is becoming increasingly difficult for children and adults to develop ties to the land and the cultural resources that represent their and other people's heritage. All who encounter archaeological and historical sites should leave with *positive* messages regarding the intrinsic value of our irreplaceable cultural resources. In this way will we secure the future of our past.

Chapter Seven

Sites Without Sights:
Interpreting Closed Excavations

Introduction

Few subjects excite the imagination and evoke curiosity like archaeology. Who is not familiar with the Hollywood images of archaeologists—pith-helmeted professors opening up cursed tombs or treasure-seeking adventurers? With these images in mind, a first visit to a real archaeological site is likely to be a disappointment. Bits of broken pottery and chipped stone tools are perceived as poor substitutes for golden chalices. Indistinct changes in soil cannot rival vine-covered pyramids.

While objects recovered from archaeological sites may not match those envisioned by Hollywood, the process of discovering the past creates its own excitement if archaeologists and museum professionals provide visitors with the tools to actively participate in the discovery process. An active archaeological excavation is a wonderful interpretive tool to show visitors the techniques of archaeology. But what happens when excavation is completed or few objects are recovered? If active archaeological excavations can be disappointing, how will people react to an empty field or pit—even one with a tantalizing story?

Staff at Jefferson Patterson Park and Museum (JPPM) in Wallville, Maryland, a 512-acre facility preserving more than 80 archaeological sites that span 9,000 years, is addressing the challenge of sites without sights through a variety of interpretive approaches. In examining philosophical and theoretical issues—such as the need to provide visitors with the skills to evaluate our interpretations and the need for relevancy—they are learning how these issues affect our interpretations.

The public programs discussed in this paper were made possible by generous support from The Maryland Humanities Council, The MARPAT Foundation, The Miller & Chevalier Charitable Foundation, Baltimore Gas & Electric Company, NCR Corporation, Mrs. Jefferson Patterson, and BFGoodrich.

Why Do Public Interpretation

Archaeologists are becoming increasingly aware of and involved in public presentation (e.g., Gibb and Davis 1989; Heath 1990; Leone 1983; Potter 1989a; Pryor 1989; Versaggi 1986). This important development warrants our attention for three main reasons. First, given the current economic climate, it is important to remember that much anthropological research is funded directly or indirectly through tax dollars. People tend not to support things they do not understand, things that do not add meaning their lives. Therefore, it behooves archaeologists to engage the general public in a dialogue regarding why we should care about and preserve the past. This is essential to developing a supportive constituency.

Second, and far more important, we are socially responsible not only for preserving the past but for making that past accessible (Davis and Gibb 1988). When reference is made to accessibility, it usually suggests physical accessibility. The term is used here in a broader sense, encompassing both intellectual and social accessibility. Despite popularizations like Indiana Jones, we have a long way to go to make archaeological research accessible. For example, I attended an engaging lecture on the archaeology of several African-American sites held in a museum of African-American culture. It would seem that everything possible had been done to make this lecture available to a diverse audience. However, the entire audience was white. This lecture was not socially accessible. Archaeology is simply not as accessible as we may want to believe. Even the word "archaeology" creates intellectual barriers as real as stairs to a person in a wheelchair. People are interested in archaeology, but most are uncertain about what archaeology is and it makes them uncomfortable. They don't want to ask stupid questions.

Finally, opening archaeological research to public view and critique adds multiple voices to archaeological interpretation. Much discussion has been engendered about archaeological research unconsciously reinforcing existing social and political values (Conkey and Spector 1984; Leone, Potter, and Shackel 1987). Well-done public interpretation initiates a variety of dialogues informing simultaneously on the present and the past. This dialogue can help make the process of archaeological research more democratic. Ian Hodder has raised the question "How can alternative groups have access to a past that is locked up both intellectually and institutionally?" (1991a:7). While only a relatively small number of academicians are involved in researching the past, there is no reason why the public cannot participate in this process through a critical evaluation of the interpretations that are presented to them. To do this we must provide the public with both the opportunity to participate and the skills needed for evaluation. Public interpretation of archaeological research is essential if we are to increase access to and input about the past.

Goals and Process of Public Interpretation

Archaeologists involved in the public presentation of their research confront new questions: (1) What are the goals of public interpretation? and (2) How, if at all, do they differ from research goals? During the interpretative process, "something foreign, strange, separated in time, space or experience is made . . . comprehensible: [interpretation requires] representation, explanation or translation. . . ." (Palmer 1969:14). This definition applies to the process of research as well as public presentation. While these two activities follow similar processes, the audiences and goals of the activities are often drastically different. Therefore, while it is important not to underestimate the public's ability to absorb the most complex of ideas, the results of archaeological research often cannot be directly presented to the public. For example, I asked an archaeologist for a title of an important research project. I was told, "A Numerical Taxonomy of Southern Maryland Redwares Based on Paste and Glaze Attributes." While many archaeologists understand why this is significant research, most people do not have the cognitive framework necessary to evaluate and make it meaningful. The issue is not just the vocabulary used, although it is important. When research is not adequately translated or made meaningful, public archaeology might result in self-satisfaction on the part of the archaeologist, but puzzled or bored expressions on the faces of the visitors. This is the consequence of differing expectations: the archaeologist wants to share facts learned, while the visitor wants to know why they are digging in squares or where the "buried city" is located. Visitors want a dialogue, but the starting points and motivations between them and the professionals are vastly different. For public interpretation to be effective, these differences must be understood and accounted for.

The goals of public archaeology differ from the goals of research. However, just as archaeological methodology is guided by well-defined research goals, public interpretation must be guided by an understanding of what it is you want to teach, and whom you will be teaching it to (Potter 1990). Ideally these goals are incorporated into the site research plan even if public interpretation will not occur until after the excavation phase of the research is completed. The ultimate goal of public interpretation arises out of the ethical responsibility we have to make the past accessible and empower people to participate in a critical evaluation of the pasts that they are presented with. The archaeologist, who sees her or his interpretive responsibility as the "simple and objective presentation of facts, often uses that position, albeit unconsciously, to reinforce a traditional view of reality" (Chappell 1989). Successful programs provide an understanding of the process of historical interpretation and establish why the past is relevant to the present.

Public Interpretation of Closed Archaeological Sites

At an ongoing archaeological site, the relationship between the artifacts and their context can be made directly. When active archaeological sites are not available, teaching the process of interpreting the past must be more indirect. For ethical and pragmatic reasons very few of JPPM's sites have been excavated. Since our mission is to interpret the cultural resources of the property, other interpretive approaches, including exhibitions, tours of the property, and signs at archaeological sites, are used to teach interpretive process and to establish relevancy.

Exhibitions as Interpretive Media

Exhibits are second only to Hollywood as providers of public information regarding archaeology and interpretations of the past. However, the medium has several disadvantages over other forms of public interpretation for closed archaeological sites. People don't always read text and even if they do, it may not answer specific questions. Also, it is hard to re-create in exhibits the immediacy and thrill of discovery associated with site visits. This emotional attitude toward the past is extremely important, for it often provides the motivation for a more critical examination of the subject. Exhibitions are a poor substitute for ongoing excavations when it comes to teaching archeological techniques. Seeing something done is second only to doing it yourself as an educational method.

Exhibitions as interpretive medium also offer many advantages. There is no time constraint. The archaeologist has time to complete the analysis of the site, and visitors can move through the exhibition at their own pace without feeling rushed or trapped. Exhibits can present both the artifacts and visual interpretations derived from their analysis. Thus, exhibits can more effectively make the connection between data and its interpretation than even tours of archaeological sites or publications. During site tours, visitors see only one point in time and may find it hard to visualize the larger picture—that is, how the accumulated bits of information are put together to form a greater whole. Understanding this epistemological connection is far more important than knowing archaeological techniques in reaching the goals of pubic interpretation. The use of hierarchical text in exhibitions can help reach an audience diverse in background and interests. A well-designed exhibition should be meaningful even if visitors simply walk through, reading only the titles. Secondary and tertiary texts provide more detailed information for those interested.

JPPM's orientation exhibit, *12,000 Years in the Chesapeake: An Archaeological Story,* contains artifacts from archaeological surveys and excavations on the property.

The exhibition describes and explains changes in human/land relationships from the Paleoindian period to the present and fulfills several important functions. It provides visitors with an informational starting point, addresses common misconceptions about the past, and illustrates the process of historical interpretation. Modern theories of education indicate that prior knowledge, belief, and experiences strongly influence learning (Shetel et al. 1968), and learning occurs when information gained requires a shift of "cognitive framework" (Borun 1991). Therefore, the orientation exhibit provides visitors with a starting point for examining their ideas about the past.

12,000 Years in the Chesapeake also introduces the language of archaeology—the vocabulary associated with cultural time periods, archaeological methods and techniques, and so on. Introducing a common vocabulary is essential to initiating a dialogue about the past. Conversations in museum settings are highly patterned and object oriented (Hensel 1987, 1991). Groups converse only as long as questions can be formulated and answers provided. Therefore an orientation exhibit must provide the information and vocabulary necessary to sustain and expand those conversations.

Since people do not talk about things they are not interested in or that have no meaning in their lives, a final function of the permanent exhibit is to illustrate how the past is relevant to present concerns. The following examples illustrate how the exhibition fulfills these functions.

The introductory text lets people know what they will see in the exhibit and indicates the theoretical or philosophical orientation—the often—passive voice of the curator. Placing the curator's name at the beginning of the exhibit can help make this voice more active, reinforcing the idea that the past is not just written down but pieced together by individuals. The introductory text to *12,000 Years* states:

> Stone tools, bits of pottery, bricks, . . . and other remains testify to the presence of people in the . . . Bay Region during the past 12,000 years. This vast period has been one of change in the land and in the lifestyle of the people. . . . This exhibit tells the story of how these people lived. It is an archaeological story pieced together from the bits of garbage and soil stains that are the starting point for archaeological interpretations. . . . It is also a modern story for our lives continue to be influenced by the bay environment. And, in turn, the environment continues to be impacted by our behavior.

This makes it quite clear that the objects people will be viewing are largely garbage in the literal, if not the figurative, sense. This is imperative to avoid disappointing an audience whose idea of archaeology is often based on the media image. The text also establishes a connection between the past and present. Human groups in the past affected and were affected by the Chesapeake Bay environment. The media has focused public awareness on environmental issues, and the exhibition framework takes advantage of this awareness. The past becomes relevant because it is interpreted in terms of modern concerns.

This connection between past and present is also made graphically. A section of the introduction panel illustrates two healing ceremonies with a photograph of a modern hospital and an artist's reconstruction of a Woodland Shaman healing ceremony

Figure 7.1. Introduction panel illustrating two healing ceremonies (courtesy Jefferson Patterson Park and Museum).

(Figure 7.1). These graphics show the similarity of human needs while at the same time illustrating that not all segments of our modern culture are equally familiar. In fact, some things, such as the hospital photograph, seem quite strange to most of us. The juxtaposition of these two images tends to make the Woodland healing ceremony seem more familiar, acceptable. When the image is encountered later in the exhibit, it is less likely to be misinterpreted even if the associated text is not read.

Americans have a strong belief in what they read, and seeing something written or presented in a museum gives it an aura of absolute truth that is hard to combat. If the goal is to get people to examine interpretations of the past critically, then they must know this is possible. Interpretations of the past, however presented, must not be

Figure 7.2. Artist's reconstruction of Paleoindian life illustrating different interpretations (courtesy Jefferson Patterson Park and Museum).

perceived by the public as having absolute authority. One way of encouraging critical evaluation is to present multiple interpretations of the data. The exhibit panel dealing with Paleoindians (Figure 7.2) contains an artist's reconstruction of the environment based on the most recent paleobotanical studies. This raises the unstated question, how did the people of 9,000 years ago fit into the landscape? Two visual interpretations of the archaeological data are then presented: humans as specialized big-game hunters and as more generalized hunters and gatherers. Note that, contrary to most depictions of Paleoindians, the later illustration depicts females as well as males.

The descriptive data about human/land relationships presented in the exhibition provides visitors with a common starting point for a critical examination of the interpretations. The explicit statement of relevancy helps people realize that the past does not exist independently of the present, thus providing a reason for caring about the past. Presentation of multiple interpretations reveals that our understanding of the past is not static but rather is open to critique and change. However, if the goal of public interpretation is to encourage a dialogue, then the process of historical

Early Plantation Life

Adjusting to the Chesapeake took time.
Many Colonists died of disease.
Plantations were isolated but they
maintained ties with England, trading
their tobacco for manufactured goods.
Like the Native Americans, the early
Colonists' diet consisted mainly of corn,
meat and seafood.

Archaeological excavation of early
Colonial sites reveals evidence of the
post-in-the-ground construction method

a. Excavation views

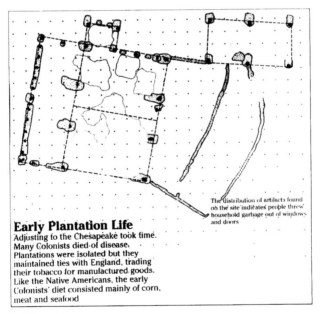

The distribution of artifacts found
on the site indicates people threw
household garbage out of windows
and doors

Early Plantation Life

Adjusting to the Chesapeake took time.
Many Colonists died of disease.
Plantations were isolated but they
maintained ties with England, trading
their tobacco for manufactured goods.
Like the Native Americans, the early
Colonists' diet consisted mainly of corn,
meat and seafood

b. Site map

Figure 7.3. The process of archaeological interpretation
(courtesy Jefferson Patterson Park and Museum).

c. Artifacts and house model

d. Artist's reconstruction showing artifacts in context

Figure 7.3. (Continued)

interpretation must also be presented. This is accomplished through a variety of techniques.

Segments of the exhibit entitled *Unpuzzling the Past* deal explicitly with an archaeological method that addresses the research issues raised in this section. The process of interpretation of archaeological data is also presented graphically throughout the exhibit. While exhibits cannot capture the immediacy of archaeological excavations, they can show the entire interpretive process, since much of this goes on after the excavation phase is completed and involves increasingly abstract extrapolation from the data. Exhibits can graphically show this extrapolation. For example, the section dealing with early plantation life (Figure 7.3) presents information on colonial house types in four ways. First, the data is presented through photographs showing the site excavations. These provide visual information about archaeological techniques. Artifacts from the excavations contribute additional primary data. Second, a site map showing features provides the first level of extrapolation from the data. A model of the house and an artist's reconstruction illustrate the relationship between the house and artifact use, supplying additional levels of abstraction from the data.

Tours as Interpretive Media

After viewing the exhibit, visitors are encouraged to continue their investigations on the "Trail of Archaeology." This self- or interpreter-guided trail incorporates visits to several of the sites discussed in the *12,000 Years* exhibition. While the information presented during the tour builds on that introduced in the exhibition, as an interpretive medium, tours offer distinct advantages and disadvantages. First, tours have broad appeal. JPPM attracts many visitors who would not normally choose to spend their leisure time in museums. For them the tour is an accessible medium often initially viewed simply as a fun way to see the property. Conversely, veteran museum-goers often choose the self-guided option, perhaps having been "trapped" on poorly organized tours in the past. Tours of archaeological sites, active or closed, provide a sense of place and immediacy that is often impossible to capture in exhibitions. However, tour groups are often comprised of very diverse individuals. Since the agenda of the tour is predetermined to a greater or lesser extent, people lose the control over timing and information they had in the exhibit. With good planning, this is counterbalanced by the opportunity to ask the interpreter questions.

Many visitors to JPPM are very much interested in the Pattersons. Questions such as "how did they use the property?" and "why was it given to the people of Maryland?" are common. The tour of the property capitalizes on this interest. Starting at the Visitors Center, which formerly was Mr. Patterson's show barn for his black Angus cattle, the environmental and cultural impacts of the Pattersons' occupation of the site are addressed. The tour proceeds around the property, going back in time, ending at the Stearns site—a late Woodland farm hamlet.

"Time traveling" is a much used and often abused approach to interpreting sites spanning long periods of time. The public is often asked to "imagine away" the present, replacing it with some reconstructed past. This removes any relationship between past and present, reducing the past to quaint nostalgia. However, when well done this approach is very effective. It maximizes the interpreter's ability to draw on commonality of experience, guiding visitors from the known to the unknown. At JPPM, visitors are guided to see the present in terms of ongoing processes resulting from decisions made in the past. Since we all have made decisions, the framework of examining choices—together with understanding the social, technological, and environmental constraints operating on those choices—provides ready access into the interpretive process.

Guided tours have the additional advantage of incorporating sources of information about the past that are not easily presented in exhibitions. For example, landscape modifications and buildings are common features in people's lives, but seldom are seen for what they are—informers on the past. During the site tour at JPPM, visitors are provided with interpretations drawn from a wide variety of sources: oral histories, standing structures, documents, and landscape modifications. As the tour progresses "back in time," the visitors realize that the sources of information decrease, leaving the interpretation of the Woodland period site totally dependent on the archaeological data.

Signs as Interpretive Media

Signs are probably the most common form of interpretation at closed archaeological sites. However, when used alone, they are probably the least successful in meeting the interpretive goals of making the past accessible and empowering our audiences. Signs usually are simple descriptions of the lifestyles of the people who lived on the site. Often there is no, or little, connection between what the people are seeing on the ground—actual archaeological remains or reconstructions—and the story told in the signs. Thus the process of interpretation is lost and relevancy is not established.

At JPPM signs are used at several closed archaeological sites. While designed to stand alone, the signs are incorporated into the overall site interpretation, which includes the exhibition and tour of the property. The most successful signs are at the Kings Reach Site, a late-17th, early-18th century tobacco plantation. When site excavations were completed, modern hand-hewn posts were placed into the excavated postmolds, outlining the house, slave quarters, and fence. Since relevancy of the site is addressed in the archaeology trail brochure and historical context provided in the exhibit, the signs focus on the process of site interpretation. Five signs (Figure 7.4),

a. Site discovery

b. Excavation

Figure 7.4. Signs at Kings Reach site (courtesy Jefferson Patterson Park and Museum).

c. Features

d. Artifact

Figure 7.4. (Continued)

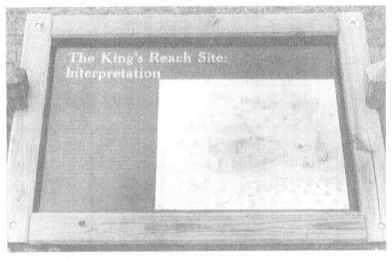

e. Interpretation

Figure 7.4. (Continued)

entitled "The King's Reach Site: Discovery," ". . . Excavation," ". . . Artifacts," ". . . Features," and ". . . Interpretation," were designed to lead visitors through the interpretive process and build anticipation for what came next. The text addresses both common questions about the site and misconceptions about the past. Graphics from the exhibit are used, showing the same information in a new context, reminding the visitors of what they learned in the exhibit about colonial life. The summary text of the final sign refers back to information provided in the preceding signs, reiterating the relationship between data and interpretation.

Conclusion

The interpretive approaches at JPPM make archaeological scholarship accessible and relevant to a broad audience. Few will have the opportunity or interest to develop an interpretive program as diverse as this. However, state and federal agencies are increasingly making public interpretation part of their scopes of work. Because the greatest challenges to closed archaeological site tours remain (1) how to keep visitors from being disappointed, (2) how to teach critical evaluation, and (3) how to illustrate the relationship between data and higher-order interpretations, the goals of your programs, whether tours, signs, brochures, or exhibits, must be carefully considered. Is the material physically, socially, and intellectually accessible to your targeted audience? Is it relevant? Can you clearly and succinctly tell people why they should care about what you are doing? Have you empowered your audience by providing them with the skills and opportunity to participate in a dialogue regarding your research questions and interpretation? Or, have you only provided disconnected facts that will be immediately forgotten? Only by answering these questions honestly can we hope to effectively interpret sites without sights.

▪ *Part Three* ▪

Interpreting Archaeology in Cities

Chapter Eight

The Past Through Tomorrow:
Interpreting Toronto's Heritage to a Multicultural Public

Science fiction buffs will recognize the shameless borrowing of the title of this article from a book by the great Robert Heinlein. I could not think of a better way to describe what archaeologists who work for and with the public on excavations, in labs, in classrooms and museums, and at heritage sites do—they are making archaeology a living and vital part of the present for the sake of the future.

Public education in the field of archaeology seems to be the new wave of the late 1990s. At every conference and symposium there are presentations, discussions, and working groups dealing with "taking archaeology public." It is an incredibly dynamic and exciting time for our profession.

No longer are public archaeologists constrained to explaining why popular interest and understanding of heritage issues are crucial to the conservation of the resource. Rather, with everyone talking at once, we are brainstorming new and better methods for marketing our own professional goals and standards to an extremely interested, if sometimes unenlightened, audience—the ordinary people to whom the heritage resources belong.

As archaeologists, however, we tend to think in terms of how public archaeology serves our own profession. Common arguments for popularizing archaeology range from increasing ordinary people's interest in heritage conservation, to the possibility of reducing site looting and vandalism and slowing the trade in antiquities robbed from sites, to the distinct and tangible benefit of an augmented public purse dedicated to archaeological salvage and research. This is, of course, the bottom line.

Editor's Note: After more than 100,000 children and members of the public had participated in hands-on learning on historic urban sites and in the A.R.C. labs, and after servicing as the model and inspiration for several other similar A.R.C.'s around the world, the Toronto facility was recently closed due to budget cuts. However, Karolyn E. Smardz has once again joined forces with Peter Hamalainen, who co-founded the A.R.C., to put together a charitable organization call "PastQuest" to revitalize the hands-on programming. A big success, PastQuest is a community-based effort, in coorperation with the University of Toronto, that utilizes off-hour, donated time from the Former A.R.C. staff. Perhaps Toronto public archaeology, despite the failure of support from the bureaucracy, is "going to rise like a phoenix from the ashes."

On the other hand, comparatively little has been stated on the possible benefit to the public of knowing more about archaeology. Archaeology is a "Good Thing" so, of course, people are fascinated by it. Aren't they?

Well, yes, most people find archaeology interesting. The sense of discovery, the romance of reaching out to touch the past, the exotic flavor of foreign lands and ancient cultures draw people of every age. Unfortunately, the very qualities that make archaeology relatively easy to market are those promoted by Hollywood films and popular novels, not by archaeologists. Still, we all benefit from Indiana Jones and company simply because the "adventure of archaeology" stimulates the popular imagination.

Public archaeology programs are growing up all over North America. These vary from simple talks for schoolchildren about "what I dug up last summer" to elaborate and extensive efforts by government agencies to teach an entire population why the destruction of irreplaceable heritage resources hurts everyone.

But how we communicate archaeological information to our target audience depends very much on the context in which public-oriented archaeologists find themselves. Different approaches are required, according to the type of heritage resource that characterizes a local area. Furthermore, demographic, economic, social, and geographic factors influence the form a marketing campaign must take. Advertising and public relations companies specialize in developing campaigns to sell their products in different ways to varying types of audiences. Age range, ethnic background, anticipated consumer resistance, economic levels, and whether the population is rural or urban all come into play. So too, public archaeology has to take these variables into account to be effective. We are, in a very real sense, attempting to sell the *concept* of heritage research and conservation. And we are trying to convince everyone at once. The only trouble with this approach is that populations are neither stagnant nor homogenous.

In Toronto, it has been the municipal school system that has for the past nine years administered and funded the city's public archaeology programs through a completely unique facility called the Archaeological Resource Centre (the A.R.C. or the Centre). Archaeology has been considered an integral part of the educational process in the city. Excavations, analyses, teaching programs, and research projects have all taken place within the incredibly complex and highly political milieu of metropolitan government. Archaeology in Toronto is paid for by the taxpayer and has been so designed to provide a direct public service.

To function effectively within the larger institutional, bureaucratic, and political structure of a school board, public archaeology in Toronto has had to assume a character very different from the discipline's traditional and familiar forms. It has evolved to fit the requirements of modern educational theory while fielding the changing political, social, demographic, and economic factors influencing Toronto's downtown neighborhoods.

The A.R.C.'s operation, then, is a combination of educational, marketing, community, and social services. Archaeology in this instance was re-created so as to serve the public that pays for it, and, in so doing, its public character has transformed urban archaeology in the City of Toronto into an entirely new type of pursuit.

The Toronto example provides an interesting model for what can happen when archaeologists stop taking archaeology to the public for archaeology's sake and start doing it to meet the general public's educational, social, and cultural needs.

What Archaeology Can Do for the Public

When one is asked what the function of archaeology is in a modern society, the old "quality of life" line simply doesn't work anymore. There are too many equally worthy causes requiring both political attention and a chunk of the taxpayer's money. But archaeology can do a great deal of real good in terms of both education and social service. The possibilities are only limited by one's imagination. Archaeology per se can be presented to the public through handson artifact lessons, dig experiences, displays, and lectures, though the discipline and its inherent mystery and romance can also make it a remarkably effective vehicle for teaching math, a form of therapy for hyperactive children, or even a valuable outdoor education experience for the physically challenged.

To make archaeology a viable, integral part of ongoing cultural and educational activities, the discipline needs to be marketed aggressively to an increasingly knowledgeable and demanding public. Archaeologists must show politicians and educators, as well as the average truck driver or garment worker who also votes and pays the taxes that support archaeological research, how the conservation of heritage remains benefits them directly in a modern world. To do this, we archaeologists have to divest ourselves of some dearly held notions. For example, knowing a site's minimum vessel count may cause our hearts to beat faster, but rarely does this have the same effect on anyone else. Take a group of schoolchildren onto a site and provide them with a (closely supervised!) opportunity to participate in seeking, uncovering, and recording evidence of past cultures, and you'll have archaeological converts for life. It is the excitement and romance of archaeological discovery that makes people think archaeology is worth doing and learning about. Of course, the *process* of archaeological research—that digging is *not* the point—must be meticulously conveyed to avoid the "treasure hunter" message. But this is the task of archaeological educators, as well as their greatest challenge.

In other words, it is not archaeology's ability to help all of us gain a better understanding of how people lived in the past that makes archaeology marketable, it is also that mysterious, romantic, exotic sense of delving into the unknown—ergo, the very process of archaeological research. Over the decades, archaeologists have borrowed from just about every other science and humanity to investigate the past. So, why shouldn't they borrow from the modern fields of marketing, communications, and public relations to help speak to and "sell" a modern and multicultural public? The highly multidisciplinary character of archaeology makes it an ideal mechanism for opening up whole new vistas of popular understanding, even in areas not directly archaeological.

Teaching Archaeology in Schools

Schoolteachers today have an awful lot on their plates. Imagine trying to keep up with computer technology, deal with issues such as the breakup of the Soviet bloc, pat down students for weapons, and keep a group of kids interested in a grammar lesson after they have played "Super Mario Brothers III" on Nintendo the night before. Now you have some idea of what the average Grade 7 teacher deals with in the course of a single day.

Preparing children for life in the 21st century is a formidable task. Classroom teachers are looking for new and different ways to stimulate the jaded imaginations of upward of 40 ten-year-olds at a time. Just about everyone finds archaeology intriguing; most students are turned on by the very idea. One of archaeology's most attractive features for the educator is that it can be a vehicle to teach other subjects. In marketing terminology, this is the "hook."

The only problem is that teachers have more than enough to do without "boning up" on an entirely new field of study. Although this is changing, the majority of archaeological information is not available in an accessible form for non-archaeologists. To introduce archaeology into the classroom, then, archaeologists need to make their product as easy to use as possible. Providing a user-friendly educational package—a "canned class" for teachers to use—obviates the marketing problem of consumer resistance. So does going into the classroom yourself to teach an archaeology lesson, or inviting a group of schoolchildren to visit or even dig at your site.

The average school system these days is doing a great deal more than teaching reading, writing, and arithmetic. Boards and departments of education confront an ever-changing kaleidoscope of problems owing to their position on the front lines of social and economic change. Immigration issues, poverty, and child abuse or neglect all have a direct impact on the kind of students sitting in front of a teacher in the classroom.

In Toronto schools also provide a broad spectrum of adult education, including English-as-a-Second-Language courses, citizenship programs for recent immigrants, basic education to combat illiteracy, job skills upgrading, night school, summer school, French immersion, and seniors and parenting classes.

In 1985, the archaeologists who began the A.R.C. tossed archaeology into the Toronto Board of Education's curriculum pool and learned how to make it swim. We found new and different ways to do archaeological research within a completely public setting, and discovered how to make the process of research a form of educational and social service within a dynamic urban environment. Most importantly, we learned to make archaeology both easily accessible and fun.

We did this by breaking archaeology down into its component parts. We asked, for example, what aspects of archaeology can be used to teach science or math, or to help students understand Native cultures? These are some of the ideas our staff has come up with so far:

- Use archaeological techniques and methodologies to teach students about science.

- Help immigrant adults feel more comfortable in their new land by showing them artifacts left behind by earlier generations of Italians, or Chinese, or Poles who made their homes in 19th century Toronto.

- Ask senior citizens to contribute a few hours to help a historical archaeologist understand what some of those homemade pioneer tools were used for.

- Combine French immersion lessons with an introduction to Canadian prehistory by setting up classes where students learn vocabulary while cooking and eating traditional foods of Canada's First Nations communities.

- Take cases full of dinosaur bones into The Hospital for Sick Children and run paleontology programs for chronically and terminally ill youngsters.

The A.R.C. staff has gone far out of its way to make archaeology easily available to teachers, students, and the public. They have accomplished this by learning how to teach specific subjects from educators specializing in them and then by producing, testing, and offering the programs themselves. Information packages, teaching kits, and a large resource library of slide sets, videos, books, and lesson plans are provided throughout the school system so that teachers can bring archaeology into their own classrooms. But the most important resource that teachers can access has always been the A.R.C. archaeologists, together with their personal knowledge and experience. The impact of working on a real excavation alongside professional archaeologists has an effect no classroom lesson, book, video, or simulated experience can match.

The Archaeological Resource Centre: Archaeology for, by, and of the People

The Toronto Board of Education has been involved in public archaeology for more than a decade. In 1985 the A.R.C. was formally created with seven professional archaeologists employed as full-time archaeological educators. For six months of each year, the A.R.C. has operated public excavations in the downtown core. Annually, they have introduced more than 12,000 people to the world of archaeology and developed new programs on an ongoing basis, and at a furious pace.

The A.R.C. is the only public archaeology facility in the world run by a municipal school system. Furthermore, Toronto is a city with a complex past, a rapidly changing present, and a remarkably promising future. Being inside a school system in a large urban center means that the A.R.C. archeologists have had to respond to the changing needs of the city's population just as quickly as schools do—that is, immediately, if not sooner.

When my colleague Peter Hamalainen and I first conceived the idea of an archaeological education facility for Toronto, we had one stated goal: to raise a generation of Torontonians who would consider archaeology a real, vital, and intensely valuable part of what they liked about their city. We also intended to prove to the archaeological community at large that good, scholarly archaeology could be carried out in a fully public context. And we succeeded. For nine years the A.R.C. was staffed by seven archaeologists who have dedicated their careers to increasing public awareness of, and protection for, heritage resources. This remarkable group devoted itself to developing new and better mechanisms for teaching archaeology, and teaching *with* it. These are public servants in the truest sense of the term.

Because the A.R.C. has always conducted its work within the institutional requirements of a large urban school system, it has been forced to meet a complex set of criteria to carry out both research and education effectively. However, this system has also provided the Centre archaeologists with an enormously valuable resource base— the 15,000 employees of the Board of Education who make up the infrastructure of an urban school system.

There are authorities within the Board on every subject imaginable. Curriculum specialists in every conceivable area of knowledge, race relations advisors, social workers, educational psychologists, English-as-a-Second-Language instructors, French Immersion teachers, specialists in the education of variously challenged children—all have contributed time and energy to helping the A.R.C. develop and implement its programs. The Board's support staff also includes extremely helpful people ranging from computer analysts, telecommunications experts, architects, and urban planners to ironmongers, carpenters, locksmiths, and bulldozer drivers. Just imagine the possibilities!

Because the city's archaeology programs are operated by the public school board, access has always been provided directly to the people of the city. There is a built-in market, though one of a highly heterogeneous kind. It is not limited or targeted or systematized. Since 1985, archaeology in Toronto has been open to anyone who comes into contact, in any way, with the school system. The Centre ministers to an enormous and enormously varied public. The Board of Education has more than 100,000 students in regular day school. Its continuing education programs serve another 200,000, a good proportion of whom are immigrant adults.

It is endemic to the Centre's philosophy that we serve as many different needs as are evident within the school system. Thus, when it became apparent that there was a need for African-Canadian history programming in schools, the A.R.C. worked with the Department of Social Studies and developed an archaeology class and a teaching kit on that subject. Most programs have always been available in French, since

Canada is a bilingual nation and Toronto has a growing French Immersion program in several of its elementary and secondary schools. When educators working with hearing disabled children asked for archaeology programs at the Centre, one of the staff learned sign language and developed a fascinating field and lab program geared to those children's special needs.

Of particular note are programs offered in cooperation with social service agencies. Recently, a series of outreach classes was designed so that children institutionalized for emotional and behavioral reasons can also learn about Toronto's prehistoric and historic past through archaeology.

Curricula grow and evolve with time. Since the school board is immediately impacted by any change in the city's makeup, so are the A.R.C. programs. And we've done a considerable amount of actual archaeological research at the same time. It is a heady and exhausting and extremely exciting place to be.

Digging into the Past

The A.R.C. has always conducted its annual six-month excavation in Toronto's downtown core. Each site is chosen not only for its archaeological research potential, but also for its suitability for public education programs. Access to local transit systems, for instance, is a major criterion. Potential community involvement and support is another.

Each spring, long before a dig begins, relationships between the archaeologists and community organizations, local schools, and area social service agencies are established. This creates an "image" for the dig, which is, in a real sense, the neighborhood's exploration of its own heritage. Thus, a cooperative spirit and a true feeling of ownership in the site and its findings are created in advance. This community-based sentiment in favor of heritage discovery and conservation endures well after the bulldozer has filled in the excavation units on the last day of digging.

Press releases issued before the excavation commences invite everyone in the city to the opening ceremony. Brochures are produced in the languages of the area's largest ethnic groups. Whenever possible, the formal site opening—complete with ribbon cutting—is held as part of an already established community festival. One project took place in a largely Portuguese area of the city; the invitation for everyone to participate in the dig was announced in Portuguese, English, and Italian just before the *Portugal Day Festival Parade* arrived in the area. Some 150,000 people came out for that occasion. Marketing!

To maintain popular interest in each season's dig, an intensive public relations campaign is conducted throughout the entire six-month period. This includes maintaining strong media contacts; distributing brochures, site buttons, and handouts in schools and community centers; and providing speakers and displays at public locations.

Cooperation with community groups has always been a major factor in the A.R.C.'s success. Special interest groups that operate site tours, charities that bring day camps or seniors to participate in dig programs, social service agencies that arrange excavation field trips for underprivileged youth—all help spread the word that archaeology is fascinating and enjoyable. Literally anyone can come and book a program to help dig into their own city's past. And it's all free of charge. Coverage of public archaeology projects in Toronto by ethnic television, radio, and newspapers has ensured a steady stream of visitors to the sites each year. Even if the archaeologists' command of Mandarin or Swahili may be limited, artifacts and structural remains in the soil are self-explanatory. So are maps, historical photographs, and soil layers tagged with dates.

Which brings up another criterion for the type of site excavated by the A.R.C. We choose sites where we can reasonably expect both demolition debris and/or fill in the upper levels and a significant amount of below-ground architectural remains. The presence of demolition levels ensures that hands-on digging programs—with every artifact mapped in place and all dirt screened—can be conducted for even very young participants with minimal impact on the resource. Field-trip classes and inexperienced volunteers learn the principles of archaeological excavation—and experience the thrill of heritage discovery—in a context that is already highly disturbed and of minimal archaeological significance. (Of course, we don't *publicize* this; it would undermine the educational and experimental impact.) A ratio of six-to-one students to archaeologists is maintained at all times, and a strict lesson plan is followed throughout the programs. Because historical debris is rich in "old stuff," we can just about guarantee that everyone who digs finds something. That's pretty important when you think of the attention span of the average nine-year-old.

High school students take part in two 6-week credit courses each summer. Because the field schools provide a sufficiently comprehensive understanding of archaeological method and theory, much of the work on undisturbed levels is done by students enrolled in the summer courses. Experienced volunteers and staff members themselves undertake the more delicate, research-oriented excavation.

Another criterion for site choice has a public purpose as well. The presence of structural remains at deeper levels provides us with the perfect "textbook" for teaching archaeology. Walls, staircases, basement floors, and bits and pieces of architectural hardware are comprehensible and familiar to just about anyone who visits the site, even if the archeologist on site cannot explain the importance of such features in each visitor's mother tongue. Interesting stains in the ground are much harder to explain by pointing and gesturing!

The research design for all A.R.C. projects has always taken into account the public nature of our work. At the time the Centre was founded, it was decided that excavations should explore an aspect of our city's past that had hitherto been neglected. This was the archaeology of Toronto's ordinary people, their homes, businesses, and pioneer farms. The impact of this decision has been twofold. First and of primary importance, we are building up a corpus of new information about the life-ways of Toronto's immigrant neighborhoods during the 19th and early-20th centuries. Second, our findings are immediately comprehensible, at least in a general sense, to the majority of site visitors and program participants. Third, since many visitors are new Canadians themselves, the 19th century immigrant experience is not unfamiliar; they can identify with what earlier new Canadians went through.

Also intrinsic to the Centre's work is that all discoveries are fed immediately back into the realm of public knowledge. In addition to the production of the annual site report, booklets, and handouts written in clear language in various tongues are distributed to provide information to the public about what was learned from digging "their" site. After the analyses are completed, displays of findings are developed and mounted in the local schools and community centers.

A critical product of the community involvement engendered by public archaeological projects is site protection. For example, the A.R.C. digs are run in the inner city. Although security is provided, there is very rarely a problem. Local residents, children, are even the local derelicts have been known to scare off potential vandals after dark.

Teaching Archaeology in the Classroom

Over the winter months, one of the archaeologists' tasks is the development of new curriculum packages. The results of each excavation are included; hence, the research conducted by the Centre augments the corpus of heritage education material available in classrooms and resource libraries.

A wide variety of programs are offered through the A.R.C. between November and May. The facility has its own classroom and laboratory. Half-day field trips for school groups provide teachers with choices ranging from "The Archaeology of Toronto's Black Heritage" to First Nations cultural programs, Native pottery making, and a dramatization of Greek myths (in French!).

Given enough notice, the Centre staff will also design classes for students with special needs or interests. These might include a program on artifact conservation for a high school science class or a hieroglyphics lesson for Grade 4 students studying ancient Egypt as part of their social studies curriculum. (After all, when most people think of archaeology, what they envision is hardly confined to this continent.) As a result of this policy, the teaching archaeologists do a lot of last-minute cramming. Fortunately, the staff has sufficiently varied training and experience to cover most periods and geographic areas, at least for teaching elementary- and intermediate-level classes.

In addition to regular classroom programs, each year the A.R.C. offers four general-interest courses for adults in night school. A wonderful by-product of this is an evergrowing and faithful group of volunteers who devote afternoons to processing artifacts from the previous season's dig. With only seven permanent staff, the Centre has always depended heavily on volunteer and student help to complete necessary, if mundane, laboratory tasks. Many of the most regular participants in our volunteer corps are senior citizens. Their help and the richness of their own memories add immeasurably to the discussion around artifact-washing basins.

Winter is also a time when new initiatives can be undertaken. One interesting development resulted from a discussion with instructors at the Board of Education's English-as-a-Second-Language Department. Drawing from historical and archaeological research conducted by the Centre, a cooperative program was created for citizenship classes aimed at new immigrants. The program focused on teaching about Toronto's 19th century ethnic heritage while students improved their language skills.

Marketing Archaeology to a Multicultural Public

It has been said that an effective teacher is a combination of a ham actor and a used-car salesperson. It's very apt; one gets on stage and performs in front of a class. And what we're all really doing is selling ideas, ideas about archaeology.

What we see from the Toronto experience is the importance of borrowing from the fields of communications and marketing. This means tapping not only educators, but also people in advertising, marketing, and public relations. These individuals have wellhoned skills that can help archaeologists sell their own product—the preservation of the past for future generations.

Learning to communicate effectively is intrinsic to increasing public interest in work done by heritage experts. Archaeologists spend years of their lives in universities learning complex concepts and techniques, and speaking the language peculiar to their own profession. Then, most spend *more* years talking to other archaeologists on sites located miles from town. This type of training does not prepare an archeologist to explain the reason for this big "hole-in-the-ground-with-stakes-in-the-corners" to the average eight-year-old, or a passing bicycle courier, or the seniors' tour group who might venture forth to visit a public archaeology site. So we all need to learn to speak again in plain English (or whatever language seems appropriate). What's more, we have to explain to people who have never visited a site before, and perhaps never will again, that which is perfectly obvious to an archaeologist. The most important quality we have found for bridging the communications gap is actually very simple; it helps if your staff *likes* talking to the public. Not every archaeologist does, nor is every archaeology graduate going to be suited for a career as a public archaeologist. Stage fright, for instance, is a major handicap.

Public archaeology demands a whole new set of hiring criteria for site staff. The public archaeologist needs to speak and write effectively in clear English. Working knowledge of at least one other language is a definite asset. But perhaps the most important requirement for a public archeology applicant is a deep-seated desire to communicate his or her love for archaeology to just about anyone who comes along.

You can teach someone to fill in record forms or use a transit. You *can't* teach them how to be an enthusiastic ambassador for archaeology in a public setting.

To borrow a term from business, it is also vastly important to "know one's market." Interpreting archaeological concerns and information in a way that makes heritage accessible to the largest proportion of the population requires a real understanding of the political, demographic, cultural, and linguistic environment in which that area's archaeology is to be taught.

Here again the Centre benefits from its position inside the school system. Since schools are directly affected by any social, economic, demographic, or cultural change within the city, help is readily available to develop mechanisms for dealing with such changes. This is crucial with the highly multicultural, multiethnic environment in which the A.R.C. operates.

Since Toronto is both historically and currently a city of immigrants, English is not the mother tongue of a considerable number of our students; yet, they are now Torontonians. The heritage resources we are digging up are relics of their new country. One of our major objectives as a public archaeology institution is to give even the most recent arrivals to the city a sense of ownership in Toronto's wealth of heritage resources.

Designing relatively nonverbal programs that do not entail reading or writing English but that do allow participation in the archaeology process either at a site or in a classroom setting is a challenge facing archaeologists in Toronto and many other urban centers on a daily basis.

A brief look at the "top ten" nations in recent Toronto immigration patterns provides a graphic illustration of the linguistic diversity (see the following table). Obviously, all the children included in these numbers will attend Toronto schools. They and their parents are part of the Centre's ever-changing target audience.

Permanent Residents Destined for Toronto, 1990[1]	
Hong Kong	13,909
Poland	4,936
Philippines	4,264
Portugal	4,040
Jamaica	2,853
India	2,647
China	2,164
Sri Lanka	1,930
Britain	1,860
Vietnam	1,720

[1]Centre for Employment and Immigration, Employment and Immigration Canada, personal communication, Jan. 21, 1992

Conclusion

In 1992, the United Nations voted Toronto the most multicultural city in the world! This is the milieu in which nine years of *very* public archaeology programs have been operated by the Toronto Board of Education's Archaeological Resource Centre.

The Centre transmits many messages to its highly eclectic audience. The most important, however, is that everyone shares both the responsibility for and the pride in the ongoing conservation of their city's heritage resources.

Two major factors have contributed to the A.R.C.'s initial acceptance and continued success:

- The Centre was designed and marketed to the Toronto Board of Education in a form that was advantageous and beneficial to public education goals and requirements; and

- Programming at the A.R.C. is geared to meeting the needs of the students and educators that it serves.

Archeology programs in Toronto change with evolving educational, social, political, and economic trends that affect education in the city. They provide a real service in helping people deal with these changes.

Two more important factors contribute to the Centre's ongoing viability. One is the staff's deep commitment to the precepts of public archaeology. Staff members see themselves as public servants—they will find a way to teach literally *anyone* who wants to learn about the past. In fact, these public archaeology specialists make the process of learning so much fun that students, senior citizens, and adult volunteers keep coming back for more.

The other factor is good publicity, which is also a form of public education. The A.R.C. operates an intensive year-round publicity campaign to ensure that media contacts are maintained and nurtured; that interviews are regularly aired; and that the greatest number of people know about, enjoy, and follow the results of "this year's dig." Positive publicity ensures that archaeology in Toronto remains in the public consciousness and that the Board of Education's role in providing this unique learning experience to its urban constituents is recognized.

It has worked. Toronto has the largest metropolitan base in Canada. It is probably the most complex cultural, multicultural, and political environment in which to provide education of any kind in this country. The city is growing rapidly and the entire milieu in which archaeological education takes place is changing constantly with the city's demographic and immigration patterns.

Yet, archaeology has for several years been an integral and valued part of everyday life in the City of Toronto. This came about in a relatively short period of time, largely because of archaeology's role within the school system. Teaching archaeology to people of all ages, any and all backgrounds, and a huge variety of levels of ability and understanding prevents any possibility of exclusivity for this traditionally professional and scholarly pursuit.

The rewards of involving both schoolchildren and adults of all ages in the process of archaeological research are direct—more public appreciation for what archaeologists do, more political support for archaeological work, increased funds for research, reduced looting and site destruction from urban development and/or vandalism. The key is to find mechanisms for giving ordinary people a sense of ownership in their past. We archaeologists can do this by offering archaeology to all members of the public in ways that are accessible, comprehensible, and relevant to their everyday lives.

Chapter Nine

Ancient and Modern United:
Archaeological Exhibits in Urban Plazas

Introduction

In Mexico City the remains of an Aztec pyramid are incorporated *in situ* into the waiting area of a modern subway station. A diorama re-creating the temple environs during Aztec times is installed nearby. In the United States, however, it is unusual to find such exhibits in public urban spaces, even though the majority of the archaeo-logical projects in our cities are required by federal, state, or city environmental regulations. With the great increase in the number of urban archaeological projects mandated by the government in the last two decades, one may well ask how the American public benefits from this work.

Since the early 1980s, historical archaeologists have been concerned about this question and have urged, both informally and formally in workshops and symposia, that the results of these excavations be disseminated to the public through either popular reports or exhibits. Unfortunately, with the notable exceptions of those pre-pared by the Delaware Department of Transportation for Wilmington (Klein and Friedlander 1983) and the University of Arizona's report on excavations in Phoenix (Bartlett, Kolaz, and Gregory 1987), very few popular accounts of urban excavations have been produced. And although there have been a number of exhibits on urban archaeology at museums throughout the country, most of these have been temporary exhibits. In fact, the only substantial permanent public exhibit on the archaeology of a modern American city that we are aware of is the National Park Service's installa-tion at Franklin Court in Philadelphia.

Incorporating permanent archaeological exhibits into modern office buildings and plazas can be one lasting and effective way of disseminating urban archaeological information to the public. During the last decade, there have been three examples of archaeological exhibits incorporated into modern office towers in the Wall Street district of New York City: 85 Broad Street, Barclays Bank at 75 Wall Street, and 17 State Street (Figures 9.1 and 9.2). In this article, we discuss the legal issues sur-rounding the creation of these exhibits, their substance, and some of the problems

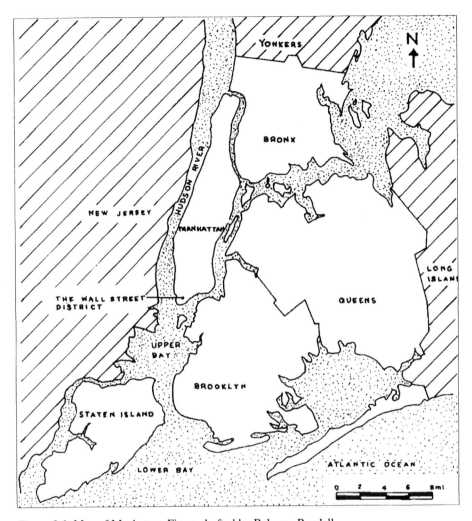

Figure 9.1. Map of Manhattan. Figure drafted by Rebecca Randall.

encountered in their execution and maintenance. Our goal is twofold. First, we want to show how, with a creative approach, archaeological exhibits can become beneficial byproducts of the delicate negotiation process between developers and government agencies. Second, we want to demonstrate how archaeological materials can effectively be included in the design of modern office towers, uniting the past and present into a pleasing visual and educational experience. The New York City exhibits can be used, we hope, as examples for other cities.

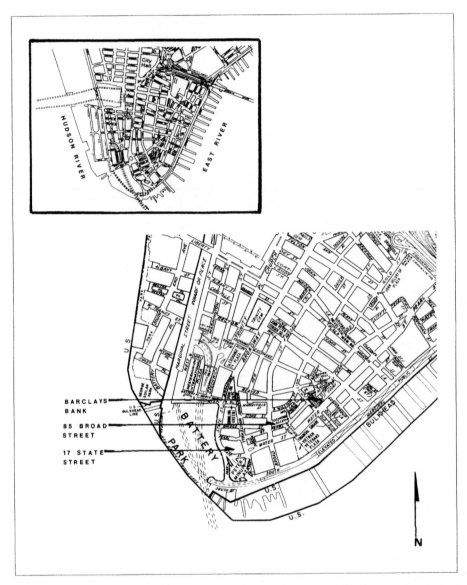

Figure 9.2. Map of the Wall Street area showing the location of the three archaeological exhibits. Figure drafted by Susan Pacek and based on maps from the New York City Planning Commission.

85 Broad Street

The Legal Issues

In 1968, Lehman Brothers, the brokerage house, requested that a New York City–designated landmark—a commercial building at 71 Pearl Street—be demolished to make way for a new office building in the financial district of Lower Manhattan. The landmark was thought to have been erected in 1700 using part of the foundation from the 1641 Dutch City Hall, the Stadt Huys. In 1826, the structure underwent major alterations resulting in its late Federal-style facade. The building was designated on the basis of the 1826 facade and the 1641, 1700, and 1826 components of the foundation (NYCLPC 1966:1). In 1970, the New York City Landmarks Preservation Commission (Landmarks Commission, or NYCLPC) agreed to allow the developer to demolish the structure if the developer would remove the facade, store it, and later reerect it at another site near the South Street Seaport Museum (NYCLPC 1966). The facade was removed and stored, and the building was torn down.

Because of economic reasons, the plan for the development was dropped by Lehman Brothers, who converted the empty block to a parking lot. In 1979, the Dollar Savings Bank, which had acquired the property in the intervening decade and wanted to sell it to a developer, had to reapply to the Landmarks Commission for a permit to build on the site because Lehman Brothers had not completed the terms of the original 1970 agreement to reerect the historic facade (NYCLPC 1980).

During the intervening decade, however, there had been several changes in preservation philosophy. Preservationists no longer looked favorably on the reconstruction of a building facade removed from its original site. In addition, although archaeologists working in other American cities had begun to show that the remains of the urban past could be found intact sealed beneath the modern city, no largescale excavation had yet taken place in New York. Because the parcel under consideration was located in the heart of 17th century Dutch New Amsterdam and was the site of the Stadt Huys—New Amsterdam's and hence New York's first City Hall—it appeared to be a prime test case for archaeology in New York City. If an archaeological site could be found in the heart of the Wall Street district, then archaeological remains could certainly be preserved in less developed parts of the city.

The Landmarks Commission therefore suggested that, instead of reerecting the 71 Pearl Street facade, the developer finance an excavation to uncover any archaeological remains on the parcel (NYCLPC 1980). The legal process requiring excavation was not part of the environmental review process; rather, it was part of the regulations regarding the recision of the designation of a landmark as covered under the 1965 New York City Landmarks law.

During 1979 and 1980, archaeologists, under the direction of Nan Rothschild and coauthor Diana diZerega Wall, excavated the site. They uncovered thousands of 17th century artifacts and many features, including the partial foundation wall of a tavern built in 1670, an early-18th century well, and the remnants of Stone Street—a 17th century thoroughfare. The Stadt Huys foundation, supposedly part of the 71 Pearl Street foundation, was not found.

In 1980, as part of the recision of the landmark designation, the Landmarks Commission required that the developer design and install an archaeological exhibit in the plaza of the new building (NYCLPC 1980:2–3). Representatives of the developer, including staff members from the architectural firm Skidmore, Owens, and Merrill; members of the Landmarks Commission staff, including Executive Director Lenore Norman, Counsel Dorothy Miner, Director of Preservation Margaret Tuft, and City Archaeologist Sherene Baugher (a coauthor of this article); and the project archaeologists, Nan Rothschild and Diana Wall, all discussed the content and design of the exhibit and how to integrate 17th century architectural elements into a modern plaza with heavy pedestrian traffic. The developer agreed to incorporate architectural elements uncovered during the archaeological excavation. The emphasis was on architecture rather than artifacts because the entire project had been proposed for the recision of the landmark designation of an historic building.

The Exhibit

The permanent outdoor exhibit—*The Archaeology of the Stadt Huys Block*—opened to the public in 1984 (Figure 9.3). It was developed by Rothschild and Wall, the project archaeologists; designed by a team from Skidmore, Owens, and Merrill, the architectural firm that designed the office tower; and reviewed by the Landmarks Commission, which commented on the exhibit's concept, text, and design. The exhibit focused on the 17th and early-18th century architecture and street plan of the site (which was on the 17th century East River shore of Dutch New Amsterdam) by highlighting elements from four colonial features: the 17th century Lovelace Tavern, the early-18th century well, the 17th century thoroughfare of Stone Street, and the 17th century Stadt Huys. The design addresses both educational needs and concerns about pedestrian flow in an open, heavily trafficked public space.

A large, free-standing vertical brass plaque introduces the exhibit and describes the excavations. The plaque is located at the border between the sidewalk and the plaza—a highly visible but relatively low-traffic area for this open urban space. The plaque includes a map of the exhibit area and a reproduction 17th century view of Manhattan's shore highlighting the first two components of the exhibit—the Stadt Huys and the tavern (Figure 9.4). The outlines of the original footprints of these buildings are marked in the plaza with contrasting colored pavers. For safety reasons, the pavers are laid flush with the surrounding pavement.

The Stadt Huys was built in 1641 as a tavern and, when New Amsterdam became a municipality in 1653, it was converted into the Stadt Huys, or state house (Rothschild, Boesch, and Wall 1987). Since no foundation walls from the Stadt Huys structure were found in the excavations, historical documents provided the information on its dimensions and location, which is outlined in modern yellow brick in the plaza.

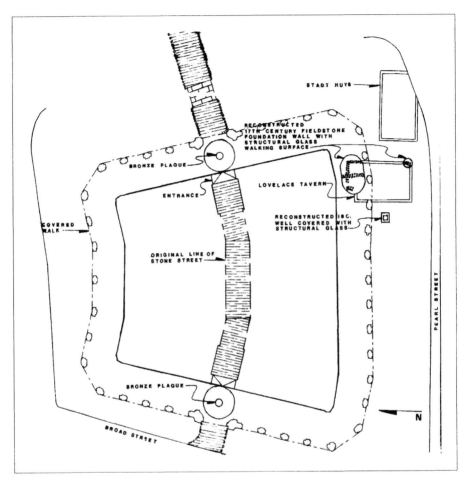

Figure 9.3. Schematic map from the exhibit at 85 Broad Street. Map drafted by Susan Pacek and based on data from Skidmore, Owens, and Merrill's exhibit designs for the plaza of the 85 Broad Street building.

The Lovelace Tavern, immediately to the west of the Stadt Huys (Figure 9.4), was built in 1670 by Governor Francis Lovelace, the second British governor of the province. It was torn down in 1706 (Rockman and Rothschild 1984:115). The archaeologists uncovered most of the stone foundation wall and thousands of artifacts associated with the tavern. The outline of the tavern is marked with gray granite pavers. There are two underground "windows" flush with the plaza floor revealing portions of the reconstructed foundation wall. One of these windows includes elements from three different structures that were on the parcel at different times in its

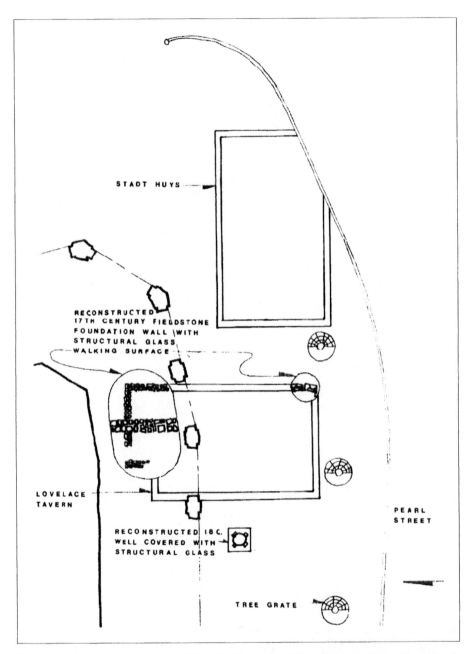

Figure 9.4. Close-up map of the exhibit in 85 Broad Street plaza. Map drafted by Susan Pacek and based on data from Skidmore, Owens, and Merrill's exhibit designs for the plaza of the 85 Broad Street building.

history: the tavern wall, a stone wall from an early-19th century building, and a support beam for the modern building. A color photograph of some of the bottles, tobacco pipes, and marbles found in the tavern is also on view in this window.

The design of the windows in the plaza raised a number of questions about safety, liability, and security. There was concern that the public might slip on the plexiglass covers, particularly in inclement weather. Waist-high railings surrounding each window solved the problem. While this solution interferes with traffic flow in the plaza, it is preferable to injuries and lawsuits. It was also originally proposed that the larger window contain some of the artifacts that were uncovered during the excavation of the tavern. A photograph of the artifacts was substituted because of security concerns.

The third exhibit component is an early-18th century well consisting of arc-shaped bricks laid end-to-end to form a circle. It was not reconstructed in its original location because that would have placed it inside the modern building. The reconstructed well, which was originally totally underground, is caped by an elevated 20-inch-high, red-brick cube with a viewing window on the top.

The fourth and final component of the exhibit incorporates the lobby of the 85 Broad Street building itself (Figure 9.3). The building's footprint encompasses portions of three separate blocks. Part of Stone Street, the 17th century thoroughfare, was demapped for the new building. The Landmarks Commission asked that the 85 Broad Street lobby align with Stone Street to retain this part of the 17th century street plan. The old street line is marked by brown pavers along the lobby floor. They extend outside the lobby to connect with the two-block stretch of Stone Street that is still intact to the east of the building. The Landmarks Commission also requested that the doors at each end of the lobby be made of glass so that one can stand inside the lobby and, looking through the doors, see the winding, narrow 17th century street. Circular plaques set flush with the ground at both entrances to the lobby proclaim the exhibit's presence. The brass plaques include a reproduction of a 1660 map of New Amsterdam showing the location of Stone Street (or the Hoogh Straat, meaning High Street, as it was then called) and indicates the viewer's position with a "YOU ARE HERE" label.

The Problems

Unfortunately, the 85 Broad Street exhibit has been beset with design and maintenance problems. The underground display cases were installed without adequate ventilation, and ever since the exhibit opened, condensation has been a continual problem. Often the plexiglass covers fog up to such an extent that it is impossible to see the displays. Maintenance is another problem. The plexiglass covers, badly scratched through the years, have not been replaced. In addition, the lights in the displays frequently burn out and are not replaced as soon as they should be. The displays often lie in darkness. Some of the cases leak, and the displays within are water stained. The color photograph of the artifacts is both water stained and faded. No one is responsible for seeing that the exhibit is properly maintained.

The Landmarks Commission has had no mandate over the exhibit since it opened. However, it has learned from this example that agreements establishing exhibits must allocate responsibility for maintenance to a museum or other institution with both the expertise and willingness to take care of problems as they arise. Finally, it is important to remember that the excavation only occurred as mitigation for the loss of a landmark building. While the exhibit in the plaza is a desirable public amenity, it is hoped that the actions, with all their legal implications, which made the 85 Broad Street project possible, not be repeated.

75 Wall Street

The Legal Issues

In 1984, Barclays Bank planned to build an office tower for its headquarters at 75 Wall Street. It requested a discretionary permit from the city to construct a larger building than allowed by law. The request triggered an environmental review, which required an archaeological excavation. This was undertaken by the firm of Louis Berger & Associates, Inc., and paid for by the developers, Barclays Bank and the London and Leeds Corporation. The excavation uncovered the remains of houses and shops from the late 18th and early-19th centuries. The archaeological mitigation required by the environmental review process included excavation of the site, cataloguing and analysis of the artifacts, and production of a site report (Louis Berger & Associates 1987). After construction was well under way, Barclays Bank asked the New York City Planning Commission if it could incorporate an archaeological exhibit into two of the plaza windows. The exhibit would be installed inside the building but viewed through the windows from the plaza outside. The bank was interested in installing the exhibit because of city restrictions on the kinds of establishments that can be viewed by the public through plaza windows. By mounting the exhibit in this way, the bank would not be bound by these restrictions and would have more flexibility in finding a tenant for their groundfloor retail space (pers. com. Marion Cotrone, Barclays Bank, 1992). The city agreed to the bank's proposal. This was the first time in New York that an archaeological exhibit was proposed and accepted as a viable use of plaza windows and first-floor rental space to fulfill a city requirement. This exhibit was displayed for over five years and was only removed when the bank found an appropriate tenant for the adjacent ground floor rental space."

The legal negotiations were conducted between the bank and City Planning Commission staff. Baugher, as City Archaeologist, participated in design discussions but could only provide nonbinding suggestions regarding the theme and text of the exhibit because the Landmarks Commission had no regulatory power in this case. The South Street Seaport Museum's Director of Museum Programs, Sally Yerkovich, and Curator of Archaeology, Diana Wall, also participated in the discussions because Barclays Bank had donated the archaeological collection to the museum.

The museum, like the Landmarks Commission, had no control over the content or design of the exhibit but accepted responsibility for its maintenance so as to oversee the condition of the artifacts. The bank staff and their exhibit designers assured the Landmarks Commission that the interior location of the exhibit would permit easy access for cleaning, maintenance, and repairs, thus avoiding the problems encountered at 85 Broad Street.

The Exhibit

The resulting exhibit at 75 Wall Street, *The Barclays Bank Site: Three Hundred Years in the Financial District,* explored the commercial history of the site, which was located in the financial heart of the city. It also interpreted one of Manhattan's earliest landfills, dating to the turn of the 18th century. The exhibit was developed by Mallory Gordon and Meta Janowitz of Louis Berger & Associates—the firm that excavated the site in 1984—and designed by Malcolm Grear, Providence, Rhode Island. Displayed on a freestanding installation, the exhibit was contained in an extremely limited space in two windows on the building's ground floor. Viewed from the outdoor plaza just to the south of the office tower, the exhibit windows face the plaza's southwest corner.

The exhibit introduced urban archaeology through text and graphics, including photographs of the excavations and a map of the archaeological features uncovered at the site. It then presented the concept of landfill, interpreted the history of a landfill lot at the site, and included a map showing the landfill history of Manhattan. The text identified Christina Veenvos, a widow, as the original developer of the parcel. In 1696, she purchased the water rights to a submerged lot and then immediately subdivided and resold most of the parcel (Louis Berger & Associates 1987[2]:C-36). She then developed the remainder of the water lot by making land through filling and then erected the property's first building, which she rented out as an investment—a true New York story (Louis Berger & Associates 1987[2]:C-37). A delft tile from this house and some yellow brick provided the artifacts for this part of the exhibit.

The second window featured archaeological materials associated with three different commercial establishments that existed on the property in the late-18th and early-19th centuries—those of a craftsman, a druggist, and a merchant. In the 1780s, Daniel Van Voorhis, a silversmith, and his family lived and worked on the property, which at that time was close to the homes of his wealthy clients (Wall 1987:320). Domestic materials, such as creamware plates and porcelain teacups, and metallurgical equipment, including crucibles for melting precious metals, were on view. Joel and Jotham Post, a druggist and physician respectively, lived and worked on the property in the 1790s (Louis Berger & Associates 1987[1]:IV–15). The exhibit incorporated drug paraphernalia from their shop, such as patent medicine bottles, vials, and ointment pots (including a creamware vessel with a transferprinted label describing its contents as a remedy for baldness). Finally, the exhibit presented materials from the countinghouse of David Dunham, a commercial merchant who occupied the property during the first two decades of the 19th century (Louis Berger & Associates 1987[2]:C-38). These artifacts included French and British liquor bottles and British-made ceramics, which Dunham was presumably importing. Taken together, these components evoked both home and work life on the site in the half century following the American Revolution.

The Problems

Because of the museum's involvement, the exhibit at Barclays Bank was spared the maintenance problems that have so beset the exhibit at 85 Broad Street. But still there are problems related to design and layout. For example, one of the exhibit highlights—a rare stoneware crock marked with the name of a local New York City potter—was obscured by the brass frame of the window. Unfortunately, neither the bank nor the design firm had had experience in designing historical exhibits, and the museum and Landmarks Commission (which both had experience) had had no control over the design. The other major problem with this exhibit was its location. It was hard to find unless you knew it was there. The windows are hidden in an arcade behind pillars, and there was no signage in the plaza proclaiming that the exhibit exists (Figure 9.5).

17 State Street

The Legal Issues

The museum exhibit in the plaza of the office building at 17 State Street was produced as mitigation for the destruction of an archaeological site (Figure 9.6). This project, like the 85 Broad Street exhibit, was triggered by legal maneuvers that we hope will not be repeated. The site developer requested a discretionary permit from the city that, in turn, required an environmental review. The Landmarks Commission advised the Planning Commission that the site of the proposed new office tower, located at the southern tip of Manhattan near South Ferry, potentially contained archaeological material from the 17th and 18th centuries (NYCLPC 1986a). While the environmental review was pending, the developer obtained an as-of-right permit, excavated the site for the building foundation, and thus destroyed any traces of the potential archaeological site (NYCLPC 1986a). A subsequent documentary study required by the Planning Commission and paid for by the developer showed that:

> ... the portion of the project area known as Lot 23 had been relatively undisturbed and was identified . . . as having had archaeological sensitivity prior to the beginning of construction excavation for this project. (Vollmer Associates 1986:[3]44)

Figure 9.5. Photograph of the exhibit, "The Barclays Bank Site," showing its obscure location in the plaza at 75 Wall Street. Photograph by Diana Wall.

Owned from 1728 to 1754 by Abraham Isaacs, a merchant and member of New York's Jewish community, this site could have been the first 18th century Jewish home excavated in the northeast. Thus it had archaeological significance for both New York and the northeast region of the country (Vollmer Associates 1986:[3]45).

The destruction of the 17 State Street site seriously challenged the enforcement of the archaeological requirement under the city's environmental review regulations. If a developer could destroy an archaeological site while its project was undergoing an environmental review and if it did not have to mitigate the loss of the site, then the whole process would be undermined. The project became a test case that went before the city's Board of Standards and Appeals—the body that, at that time, resolved conflicts between applicants and the Planning Commission. The Landmarks Commission requested some form of mitigation for the loss of the archaeological site, while the developer's battery of attorneys fought hard to avoid mitigation. Community and professional groups, including the Professional Archaeologists of New York City, supported the request for mitigation at public hearings (Wall 1986). The Board decided in favor of mitigation. The Landmarks Commission—represented by Executive Director Joseph Bresnan, City Archaeologist Sherene Baugher, and Director of Environmental Review Jeremy Woodoff—drafted a mitigation plan that included a permanent museum exhibit and a maintenance plan (Woodoff 1986). The draft was discussed with the developer's legal counsel, and some modifications were made. In 1986, the Board of Standards and Appeals, the developer, and the Landmarks Commission agreed to this plan (NYCLPC 1986).

Under the memorandum of agreement, the developer would pay for the design and installation of an exhibit on New York City archaeology and support its maintenance, management, and public education programs for five years. The developer could, however, turn over the administration and operation of the exhibit to a museum or university, which was done in 1989 through an arrangement with the South Street Seaport Museum. To ensure completion of the exhibit and avoid the problems experienced at the 85 Broad Street site, the developer could not obtain a permanent Certificate of Occupancy for its building until the conditions of the agreement were fulfilled and approved by the Landmarks Commission.

The Exhibit

New York Unearthed: City Archaeology, the exhibit at 17 State Street, opened in the fall of 1990. It is located in a small building in the plaza and is connected underground to the office tower. The museum has two floors of exhibit space: about 400 square feet at the plaza level and around 1,200 square feet at the level below. Unlike the other two exhibits, *New York Unearthed* does not examine the archaeology

Figure 9.6. Photograph of the exhibit, "New York Unearthed," in the plaza at 17 State Street. Photograph by Diana Wall.

of one particular site but rather examines many sites, interpreting the archaeology of the city as a whole. The exhibit consists of six components:

1. The first begins on street level with ten 4-foot-wide dioramas that descend along a ramp. Each diorama comprises a three-dimensional collage depicting a historical scene from the city's past; under each collage is a case of artifacts from archaeological sites directly related to the scene. The dioramas are arranged in chronological order, from the 20th century back to Native American times, so that as visitors walk down the ramp they go back through time.

2. Next, visitors go to the lower level where, upon entering, a large accordion wall offers a view of the city's shoreline in the mid-18th century and later, on exiting, a modern view of the late-20th century shoreline (including, of course, the 17 State Street building).

3. Across from the accordion wall, on the left, is the third component, a small panel exhibit entitled *Unearthing the City's Past*. Through text and photographs it describes the steps of the archaeological process: background research, excavation, and laboratory and analysis.

4. The centerpiece of the exhibit is a state-of-the-art conservation laboratory. In this glass-enclosed space, visitors can watch conservators as they stabilize the artifacts from the South Street Seaport Museum's archaeological collections. The public can interact with the conservators through large, sliding-glass windows.

5. The fifth component, *Beneath the City*, shows how archaeological remains can survive even in a heavily urbanized area. This display, a bas-relief cross-section of an archaeological site in the Wall Street district, explains how features, such as early basement floors, privies, landfill, and even the old shore of the East River, can be sealed and preserved under the relatively shallow basements of the city's smaller, older buildings. The cross-section, constructed at approximately two-thirds scale, incorporates display cases that feature real artifacts as if they were *in situ*.

6. Finally, at the far end of the space is a video theater, which is concealed behind a wall designed to resemble Manhattan schist (the bedrock of Manhattan Island). The ten-capacity theater is mounted on hydraulic fittings and simulates an elevator; it bounces and bumps and even gives the illusion of a freefall for dramatic effect. In the eight-minute video, the elevator—named UeNYSe (pronounced *Eunice*) for *Unearthing New York Systems elevator*—is endowed with "artificial intelligence." In the course of the story line, UeNYSe takes the viewer down under the ground to visit an archaeological excavation and interviews an archaeologist named Archie about his project. Archie provides a tour of his site, explains parts of the archaeological process, and shows some of his finds.

Many were involved in the creation of *New York Unearthed*. Milton Glaser, Inc., a firm hired by the developer, designed and developed all of the space, most of the graphics and signage, and some of the exhibit components (including the ten dioramas and the accordion wall). Joel Grossman, Kate T. Morgan, and Diana Wall served as the archaeological consultants. The museum joined the project only after its development was well under way. Museum representatives Sally Yerkovich and Diana Wall added some components for their programming needs, such as the panels showing the archaeological process and the site crosssection. Museum staff and Grossman were the forces behind the conservation laboratory, which in addition to being used for programs also ensures the stabilization of the museum's archaeological collections. The museum staff also helped develop and review the text for most of the exhibits. The theater and video were developed by Spiegel-Horton and SMA Video, with Grossman serving as archaeological consultant. The Landmarks Commission representatives—Baugher, Bresnan, Woodoff, and Chairman David Todd—also played an important role. They suggested, commented on, and approved the text, artifacts, and design for the dioramas, the conservation laboratory, and the underground crosssection.

The Problems

Although *New York Unearthed* was potentially a conceptual hodgepodge because of all the parties involved in its creation, fortunately, this hazard was averted. The building's new owner has voluntarily continued to support the exhibit well beyond the five-year period that was legally mandated. In fact, *New York Unearthed* is not only the most ambitious but also the most successful of the three New York exhibits. There is just one problem with the exhibit. Although the video is very popular, its sophisticated technology still has some bugs in it, and, unfortunately, the system is often closed for repairs.

Conclusion

The three exhibits, implemented under different regulatory requirements by local government agencies, provide examples of how local governments can take advantage of existing circumstances to encourage the installation of permanent archaeological exhibits in modern urban spaces. These exhibits have enhanced the public's awareness of New York City's rich archaeological heritage. They provide the public with the only permanent, tangible evidence we have of the city's numerous excavations. They are concrete reminders of the people who lived and worked in New York throughout its history.

Chapter Ten

The Evolution of Interpretation:
The Charleston Place Site

Introduction

In the United States a false dichotomy often exists between "archaeological research" and the "public interpretation" of such research. This is due in large measure to the discontinuity that occurs between the quality and/or quantity of data generated by archaeologists and how the data are ultimately presented by exhibit programmers and designers. Museum personnel and public historians often debate the way objects should be used and interpreted. As archaeology becomes increasingly self-aware and is forced to confront current social issues, such as repatriation (Baker and Thomas 1990; Messenger 1989; Pinsky and Wylie 1989; Tilley 1990), it may find a natural ally in the relatively new social history that stresses "history from the bottom up." As defined by Michael Ettema (1987:75), this phrase was intended to highlight a concern for the long-neglected masses of ordinary people, but it also points to an interest in the minute details of daily life, such as diet, hygiene, gender roles, housing patterns, work habits, and family ties. This motivation stems from a growing awareness that the way ordinary people lived their lives in the past has an effect on the way we live our ordinary lives today. Following from this is a new emphasis on interpretation through exhibits and programs. Some have argued that this new approach deemphasizes objects; interpretation becomes "books pasted on the wall." It is currently the charge of the museums and their interpretive staff to strike a balance between objects and their interpretation through the theory of the social function of objects. And it is precisely this theory that drives much of archaeological research. It is also this theoretical orientation that opens the door for archaeological research and objects to share equally in the public interpretation of the past (Blatti 1987).

One of the basic problems to be explored is the difference in perspective between technically oriented archaeologists, who often speak in jargon and never write fewer than 1,500 pages per site, and exhibit planners and site interpreters, who strive to present an uncomplicated, educational, and entertaining program (Alderson and Low 1985). One obvious result of this dichotomy is the tendency for each group to create an exclusive past based on their own perspective. According to Ian Hodder, this dichotomy separates researchers from the indigenous "owners" of the past (1991a:13). When esoteric technical vocabularies possessed only by specially trained professionals are used to describe archaeological and historical data, only those who walk that walk and talk that talk have access to this evidence. Museum visitors are either intimidated or bored by this intellectual franchise, resulting not just in unpopular exhibits but also in a cultural hegemony predicated on public non-engagement. This point is brought home to us every semester when students enrolled in one of our introductory archaeology courses at the University of Tennessee review some of our professional publications and reports (including a "popularized" booklet on the Charleston Place site that we coauthored.) Even though these students might be expected to positively temper their reviews in the interest of their grades, many are outraged that the professional articles are so obscure. It is very clear to these students who is dominating the production of the past in these publications, and they don't like being excluded. They feel cheated. They *should* feel cheated.

This is not to suggest that archaeology should present a romanticized view of the past, always subject to the will of any interested (engaged) group that happens to have an interpretive agenda. Hodder stresses that it is essential to differentiate the claims of subordinate groups seeking to establish their right to knowledge from the claims of those promoting fringe, unfounded archaeologies. (Since one of us lives and works 40 miles from the site of the Scopes Trial, "scientific creationism" comes immediately to mind.) There is more than one way to achieve "guarded objectivity," however, and a dialogue with the public can contribute to this goal. Jargon results only in monologues.

We believe the technical/interpretive dichotomy is artificial and harmful to the best interests of archaeologists and interpreters (not to mention the public). We also believe such a dichotomy can be alleviated by an interactive, interdisciplinary relation between the two groups. To exhibit and interpret archaeological research, museum personnel must receive more than a copy of the technical report. Archaeologists must strive to communicate what is unique, exciting, and new from their research. This may necessitate a long-term commitment on the part of both groups. Advances have been made on this front, as illustrated by the interpretation surrounding a large urban project in Charleston, South Carolina—a project that began in 1981 and is still evolving.

The Evolution of Charleston Place

Coordinated by the National Park Service's Southeast Regional Office in Atlanta, research at the Charleston Place site was undertaken by the Jeffrey L. Brown Institute of Archaeology, University of Tennessee at Chattanooga, and The Charleston Museum as part of cultural resource management (CRM) compliance required by the construction of an Urban Development Action Grant–assisted development project

(Figure 10.1). Located in the Charleston Historic District, the one-block project area was initially tested by the Institute to determine if any National Register–eligible archaeological remains were present. Six weeks of Institute testing and data-recovery fieldwork in 1981 were followed by weeks of demolition monitoring and salvage data recovery by The Charleston Museum in 1981 and 1985. In addition, several weeks of site-specific documentary research occurred before, during, and after fieldwork.

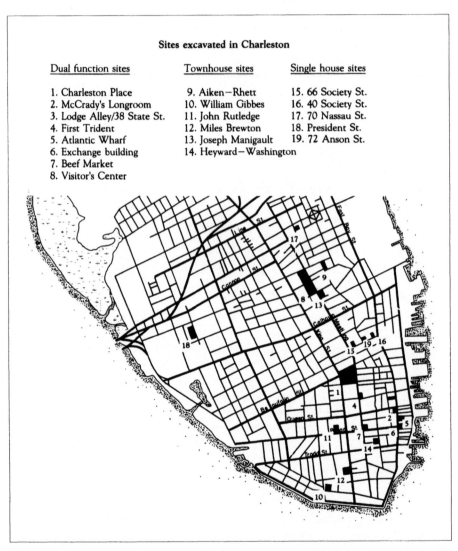

Sites excavated in Charleston

Dual function sites	Townhouse sites	Single house sites
1. Charleston Place	9. Aiken–Rhett	15. 66 Society St.
2. McCrady's Longroom	10. William Gibbes	16. 40 Society St.
3. Lodge Alley/38 State St.	11. John Rutledge	17. 70 Nassau St.
4. First Trident	12. Miles Brewton	18. President St.
5. Atlantic Wharf	13. Joseph Manigault	19. 72 Anson St.
6. Exchange building	14. Heyward–Washington	
7. Beef Market		
8. Visitor's Center		

Figure 10.1. Map of peninsular Charleston, showing the location of Charleston Place and other excavated sites. Map by Martha Zierden (courtesy The Charleston Museum collections).

Documentary data indicates that the site was originally occupied by a small number of domestic structures in the early-18th century. Located on a main thoroughfare in early Charleston, combination domestic/commercial structures almost completely covered the site by the mid-19th century (Figure 10.2), and numerous building, demolition, and rebuilding episodes were reflected in both the documentary and archaeological records. Over 300 square meters were excavated at the site (Figure 10.3), resulting in the recording of more than 165 features and the recovery of more than 15,000 artifacts dating to the 17th through 20th centuries. Besides establishing the existence of an extensive, coherent archaeological record, researchers successfully investigated a number of important issues concerning site structure and function. Research themes included the following:

- Settlement: the documentary and archaeological correlates of settlement patterning changes and use of urban space through time;

- Function: the delineation of site function, particularly domestic versus commercial activities as monitored by artifact type;

- Resources: the testing of a regional model of resource utilization through the application of biomass and MNI (minimum number of individuals) determinations for the faunal assemblage (187 kilograms of bone were analyzed); and

- Change: the impact of three centuries of changes in trash, waste, and water procurement practices on the site (Honerkamp and Council 1984; Honerkamp, Council, and Will 1982; Zierden and Hacker 1987).

Institute researchers originally proposed these topics specifically for this site. The Charleston Museum later produced a City Research Design that incorporated and expanded the topics, which were then explored at several other urban sites (Zierden and Calhoun 1984).

Following completion of the fieldwork by the Institute and the first phase of salvage work by the Museum, a small exhibit was prepared by Museum staff. It was one of five archaeological exhibits located in the anthropology hall of the museum (Zierden 1984). All five exhibits were project-specific, descriptive, and designed to teach basic lessons about urban archaeology, such as the following:

- Cities do contain archaeological remains that can provide important information on the past.

- The importance of these remains lies not in the artifacts themselves, but in their association and context.

- Large-scale development projects (the impetus behind all urban projects at that time) would destroy these fragile remains if they were not excavated in a controlled manner.

These were, and still are, important points to make to the public. They can remain integral to interpretation yet be presented subtly, along with broader interpretations of the past, through a consideration of archaeological material culture.

For the most part, the exhibits showed a number of artifacts that were aesthetically pleasing but minimally interpreted within the context of urban development. This was partially rectified in 1983 by the preparation of an introductory panel on "Urban Archaeology in Charleston" and by an attempt to have each project exhibit address two general research themes—the determination of socioeconomic status and site function on dual residential/commercial sites. While this served as a first step in presenting a unified approach to archaeological research, the exhibits and their material culture still seemed distant, removed from the general flow of history as presented in other media. The situation, in a way, epitomized the position of urban archaeology in relation to more traditional disciplines.

The archaeological project at Charleston Place resulted in two lengthy technical monographs and the accumulation of nearly 300 cubic feet of cultural materials. This large project thus became the cornerstone of archaeological research in Charleston. Likewise, the newly constructed hotel/shopping/convention complex became the cornerstone of Charleston's downtown revitalization. The project thus became a logical vehicle for a greater dissemination of information on the history beneath the now-central complex. A smaller booklet summarizing the studies was envisioned and the project was enthusiastically endorsed by the city of Charleston. City government personnel suggested that the principal developer, a business magnate from Baltimore, might be delighted to fund this very modest project ($2,500). Having already completed his work in Charleston and moved on, he declined. The booklet project languished for lack of funds. Finally, an impetus came when the city of Charleston and Mayor Joseph P. Riley, Jr., hosted the National Conference of Mayors in 1989. The city was spruced up to be seen at its best, and Charleston Place was to be the focal point of the conference, both as the hosting facility and a hallmark of municipal accomplishment. To this end, the city funded publication of the booklet and requested an on-site exhibit for the duration of the conference (Figure 10.4). The city retained half of the 500 booklets published to distribute to the attending mayors and visiting dignitaries; the other half were to be sold by The Charleston Museum (Honerkamp and Zierden 1989).

The booklet was published as part of The Charleston Museum's *Leaflet Series,* which includes occasional publications dating from as early as 1925. Like the booklet, other publications in the series are short summaries of research that are designed for the general reader. The Museum has long-range plans to expand and continue this publication program, and other archaeological leaflets are envisioned.

Figure 10.2. King Street in 1902, in the vicinity of the Charleston Place site (courtesy The Charleston Museum collections).

Figure 10.3. Mapping and excavating a brick-lined well. Photograph by Nicholas Honerkamp (courtesy The Charleston Museum collections).

Figure 10.4. The archaeological exhibit at the National Conference of Mayors, 1989. Photograph by Martha Zierden (courtesy The Charleston Museum collections).

The Evolution of Museum Interpretation

During this period of evolution in the Charleston Place project, the face of The Charleston Museum was also changing. In 1983, the mission of the Museum shifted from a worldwide, all-encompassing focus to a concentration on the preservation and interpretation of Low Country social and natural history. A long-term plan was developed for the Museum, its historic houses, and its wildlife sanctuary. As part of these changes, the archaeology program and its staff were converted to a permanent curatorial department at the Museum, and the archaeologist and historian began to work with other curators on projects integral to the Museum mission, including exhibition, the upgrade of curatorial facilities, conservation, and long-range planning.

Most ambitious were plans for new permanent exhibitions in three galleries, two focusing on social history and the largest covering natural history. Extensive planning resulted in exhibitions that were thematically inclusive and exhaustive.

The history halls, designed to present the panorama of human experience from prehistory to the 20th century, were organized by topic within a general chronology. During the planning process, the archaeology staff members suggested new topics and new approaches to traditional topics. When themes were narrowed and artifact selection began, a radical approach was taken. Archaeological artifacts were "treated as equals" with documents and decorative arts examples; all were exhibited in the same cases when interpreting the same concepts. In the first gallery, archaeological artifacts illustrated the colonial mercantile system and trade ties to Britain, illicit trade, maritime activities, domestic life on plantations, African-American contributions to production and material culture, and the opulence afforded some by the successes of plantation agriculture (Figure 10.5).

The success of this first exhibition gallery led to a more complete integration of archaeological research, material culture, and interpretations into Museum programs. The policy of exhibiting archaeological and historical artifacts together has carried over to the temporary exhibit program. "The Bountiful Coast," open for six months in 1988, presented an overview of historic foodways. Here, interpretation was based primarily on archaeological research, particularly faunal studies (Figure 10.6). Archaeologists designed and outlined the scope of the exhibit and wrote the label copy, while objects from both the history and archaeology departments were used to interpret the themes. Archaeological research and material culture has also been integral to "Reflections of Thine Image: Women of the Low Country," open in 1989, and "Links in a Chain: The Significance of African-American Labor," open in July 1991.

The last bastion of interpretation for archaeology to challenge was the historic house museum. The changes in interpretation at the Museum's historic houses is only symptomatic of issues facing museums nationwide. Historic house museums are traditionally the homes of men and women who were at least wealthy and white, if not regionally or nationally famous. Interpretation and material culture at these

Figure 10.5. Archaeological materials are used to interpret the evolution of Charleston in the Museum's permanent exhibition (courtesy The Charleston Museum collections).

houses has thus focused primarily, if not exclusively, on these men (or, more rarely, these women) and their families, ignoring white servants or black slaves as well as the details of a grueling daily life. Many historic house interpreters, including those of The Charleston Museum, are now striving to correct this imbalance and take an inclusive, multicultural approach to site interpretation. In physical terms, this means interpreting the work yard, kitchen, slave quarters, stables, carriage house, wells, and privies, as well as the main house and formal gardens.

The interpretive ideas first formulated with the Charleston Place project—diet, urban spatial patterning and lot layout, potable water supply and sanitation—have been expanded through subsequent excavations at both upper- and middle-class residential sites in Charleston. These have resulted in the following conclusions and new interpretations of daily life in Charleston.

1. Analyses of faunal material has demonstrated that a sizable portion of the beef consumed on Charleston's elite sites came from onsite butchery. The architectural and documentary records hint at livestock maintenance on site; the archaeological record suggests that it was very common. In contrast, it appears that sites associated with public meals and entertainment, such as taverns and clubs, obtained their meat from the market (Reitz and Zierden 1991).

2. The archaeological record suggests that yards were refuse-laden throughout the 18th and early-19th centuries. The elite site residents attempted to offset this by isolating the work yard from the formal yard. By the second quarter of the 19th century, they were also paving these work yards and moving refuse disposal further to the rear of the lot or depositing refuse offsite. Elaborate drainage systems were also constructed. By the 1850s cisterns to collect rainwater were becoming common; urban density and the proximity of wells to privies had resulted in groundwater contamination (Honerkamp and Council 1984; Zierden and Herman 1996).

3. The faunal assemblages of urban sites contain a larger percentage of commensal and vermin species; however, the elite townhouse sites exhibit a smaller percentage of these, suggesting that their efforts to clean up their yards were at least partially successful (Reitz 1986; Zierden and Calhoun 1990).

4. Palynological and ethnobotanical analyses suggest a dramatic deforestation of the Charleston area between 1760 and 1800. This is accompanied by the filling of low-lying areas and a reduction in mesic (wetland) plants. This deforestation is suggested in the documentary record through the dramatic rise in the price of firewood. This is also reflected in the ethnobotanical record through increased use of coal during these years (Reinhard 1990; Trinkley 1984; Zierden and Calhoun 1986).

Figure 10.6. Archaeological data on diet and foodways formed the basis for the special exhibit "The Bountiful Coast," (courtesy The Charleston Museum collections).

5. Trends in segmentation and privatization, as well as increasing white paranoia toward the slave population, is reflected in the construction of solid brick walls during the second quarter of the 19th century. Archaeological evidence suggests that these barriers replaced more open boundaries, often post-and-rail fences (Zierden and Herman 1996).

6. The faunal record clearly demonstrates a dependence on domestic mammals by Charlestonians, more so than by rural peoples. The faunal assemblages of upper, middle, and lower classes are remarkable in their similarity, with only subtle differences among them. It appears that elite Charlestonians enjoyed a more diverse diet, a diversity supplied by wild birds, reptiles, and fish (Reitz 1986; Zierden and Calhoun 1990).

These ideas have been incorporated into the recently overhauled interpretation at the museum houses (Varnado 1991; Zierden 1991). The new interpretation also emphasizes the resident slaves, the placement of the properties within the larger social and temporal context of the region, and the gritty reality of daily life at the outbuildings. This is balanced with deemphasis both on individual pieces of furniture and other artifacts as well as on the social and political accomplishments of the patriarch (or matriarch). To say that the house interpretive staff rushed to embrace these new ideas would be to paint an overly rosy picture. Archaeologists are perceived by many as obsessed with things filthy and scatological. Our meeting point has been the idea that the grim hardships of daily life in colonial and antebellum cities made the elegant lifestyle of the elite all the more notable.

The involvement with and interpretation of ordinary people in Charleston particularly focuses on the city's African-American population. In 1987, the archaeology program began research on these groups, as well as the white working class, by conducting documentary research and amending the City Research Design (Rosengarten et al. 1987). The project also became a public history project when leaders of the African-American community wanted to know why they weren't asked to be involved. We quickly moved to correct this by forming an advisory committee of local scholars and residents. These people read draft reports, spread the word and provided contacts, and suggested topics of interest to the community. The project was successful, particularly on the "public" front. Since that time, we have worked on a regular basis with the staff of the Avery Research Center for African-American History and Culture at the College of Charleston. They are willing to review projects, exhibits, and interpretations concerning Charleston's African-American population and make candid suggestions concerning approach and content. They interface with the black community, making our attempts at multicultural interpretation and exchange more successful.

Interdisciplinary Interpretation

"Integrated," "interdisciplinary," and "multicultural" are terms that have become popular in the archaeology and museum fields; the terms aptly describe the goals and realities of public archaeology. The Charleston Place example has demonstrated the evolution of an archaeological project from site-specific CRM-driven research, to site interpretation, and finally to an integrated museum interpretation program. The most successful archaeological projects are usually interdisciplinary, involving scholars from a number of fields exploring long-term research questions. Successful public interpretation programs must also be interdisciplinary. The mechanistic approach of the recent past—handing a technical site report to museum interpreters, expecting them to somehow transform sherd counts and MNI tabulations into meaningful and interesting displays—is now obsolete because it doesn't work. In our view a truly "interdisciplinary" interpretation must be free of jargon, be sensitive to subordinate groups' right to knowledge, and be able to combine archaeological research approaches, concepts, and results with those from more traditional disciplines.

At the same time, archaeologists must emphasize the unique and nonrenewable nature of the archaeological record, stressing that it is an integral element of a historic property and, like the buildings and grounds, requires special care and handling to preserve it and revise ongoing interpretations. Finally, we must be open and honest, admitting what we know and do *not* know. We must share with the public what excites us—cow bones, for example—until they too feel the excitement. And we must come to know what is interesting and worthwhile to those whose heritage is being exhibited (Leone and Potter 1992). Only then will archaeology be looked upon as integral to knowing the past.

▪ *Part Four* ▪

Interpreting Archaeology at Museums, Parks, and Sites

Chapter Eleven

Public Archaeology at Cahokia

Just eight miles east of St. Louis near Collinsville, Illinois, lies the largest prehistoric site north of Mexico—Cahokia Mounds. Occupied from Late Woodland (A.D. 700) through Mississippian (A.D. 800–1400) times, the site at the height of its development (A.D. 1100–1200) covered nearly 4,000 acres with more than 100 mounds and was populated by an estimated 20,000 inhabitants.

In 1925, the state of Illinois purchased the initial 144 acres and built a pueblo-style rangers residence with a "relic room" for the display of private and other collections. Over the years, a total of 2,200 acres of land in the central section of the original site were acquired. First managed as a state park under the Illinois Department of Conservation (DOC), in 1976 the lands were reclassified as Cahokia Mounds State Historic Site. At this time, management goals shifted from an emphasis on recreation to cultural resources.

From 1971 to 1976, DOC undertook a joint venture with the Illinois State Museum to develop an interpretive program at the site and establish a museum using the old building. A Master Manager Plan, originally written in 1980 and updated in 1992, was developed to provide goals and guidelines. Listed as a World Heritage Site by UNESCO in 1982, Cahokia Mounds was the first state-owned property thus designated in the United States. In 1985, the Historic Sites Division was split from DOC to combine with other cultural units to form the Illinois Historic Preservation Agency, which today manages the site.

Over the years, a small staff installed more than 30 exhibits, a minitheater, a gift shop, outside reconstructions, and many other features. A variety of programs, activities, exhibits, and interpretive techniques have been employed to reveal to the public the nature of this unique Mississippian center and the culture of the people who built it. Guided and self-guided tours, slide shows, special events, craft classes, lecture and film series, experimental archaeology projects, and archaeological field schools were developed. Even a volunteer organization and a nonprofit support society were organized. In September 1989, a new, world-class interpretive center opened. (Funding was approved by the governor of Illinois in 1984.)

As public awareness and site visitation grew and interpretive facilities changed, programs were modified, dropped, or initiated to meet the growing needs of visitors, educators, and students of all ages. These changes reflected current thinking in archaeological interpretation as well. Often working with limited budgets, almost all of this was accomplished in-house.

Educating the Public

Public misconceptions about Native Americans—prehistoric and historic—and the field of archaeology have been fostered by the myths and stereotypes presented in films, television, and books. Even the educators of our children are widely misinformed on these subjects.

Archaeological museums should strive to dispel this misinformation by providing up-to-date material on Native American cultures of all periods, and on the procedures of proper archaeological technique. Because most archaeological museums are site-specific, information generated by archaeological research at the site and in the local area can be used to accomplish this. While the possibilities for interpretation are numerous, much of what can be done depends on site budget. Attempts should nevertheless be made to reach people of all backgrounds and levels of interest, at least to some degree.

Levels of Public Interest

There are several levels of public interest and knowledge concerning archaeology and prehistoric and historic Indian cultures. The following represent most visitor categories, which are not mutually exclusive.

1. *Professional archaeologists and anthropologists* with academic training and field experience are usually intimately familiar with the information being presented.

2. *Amateur or avocational archaeologists,* employed in other fields, pursue archaeology as a hobby. Often self-educated in the discipline, they have a basic knowledge of archaeology and have perhaps worked some with professionals.

3. *Collectors* are those who field-collect artifacts for personal collections; they can include amateur or avocational archaeologists. They have a working knowledge of artifact types and categories and cultural periods. Collectors may or may not participate in the trading, buying, or selling of artifacts.

4. *Academics* with college degrees in other fields have an interest in archaeology, cultures, and museums in general. They are often knowledgeable to some degree about archaeology.

5. *Tourists* tend to stop and see points of cultural, historical, or natural interest. They may or may not have a knowledge of archaeology. Many choose a particular site for their destination; others are drawn by road signs or other sources of information that may have piqued their interest.

6. *The general public* or locals, like tourists, either tend to visit museums and attractions or come out of curiosity. A large number accompany their out-of-town relatives or friends who want to see a particular site. Publicity about the site or its activities may lure them in.

7. *Educators* of all levels, preschool through college, consider the site a resource. They may be teaching courses or using textbooks that include topics on Indians or archaeology. Some accompany their classes on field trips, others come for personal enrichment.

8. *Students* come on field trips. The visit can be either a direct learning experience or an enjoyable day away from school, depending on the orientation of their teacher. As individuals, students may come seeking information for a research project or for personal enrichment.

Exhibits

At Cahokia the new Interpretive Center accommodates most of these levels without favoring a particular one. The exhibits are designed so that all visitors get something out of them, whether the visitor is a "30-minute-walk-through" person, one who stops to look at major objects and texts of interest, or a "reader" who does not miss a thing, often spending a whole day.

We were fortunate to have a budget that allowed hiring professional exhibit design and fabrication firms, although we monitored all stages of design, text writing, and image production, and had right of refusal. The displays are set up on seven exhibit islands, each with a different theme or topic:

- *Time* or where Cahokia fits into the cultural sequence
- *Culture* focusing on the Mississippian tradition
- *City* stressing Cahokia's urban characteristics
- *Structures* discussing mounds, Woodhenge, the stockade walls, houses, and other structures
- *Life*, treating such topics as beliefs and customs, symbols, agriculture and food gathering, rank and status, ornaments, games, and death
- *Products* or objects, their acquisition and processing from stone, bone, wood, pottery, shell, and fiber
- *Knowing* or the archaeological process

We use a variety of media to present the information on the islands and elsewhere, as detailed next.

Artifacts

Most visitors expect to see artifacts. We display a number of them at each exhibit island. Drawers installed in the display bases hold additional artifacts for demonstrating the range and variety of shapes and styles without cluttering the space. When possible, we use specimens found at the site or nearby. Casts are used only when originals are not available. Replicated specimens are sometimes used to demonstrate the manufacturing process and hafting techniques. Most artifacts or artifact groups are identified with labels.

Models and Dioramas

Our full-scale diorama incorporates seven structures. Eighteen mannequins, cast from living Native Americans, represent different ages, sex, and status and are posed performing daily activities, such as making crafts, cooking, or trading. Enclosed in a 60-by-40-foot room with two-way mirror walls, the scenes repeat as in an infinity box. One sees scores of structures and people. Designed to give one the impression of being in one of Cahokia's neighborhoods, the diorama in effect reinforces the urban nature of Cahokia.

Another full-scale setting simulates an archaeological excavation complete with archaeologists. Small-scale dioramas on the islands illustrate different seasonal activities. There are also models of Monks Mound, Woodhenge, several mound types, and the portion of the central Mississippi Valley that includes the American Bottom and Cahokia.

Artwork

A variety of artists created the line drawings, paintings, and graphics seen throughout the gallery. Their work includes enlargements for murals and images featuring individual topics on each island. The art is very effective in re-creating daily life scenes, tool manufacture and use, and overall images of the city and its structures.

Audiovisuals

An award-winning orientation show uses 13 slide projectors on a 40-foot screen in a special theater. Video (disc) monitors in the island areas show the flintknapping process, the use of computers in archaeology, and the archaeological process in the field and lab. An ambient sound system permeates the gallery with sounds of nature and village activities.

Text and Labels

Each island has a major introductory text, minor texts, and subtexts, presenting the subject(s) under discussion in a progressively more specific or detailed manner. To provide even more information, the designers developed "pull-panels" that emerged from the sides of the island walls. There was one design flaw, however. The panels were often abused by children using them like a Nautilus machine, and they have been removed.

Labels are provided for most artifacts or classes of artifacts, and cast items are identified as such. Some labels merely identify a subject, others provide more information. All have the same typeface and ink color.

Temporary Exhibits

Near the exit of the exhibit gallery, a small area was designed as a temporary exhibit hall. Creating or bringing in a variety of new exhibits helps lure visitors back to the site. Both archaeological and art exhibits are displayed, usually for three-month periods. The temporary exhibits, which have been very well received, keep the museum looking fresh.

Educational Programs

We have implemented a variety of interpretive and educational programs, activities, and special events. Some of these were restructured to take advantage of the facilities at our new Interpretive Center and provide a greater educational experience for participants.

Previously, we provided on-site guided tours to school, scout, and adult groups. However, to avoid serving as "baby sitters" for many groups, we adopted an educational program format that better utilizes staff and volunteer time. Now, before scheduling, teachers must attend a workshop so that they are knowledgeable about the site and the program. Scheduled groups receive a packet that includes pre- and post-visit activities. The actual visit consists of viewing the orientation show, visiting the exhibit gallery, and participating in a hands-on experience.

Programs with different themes are offered several times during the year. Some are geared to certain age or grade levels. Themes include: Mound Building, Wattle and Daub (house construction), Indian Games, Clothing and Ornament, Indian Foods, and Tracks and Traps. The Mound Building program, for example, includes digging soil with a chert hoe, carrying the soil in baskets to where a small mound is built, or repairing erosions on existing mounds, and then tamping the soil with poles and feet. Baskets are counted and weighed to project the quantity of earth moved and needed. Thus, both physical and mental exercises are involved.

These programs are very popular and booked months in advance. Teachers and students alike learn from the experience, gaining insight into the daily lives of the American Indians.

Site Tours

Site touring at Cahokia is primarily self-guided. Some of the educational groups tour on their own, as do those unable or unwilling to participate in the educational programs. Three tour trails are open to the public. Hikers can borrow a companion cassette with a cassette player or buy an inexpensive guidebook.

Seasonal guided tours are led by volunteers and offered daily from June through August, and on weekends in April, May, September, and October. These are primarily for the random visitor or member of the general public, although small groups may join in. Morning tours follow one trail, afternoon tours another. On these tours, information is provided about the visible site features and any excavations or other research that has been conducted in the area.

A 6-mile (10-kilometer) Nature-Culture Trail leads hikers through some of the more remote areas of the site where one encounters several ecological and archaeological zones. A guidebook for this trail is also available. In the spring and fall, site staff lead visitors and provide an ecological and archaeological dialogue on an all-day hike.

Experimental Structures

A number of experimental projects have been conducted at the site. Most involved the construction of Indian type dwellings. These projects have several important functions.

- *Practical learning experiences.* Participants gather native materials and learn first-hand how to prepare them for use in construction (sometimes with the assistance of modern equipment). Trees are cut, trimmed, and debarked; grass is cut and tied into bundles for thatching; proper-sized saplings are cut and intertwined between wall posts for wattle; and daub is prepared by mixing clay, water, and grass, and then applied properly over the wall structure.

- *Interpretive tools.* Staff members employ the projects to explain to the public how such houses were built and used as single-family dwellings, as storage buildings, and for other purposes. With the construction materials readily visible, the building process can easily be explained. This helps dispel the myth that Indians only lived in tepees.

- *Functional structures.* When finished, the buildings can be used for overnight "live-ins," storytelling programs, and mini-classrooms. Depending on how secure the reconstruction site is, an assortment of furnishings and replicated artifacts can be included to create the atmosphere of a home.

Building a structure of any size is very time-consuming, and it is best to have all the materials on hand. This is not always possible since some resources, such as prairie grass, are only available in certain seasons. Because it takes several people to accomplish many of the procedures, incorporating the project into a scheduled group activity usually works well. We built one house in this manner and constructed others piecemeal, sometimes profiting from the house-building educational program activities. Site staff and members of our volunteer organization perform the majority of the work, letting the classes assist with some of the less crucial procedures.

To demonstrate other types of structures, provide additional security for the reconstruction area, and create an ambiance for the entire reconstructed complex, we also built stockade/palisade walls and fences around the houses and garden.

Although not always possible, it is desirable to use replicated tools. These leave the proper tool marks, give an idea of the time and labor involved in using them, and provide subjects for comparative use-wear studies.

Modern fasteners such as nails, screws, and wire are avoided. For lashings, we primarily use bailer's twine, which approximates native cordage, and rawhide or bark strips. A properly pitched and thatched roof protects from most kinds of weather. For others who would like to build experimental structures, unless there are interior dioramas and climate controls, plywood or sheet metal under grass roofs should be avoided, as they are obviously modern and a detraction.

Experimental Gardens

Few people realize how many Indian societies were agricultural. We have found that cultivating gardens with traditional crops helps get the message across. We grow varieties of corn, pumpkin, squash, bottle gourds, sunflower, tobacco, and Jerusalem artichoke. Sometimes we do the groundwork with hafted flint hoes and digging sticks, letting people watch or even use these tools to see how they work.

Craft Classes and Workshops

A direct way to involve the public in prehistoric technologies is to offer, throughout the year, a selection of classes such as pottery making, flintknapping, hide tanning, and basket and mat weaving. Craftspeople to teach the classes are available in most areas of the country. Some will be local, others must be brought in. We have tried to engage as many Native American craftspeople as possible. A nominal tuition covers costs and ensures that enrollees show up. Staff and volunteers also participate in the classes developing skills for their own on-site demonstrations and events.

Special Events

To maintain public interest in a site, special events can be offered several times a year with different themes. At Cahokia we have two major events: *Kids Day* in May and *Heritage America* in September. *Kids Day* is a one-day, primarily hands-on event that permits children to participate at a basic level in various crafts. Demonstrators show the more sophisticated techniques. Indian dancing, storytelling, games, and other activities complete the program.

Heritage America is a more involved, 2-day event that includes the participation of Native Americans. We focus on demonstrations and have constructed an arbored dance circle for intertribal dances and activities. Our volunteers show prehistoric crafts, and various Indian individuals and groups demonstrate historic and contemporary crafts.

Involving the American Indian community was an important step. In 1990, when the first *Heritage America* was held, many of the Indians were apprehensive. This was, after all, the first such Indian gathering at a major archaeological site. However, they were so pleased with the new Interpretive Center, its depiction of Indian life, and the way the event was organized, that they requested to participate again in 1991 and spread the word for others to come, and the event has grown in subsequent years.

We also hold several half-day events throughout the year. These have included:

- *A Native Harvests Festival*, where people can grind corn, crack nuts, taste traditional Indian foods, and view special exhibits;

- *Native Animals*, where rehabilitation centers bring in raptors, and children learn about animal tracks, observe mounted specimens or furs, and examine a comparative bone collection; and

- *Storytelling and Stargazing*, with stories relating to the cosmos and observations of various constellations.

- *Indian Dance and Music*, with explanations, demonstrations, and participation in traditional dance steps and music.

Archaeological Field Schools

For years we had a public field school program that focused on exploring the stockade wall system and the prestockade residential features at Cahokia. Sponsored by our support group, the Cahokia Mounds Museum Society, a professional archaeologist directed the project. Participants came from diverse backgrounds, but they all shared a genuine interest in learning proper archaeology. Many have gone on to pursue degrees in the field.

Management of this popular and well-received field school has shifted to Southern Illinois University at Edwardsville. Better equipped and staffed to handle such a program, the university has since conducted several field schools for both academic credit and noncredit participants. Research goals are designed to accommodate proposed site development projects and to reveal crucial information about areas of the site that are not well understood. In the process, several nondestructive approaches, such as controlled surface collections, soil coring, and remote sensing with magnetometers have been used. On occasion, traditional excavations have been conducted as a result of some of the above-mentioned testing procedures.

An accredited, field-school course for teachers was added to instill an appreciation for the past and present cultural resources through curriculum-based activities and lessons. Teachers are exposed to the principles of archaeology by re-creating a site-formation process. They participate in activities that would have taken place during prehistoric occupation, such as mound building, toolmaking, cooking, construction, and pit digging and use. They also learn to map and record the resulting features and debris. In subsequent field schools, teachers will excavate and evaluate this "site" using basic archaeological techniques and see if their interpretations of the data are accurate. Based on these experiences, supplementary lectures, hands-on activities, and demonstrations of prehistoric crafts, teachers create lesson plans for their classrooms. Thus archaeology can be taught without endangering an actual site, and, overall, the field school courses are much more effective than a simulated dig.

Conclusion

We have been fortunate at Cahokia in recent years to have received sufficient funding to construct a facility that reaches the public in many ways. It is important to have a well-rounded interpretive program, efficiently utilizing staff and volunteers. I encourage any museum, regardless of size, to develop a volunteer corps, as it greatly contributes to what can be accomplished. Without our volunteers at Cahokia, we would not be able to operate. After all, with all the exhibits and audio-visual programs, it is still the personal touch, the human contact, that is most effective in educating the public.

Chapter Twelve

Interpreting Cultural Resources:
*Hatzic Site**

Introduction

East of Mission, in southwestern British Columbia, a large boulder lies partially exposed in an open field on the north bank of the Fraser River (Figure 12.1). In a geological context, it is a glacial erratic deposited approximately 15,000 years ago. To the Stó:lo Coast Salish First Nations[†] of the lower Fraser River valley, the boulder—named X̱á:ytem (or the Hatzic Rock)—is a "transformer" site, a spiritually significant landmark where three chiefs were transformed to stone for their act of defying the Creator.

Since its discovery in the fall of 1990, X̱á:ytem has been the focus of considerable academic research interests. It has also been a source of concern for First Nations communities whose spiritual and political values reflect contemporary uses of the archaeological record that can be quite distinct from those suggested by academia. In addition, the site has drawn wide media attention, generating diverse public opinion about archaeological resources and their preservation. Combined, these factors might well have set the perfect stage for merely controversy (see McGhee 1989). Instead, they laid the foundation for a collaborative research and interpretive project that continues to the present. From planning to research to interpretation, the

---

* Adapted from a paper originally presented at the 1992 Annual Meeting of the Canadian Archaeological Association, London, Ontario, May 1992. Earlier versions of the paper were read by Michael Ames, Linnea Battell, Michael Blake, R.G. Matson, Gordon Mohs, and Brian Thom. The UBC Dean of Arts Office provided supplementary funding to enable the archaeological field school excavations at X̱á:ytem. The British Columbia Heritage Trust provided funding of the public interpretation program, and the Stó:lo Nation and Archaeology Branch, Government of British Columbia, assisted with the funding of the 1991 Stó:lo field crew.

† Names are a problem and, in the case of Canadian Aboriginal people, have changed with the times. Although the Indian Act remains in force in Canada, the term "Indian" is widely disfavored by those the term is used to describe. "Native" (but not "Native Canadian") and "Aboriginal" are occasionally used in self-reference, but "First Nations" and "First Peoples" are more commonly accepted at present. These four terms will be used interchageably in this paper.

Figure 12.1. View of X̱á:ytem. Photograph by J. Vinnick.

work at X̱á:ytem provides a model of collaboration between archaeologists and local communities.

X̱á:ytem Project History

The site of X̱á:ytem (Figure 12.2) was discovered in October 1990, by Gordon Mohs, a heritage consultant for the Stó:lo Nation. Soon after its discovery, the site suffered extensive damage from bulldozing in preparation for a housing subdivision development. The initial concern was preservation of the rock itself, situated in the center of the planned subdivision and slated for blasting. Mohs and a small field crew carried out emergency investigations during October and November to salvage what information remained in the bulldozed land surface. This work led to the discovery of deeply buried archaeological deposits that indicated a semisubterranean dwelling structure, radiocarbon-dated to approximately 5,000 years ago.

When the developer, Harry Utzig, was informed of the archaeological results, he agreed to consider alternative plans to preserve the rock in the subdivision, and to postpone any further development until mitigation could be carried out the following spring. Utzig's commitment to heritage conservation is exemplary and he deserves special recognition for his efforts, which he undertook at his own considerable financial expense.

During the winter of 1991, representatives of the Stó:lo Nation and the University of British Columbia (UBC) met to discuss how both institutions might collaborate to salvage the remains of the house structure before further construction continued. Arrangements were made to incorporate the 1991 UBC Archaeological Field School in the investigations.

From mid-May to the end of July 1991, most of the entire house structure was uncovered, and evidence suggesting an earlier occupation was discovered nearby. In further assessment of the site in September, evidence of more extensive occupation was also discovered (Pokotylo 1991; Wilson 1991). This research has furthered our understanding of the origins of settled village life on the Northwest Coast—extending back to at least 5,000 years ago—and the early development of complex societies in the region (see Mason 1994). The evidence from X̱á:ytem indicates that early inhabitants were semisedentary hunters and fishers who had a well-developed woodworking industry, led a complex ceremonial life, and participated in regional exchange. From a scientific perspective, the findings at X̱á:ytem are highly significant. More importantly, they reaffirm Stó:lo oral traditions that assert that the Stó:lo and their ancestors have lived here for thousands of years (Mohs 1992).

Of equal importance to the scientific results was the unprecedented public interest, from both Euro-Canadian and First Nations communities, in the excavations and the preservation of the site. A public interpretation program was developed to run concurrently with the excavations. Native students conducted guided tours of both the

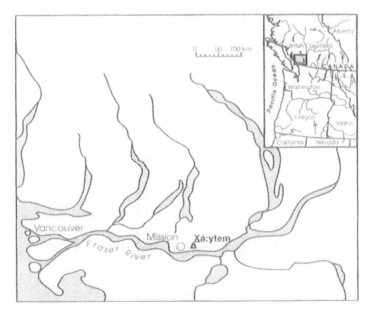

Figure 12.2. Map of X̱á:ytem site location.

rock and the excavations and described the spiritual and scientific significance of the site. An estimated 7,000 people visited X̱á:ytem during the 1991 excavation period.

The high level of public interest also resulted in the formation of the Friends of the Hatzic Rock Society, an organization with a mandate to promote preservation of the site and whose membership encompasses both Euro-Canadian and First Nations local communities. The Society took over the management of the interpretive program to extend it from August to early October 1991, and continued to present public programming at the site from 1992 to 1994, when the Society was formally dissolved. In addition to the general public interest, many Native elders and spiritual leaders visited the site, and numerous events were held to acknowledge the spiritual significance of the site to the Aboriginal community.

The widespread concern for X̱á:ytem led both the federal and provincial governments to formally recognize the site's significance. The government of Canada designated X̱á:ytem as a National Historic Site in July 1992—the first Aboriginal spiritual site in Canada to be formally acknowledged in this manner. The government of British Columbia designated X̱á:ytem as a Provincial Heritage Site and acquired the site property in the April 1993, to be held in trust by the B.C. Heritage Trust. Since then, the site has been comanaged by a committee of Stó:lo Nation and provincial government representatives.

Public Interpretation of X̱á:ytem

Recent public opinion surveys in the greater Vancouver region indicate that people interested in archaeology would prefer to learn more about the subject by visiting an archaeological excavation, but they also have a very limited idea of Native antiquity in British Columbia (Pokotylo and Mason 1991). X̱á:ytem provided a unique opportunity not only to increase public understanding and awareness of prehistoric archaeology, but also to show the links with contemporary Aboriginal populations in the region.

The public interpretation program was developed with the assistance of the UBC Museum of Anthropology staff and the Stó:lo Nation. The program's initial objectives were as follows:

1. To describe the role of X̱á:ytem in the cultural history of the lower Fraser River valley, and show continuity in land use in the region. This incorporated both academic and Aboriginal perspectives and covered both the precontact and historic periods. A critical element was to show how spiritually significant the site is to the Stó:lo community, and to emphasize that their concerns in interpreting the site are just as significant as those of academia.

2. To increase public awareness of heritage conservation issues by using the excavations to stress the nonrenewable nature of archaeological resources, and the need for their conservation.

3 To increase public understanding of the nature of archaeological field research and the need for scientific excavation methods to collect and interpret archaeological data, by providing an opportunity to observe firsthand the archaeological field research process.

There was a mutual concern that the interpretive program should address the issue of representation, particularly the aspect of continuity of Aboriginal occupation in the region from precontact to contemporary times, and First Nations' perceptions of their antiquity. The First Nations community took an active role in presenting both the archaeological and spiritual significance of the site to a larger audience. Greg Brass, a UBC Native student, was appointed as on-site supervisor, and two Stó:lo college students were hired as site interpreters. They were given a week of training that included sessions with UBC resource people and Stó:lo elders.

Visitors to the site were immediately greeted by one of the interpreters, who initially presented the entire program. The interpreter would first guide visitors to the rock and relate its spiritual importance to Stó:lo myth and tradition, and then escort them around the excavation area. When Native interpretations differed from academic ones, *both* perspectives were presented. After the presentation, visitors were free to view the exhibit, ask questions, and examine "touchable" artifacts collected from disturbed surface areas of the site.

The on-site exhibit consisted of four panels mounted on a free-standing framework at the entrance to the excavation (Figure 12.3). The exhibit outlined the history of the X̱á:ytem excavation, archaeological data, traditional Stó:lo culture, and cultural heritage issues. The portable design of the exhibit facilitated it's circulation to local schools, museums, and Native cultural centers. The exhibit was forwarded to the Stó:lo Nation at the completion of the field project for this purpose. Recent finds from the excavation were placed in a small display case that was constantly updated.

A brochure was also created, outlining the history of the discovery of X̱á:ytem, research objectives of the excavation, the relationship of X̱á:ytem site to southwest British Columbia prehistory, and current heritage conservation measures for archaeological sites in the province.

The interpretive program at X̱á:ytem was very successful in a number of aspects. Public interest was overwhelming. The site received a high profile in the media, with printed press, radio, and television coverage at the local, national (see D. Wilson 1991), and international level (see Steiner 1991). Media attention was undoubtedly responsible for the site's high profile; raising public interest sufficiently to encourage more than 7,000 people to come out and view the site. For most visitors, this was their first encounter with prehistoric archaeology and Aboriginal culture. The program elicited many favorable comments, particularly regarding the First Nations interpreters who combined both scientific and spiritual perspectives in the presentations.

Figure 12.3. On-site exhibit at X̱á:ytem during 1991 excavations. Photograph by David Pokotylo.

How the X̱á:ytem story has been treated by the media would make a revealing study of how news is constructed, rather than merely reported. Local papers throughout the lower Fraser Valley were the first to cover the story. "Beating the [bulldozer] Blade" warned of the potential threat to a "stone-age" archaeological find by residential development (Robbins 1990). Later, a story printed in the Stó:lo newspaper (Ned 1990) treated the find of a dwelling as proof of Stó:lo antiquity in the Fraser Valley. Articles written in the spring and summer of 1991 elaborated much more on the cultural significance of the rock. In particular, a Vancouver newspaper article (Glavin 1991) went into great length about the deity that created the "stone people," and described in detail the visit of a Native spiritualist to the site. Here, the archaeological significance of the site came across as secondary. Although press coverage was mainly supportive of preservation efforts, it did evoke some diverse public responses. The most extreme was a letter to the editor of a local newspaper (Mortimer 1991) in which the writer disputed the antiquity and significance of the site on Creationist grounds. How could the site possibly be older than 6,000 years, the dawn of humanity?

First Nations' Perspectives

Prominent objects and anomalous sites in the landscape frequently have cultural significance to the Stó:lo. Often they are associated to accounts of the deity X:als, the great creator who, among other things, transformed people and animals into stone formations or left physical evidence of visitation. The Stó:lo describe X̱á:ytem as a "transformer site" (see Mohs 1987, 1990, 1994:192–195), and the full name— X̱á:ytem Ihexwala Si:yam (three Si:yams turned to stone)—is associated with a time in ancient Stó:lo history when X:als, came to earth. The rock represents three great chiefs (Si:yams) who challenged the authority of X:als, and were transformed into stone. Such sacred sites are of great significance to many of the Stó:lo people, a number of whom are elderly. As one Elder expressed to Gordon Mohs in 1985:

> These places are very important for us, those that know about them. They are something that is proof of our past. But it seems that something that is proof of our past is not as sacred as things that are sacred to Europeans. These places are special. They were put here for a reason. X:als meant for these places to last for all time. They were not meant to be destroyed. But white men don't understand this (Mohs 1992:12).

Unfortunately, much of the cultural information is inaccessible knowledge that only a minority of the Stó:lo possess. X̱á:ytem posed a special problem, as documentation of this particular site was sparse. There had been a village in the area whose people were referred to as Hatzic. The population, it is reported, was completely wiped out by epidemics resulting from European contact.

To verify the spiritual significance of X̱á:ytem, a Native spiritualist from Nooksack, Washington, offered a reading or visionary interpretation of the site. The location of the initial test excavation pits was partly based on the spiritualist's description of the settlement following a vision he had while visiting the site. As for the rock, he said a song remains trapped inside and belongs to those who had been transformed. Over the course of several months, various oral accounts have emerged about the former villages in this location and nearby. All these accounts have supplemented the initial interpretations. At a Burning (a Coast Salish religious practice) held for the excavators in July 1991, the spiritualist had another vision in which the former occupants revisited their abandoned dwelling and described it to him. Also, he said these people were not angered by the disturbance to their dwelling and supported the work that was taking place (pers. com. Mohs 1992). Testing the accuracy of any of this information is difficult, because much of it depends on one's perspective or beliefs.

News about the finds at X̱á:ytem and the wide public interest in Stó:lo culture and history have had great impact on the greater population of the Stó:lo. The most immediate effect was the heightened interest and awareness they felt in their own cultural traditions. At a presentation given by the site interpreters for the Stó:lo Elders an elderly woman, who had learned about the rock as a young girl, told the more precise story about the rock's being three chiefs. At a gathering of Stó:lo Elders at the end of the summer, an 85-year-old woman had these words to say to those present:

Everybody listen. You children here, it's time you listened. Because you people are young, you don't understand why the rock is singing. Why is he singing? Can you answer that? He wants something, that's why. He wants something from somebody; somebody that used to be a relative years ago, from you children here.

You're supposed to give an offering, say a little prayer for the rock or whatever you think, just thank the rock that he's here for you children to see it. And enjoy looking at the rock. It's a great spirit that's been left behind for you children. I talked to the rock already. I thanked the rock for coming to see it. That's all I'll say.

Anything that's spiritual, you thank them and talk to them. That's the way it goes today. You just don't climb around on it. You just don't play with the spiritual things. You got to talk to them, thank them. Thank them for coming to see it. It's not something to play with. That's something that's very important to us Elders. It really is spiritual.

You children should learn all of these things. You're taking over what the Elders are doing. Very few of us are here to say these things. But I cannot talk too much and I'm tired already. OK. That's all I can say. Bow before that when you come and see that. And talk to the rock and thank him for everything, that you enjoy looking at it (Mohs 1992:14).

The Stó:lo also realized the many implications of the increased public interest in their cultural traditions. Since September 1991, the Stó:lo Nation has been developing a heritage plan for X̱á:ytem that will ultimately result in both a major Native interpretive center and a lucrative attraction for growing cultural tourism. The first significant phase of this development plan was the opening of the Longhouse Interpretive

Centre in 1994 (Figure 4). Stó:lo culture, history, and spirituality are featured along with the site's archaeological and scientific importance. Upon completion, the heritage development at X̱á:ytem will be comparable to facilities at Head-Smashed-In Buffalo Jump, Alberta, and Waneskewin, Saskatchewan.

For the many other Coast Salish First Nations throughout the Lower Mainland and Southern Vancouver Island, the finds at X̱á:ytem furthered the positions of these populations in terms of Aboriginal rights, land claims and establishing original occupation. The Assembly of First Nations National Indian Brotherhood also garnered its support for preservation of X̱á:ytem. The site has not only affirmed a sacred spiritual significance, but has acquired symbolic political significance as well.

Friends of the Hatzic Rock Society

One of the more intriguing developments in the course of the interpretation program was the establishment of the Friends of the Hatzic Rock Society, initially formed to lobby for the preservation of the site. The group, composed of First Nations and Euro-Canadian members, has used both scientific and sacred arguments to develop the site into a heritage park under the direction of the Stó:lo Nation. The membership

Figure 12.4. X̱á:ytem Longhouse Interpretive Centre. Photograph by G. Mohs.

also includes individuals who, reflecting a "new age" philosophy (Feder 1990:189–190), feel close personal connections to the site. This connection ranges from a belief in reincarnation and past lives, to picking up vibrational qualities and the memory that is contained at the site and particularly inside the rock. One individual maintains that she has projected her consciousness inside the boulder and has encountered a "grandfatherly" being to whom she has made offerings of tobacco and from whom she has received gifts in return. Although these perspectives have not been overt in the lobbying process, they reflect another role beyond those of scientific significance and Native spiritualism: the role the site now assumes in contemporary society.

A Final Reflection

The interpretation program at X̱á:ytem has been highly successful in increasing the public profile of archaeological heritage resources in British Columbia. We are confident that many more people are now sensitized to issues of archaeological preservation and First Nations traditions.

X̱á:ytem has also generated a range of feelings and concerns far beyond our initial expectation, showing that the archaeological record has a diversity of uses in contemporary society. From a scientific perspective, the rock is a glacial erratic: reflecting a Pleistocene landscape. In Stó:lo mythology, this same rock conveys a story of a powerful deity, one that can transform people and animals into stone formations. For the Stó:lo, archaeological concerns are not always paramount in preservation arguments. X̱á:ytem and other such sites are much more than relics of the past for study by academic archaeologists; they are sacred places of living power.

Clearly, the scientific and First Nations communities could have competed for authority of interpretation of the site and the rock itself. Instead, the two groups came together, compromising when necessary, to provide a broader, more inclusive interpretation. While respecting each other's perspectives and philosophies, they formed a true collaboration to their mutual benefit and to the benefit of the public—a public eagerly awaiting the stories yet to be told as the collaboration continues.

Chapter Thirteen

Putting People Back into the Landscape:
Sabino Canyon

The Sabino Canyon Recreation Area, administered by Coronado National Forest, is a unique desert oasis located near metropolitan Tucson, Arizona. The canyon is one of many that cut deeply into the foothills of the spectacular Santa Catalina Mountains that border Tucson. Rising high above the desert, Sabino Creek is fed by the spring snowmelt from the mountains, creating one of the rarest of desert habitats—a perennial stream.

Sabino Canyon draws Tucsonans and tourists alike to enjoy its rugged landscapes, running water, and lush greenery. Few visitors, however, are aware that Sabino Canyon was an equally compelling oasis in the past. Native Americans used the canyon long before Francisco Vasquez de Coronado set foot near the area that would become a National Forest bearing his name. Hispanic and Anglo ranchers and miners settled and worked in this part of the Tucson Basin when Arizona was a raw and dusty Territory. By the turn of the century, Sabino Canyon was a remote and beautiful refuge for city dwellers who traveled by wagon to picnic along the banks of the creek. Still later, the federal programs of the Depression years sponsored the construction of bridges, roads, and recreation facilities today's visitors enjoy.

Despite this rich history, current interpretive programs at Sabino Canyon Recreation Area focus on the outstanding natural environment. Its human history is far less visible, though, and presents a distinct challenge to interpreters. Sabino Canyon's archaeology—small surface sites lacking standing walls, boulders that were used to grind wild plant seeds hidden among the stream-side trees, and rock piles and alignments representing prehistoric agricultural fields—are unimpressive to the typical visitor and scarcely evocative of the canyon's history of several thousand years. Putting people back into this landscape—interpreting its human uses, past and present, in ways that are meaningful, understandable, and accessible to all visitors—is the challenge and goal of interpretive programs.

The Landscape and How It Was Used: The Natural and Cultural Environments of Sabino Canyon Recreation Area

The landscape of this desert oasis is immediate and compelling. No visitor can ignore its unique character and stunning visual quality. Perhaps the most intriguing aspect of Sabino Canyon is the richness and diversity of its plant and animal life. The canyon, which spans a wide range of elevations and topography along its length, provides a lush array of microenvironments. At least six different biotic communities have been identified here. Moreover, Sabino Canyon is a climatic island that is warmer and wetter than the rest of the Tucson area, further enriching the luxuriant plant life. The rocky slopes of the spectacular upper canyon support stands of the giant saguaro cactus—the signature plant of the Sonoran Desert—and the green-barked palo verde tree. Smaller cactus, shrubs, wildflowers, and many other plants fill out a rich and complicated tapestry of plant life. In cooler areas grassland species dominate, including ocotillo, with its flame-colored tips that flower in spring, sweet-smelling shrubs, grasses, and many members of the agave family.

The riparian community lining the stream bed provides a cool and green contrast to the thorny vegetation of the surrounding desert bajada or foothills. Of extraordinary interest to biologist and visitor alike, the riparian zone with its broad-leafed trees, dense shrubs, and stream-side plants supports an immense army of animal life. Children splashing in the pools share the waters with native fish, Sonoran mud turtles, crayfish, and even freshwater jellyfish. Javelina, raccoons, bobcats, and the rarely seen ringtail cats come for water and shelter. Over 200 species of birds populate the canyon.

Unfortunately, the desert riparian habitat is rapidly disappearing as human impacts on southern Arizona's streams increase. Sabino Canyon provides an unparalleled opportunity to educate visitors about the importance of these habitats and the need to preserve and protect them.

Although the cultural environment of the canyon is no less rich than the natural one, it is far less visible. The unusual habitat of Sabino Canyon was the factor shaping the way it was used by humans in prehistory and history alike. The human history of Sabino begins with the preceramic period Archaic hunter-gatherers, who were no doubt attracted by its abundant plant and animal life. The only traces of the Archaic people discovered in Sabino Canyon so far are projectile points that they left behind, although their campsites are found in nearby bajada and canyon areas. The Archaic folk were followed by the desert farmers, the Hohokam, who made and used pottery, built large villages along the banks of the desert rivers, and developed a complex and arresting ceremonial life focused on a semisacred ball game. The Hohokam began to live in the Tucson area some time around A.D. 700 to 800 and remained there until about A.D. 1400. The Tucson Basin also was occupied, beginning about A.D. 200, by a farming people who made pottery. Archaeologists have yet to decide whether these early potters were descendants of the Archaic people and ancestors of the Hohokam, or whether the Hohokam were an immigrant people of another culture who established themselves in the desert valleys much later.

In Sabino Canyon, bedrock mortars attest to the collection and grinding of mesquite beans, a staple wild food of the Hohokam, and associated petroglyphs encode information archaeologists have yet to decipher. A number of small rockshelters no doubt served as temporary campsites for people who came to the canyon for its rich resources. Rock piles and alignments reflect farming activities on the lower slopes of the bajada, with corn and agave among the crops that were grown. At least three archaeological sites in the canyon may represent small, probably short-term habitations where the Hohokam lived during the A.D. 1000s (Whittlesey and Harry 1990).

Some time after the Hohokam left the Tucson area, around A.D. 1400, traces of another people began to appear in Sabino Canyon as well as elsewhere in southern Arizona. These people built fragile, oval brush houses with stone cobble foundations and made rough-surfaced, brown pottery. Some archaeologists link these people to the Sobaipuri, one of the Piman peoples who were living in the Santa Cruz and San Pedro River valleys when the first Jesuit missionaries arrived in the late 1600s. Still later, pottery attributed to the historic Tohono O'odham people, which is easily identified by the black interior that results from using horse manure as temper, occurs at Sabino Canyon sites. We believe, however, that the Tohono O'odham did not use the canyon intensively, perhaps because of its proximity to the San Pedro River valley, a favorite route for the Western Apache on their raiding expeditions into Sonora.

Hispanic and Anglo ranchers began using the Sabino area in the 1860s and continued into the early-20th century. They, too, were drawn by Sabino's resources, chiefly its water, and the history of the area becomes largely one of a struggle to control and harness the waters of Sabino Creek. Bill Kirkland built the first permanent settlement along Sabino Creek about a mile south of the canyon, according to David Lazaroff (1993:86). Ranching was a tenuous enterprise, fraught with dangers from Apache raiding and the turmoil of the Civil War. In the 1880s, a struggle to control the water of Sabino Creek developed among local entrepreneurs. A scheme to build dams on Sabino Creek and nearby Bear Canyon Creek and supply Tucson with power and water for irrigation was devised by a professor at the University of Arizona; it proved unsuccessful. A similar scheme, revived in the Depression years, also failed. As David Lazaroff writes (1993:99), this failure saved Sabino Canyon, for the dam would have destroyed the stream and its unique riparian habitat. Recorded archaeological sites document Anglo use of the canyon between the early 1900s and the 1930s, with artifacts representing household refuse and construction materials (Whittlesey and Harry 1990).

During the dam-scheme years and after its failure, federal work programs sponsored construction of the recreation and administrative facilities that are today's most visible cultural resources in the canyon (Whittlesey and Harry 1990). WPA and CCC workers eventually constructed a less grandiose dam, which created Sabino Lake.

They also built a ranger station, bridges, picnic tables, and rest rooms. Today's visitors still ride over the WPA bridges, some of which bear their original date plates.

As David Lazaroff (1993:xi) tells us, Sabino Canyon is much more than the sum of its natural and cultural environments. It represents, in microcosm, virtually all the lowland habitats of the Southwest. Its cultural history is a similarly encapsulated version of the changing relationships between people and the desert. Sabino Canyon is a mirror reflecting far more than what is immediately evident.

How the Visitor Sees Sabino Canyon Today

People come to Sabino Canyon to picnic, enjoy the cool waters, bird watch, and hike its trails. The Visitor Center was opened in 1963, and although it originally housed a full-time interpretive staff and extensive exhibits, budget cuts have whittled these away (USDA Forest Service 1991:6–7). The center now is primarily office space, with an information kiosk and small exhibit area. A tram service was installed in 1978 to reduce pollution and traffic congestion in the canyon. Now providing the only motorized access, the tram is boarded at the Visitor Center.

Visitors to the canyon can learn about it in three ways. The Visitor Center houses a few exhibits and printed information, which emphasize the natural environment and the wildlife of Sabino Canyon. The Sabino Canyon Volunteer Naturalists, a group of dedicated volunteer interpreters, guide visitors on nature walks and hold informal talks. During the 1989–1990 season, almost 18,000 people attended over 400 of these interpretive events. The drivers of the shuttle trams have developed talks that provide general visitor information and interpret the natural environment of the canyon to visitors as the trams travel up the canyon. In all these approaches, it is the natural environment that is emphasized. People, past and present, are conspicuously absent from the interpretive landscape. The visitor may learn about the giant saguaro cactus, how much it weighs and how old it grows to be, without ever knowing that the cactus was a primary staple of prehistoric and historic desert people alike.

What the visitor sees, enjoys, and learns about, then, are the obvious qualities of the natural landscape—the scenery, the creek and lake, the vegetation, and the animal life. What the visitor does not discern or understand are the cultural resources of the canyon. The prehistoric archaeological sites in the area are predominantly small campsites, areas where wild plant foods were collected and processed, and rock features were used to collect rain water and divert it to fields. None have aboveground architecture or other characteristics that are recognizable as archaeological sites to the typical Sabino visitor. Even though the Visitor Center is built near one of the largest sites in the immediate vicinity, most visitors walk across its surface without even being aware that below their feet lies a prehistoric site. Because the Hohokam lived in pit houses made of poles, brush, and mud, the traces of their lives are now buried, and the sites are recognizable as such only by surface scatters of broken pottery, flaked stone tools, and the like.

Similarly, most of the historic period sites in the canyon are artifact scatters lacking standing buildings, walls, and other features that make them readily identifiable as sites. The historic value of the most obvious features, the bridges and recreation facilities of Sabino Canyon, is not emphasized and remains unnoticed by the majority of visitors.

In short, the lengthy and intimate connection between people and the landscape in Sabino Canyon is not brought to the attention of the visitor. The deeper significance of the natural beauty of the canyon is hidden, and its place in Tucson history is ignored. Both humans and the environment suffer as a consequence.

Meeting the Challenge

Existing interpretive programs clearly are not capitalizing effectively on the unique relationship between people and the environment that exists in Sabino Canyon. To remedy this, Coronado National Forest contracted with Statistical Research, Inc., a private cultural resource management firm in Tucson, to create a Cultural Resources Interpretive Plan. This plan is included in the overall Sabino Canyon Interpretive Plan developed by the Forest, which links cultural resources, natural resources, recreation opportunities, and management goals (USDA Forest Service 1991). This plan identifies two major objectives: (1) to preserve the natural and cultural features of Sabino Canyon, and (2) to enhance visitor understanding and appreciation of the canyon by providing a human perspective on the obvious natural attractions (USDA Forest Service 1991:29). The plans are consistent with the Forest Service's Interpretative Action Plan (USDA Forest Service 1989), which requires an integrated and diverse approach to increasing visitor access to and appreciation of cultural resources.

Reaching the People

To reach the people who use Sabino Canyon, we must know who they are. Sabino is one of the most heavily used outdoor recreation areas on the Coronado National Forest. Its use, which parallels the rapid growth of Tucson during the last decade, is for picnicking, hiking, bicycling, water sports, and related activities (USDA Forest Service 1976:2). Records indicate that in 1990 nearly 200,000 tram rides were provided and over 86,000 people visited the front desk at the Visitor Center. Total visitors are much more numerous, however, because not everyone uses the tram service or stops at the Visitor Center. It is estimated that more than 600,000 people visit each year, the greatest volume passing through between February and April when tourism peaks in the Tucson area (USDA Forest Service 1976:112–113).

Who are the people who visit Sabino? Although diverse, they can be divided into four groups: local residents and nonlocal visitors, both adults and children. The reasons for coming to Sabino Canyon differ markedly among these groups. For example, bicyclists are predominantly adult, local residents who do not use the tram service and are unlikely to join docented activities or stop at the Visitor Center. Older adults and families with children typically come to relax and picnic. Both groups are likely to use the tram and stop at the Visitor Center. Similarly, visitors' interest in interpretive programs varies with their age and place of residence. The out-of-town visitor is likely to want to learn as much about the area as possible, including its natural environment and its history. Locals, with the exception of schoolchildren who come specifically to the canyon to participate in the docent-conducted activities, are less likely to seek interpretive information. The entire audience cannot therefore be reached by one interpretive avenue; interpretation must be tailored to meet the public's diverse interests and abilities. The diverse audience at Sabino Canyon Recreation Area provides a unique opportunity to experiment with a multilevel approach to interpretation.

Goals for Interpretation

The Cultural Resources Interpretive Plan has four goals that take into account the unique character of Sabino's physical and cultural environment and the diversity of its visitors.

Goal 1: A New Perspective

The unique natural environment of the Sonoran Desert is readily interpretable, for it is, after all, the desert that draws visitors to southern Arizona's outdoor recreation areas. Public interpretation at most of the popular visitor centers (Saguaro National Monument, Arizona Sonora Desert Museum, Catalma State Park) emphasizes these qualities. By contrast, there are no equivalent opportunities to interpret and highlight the richly diverse cultural heritage of the Tucson area. We believe that in continuing to emphasize the natural environment over the cultural one in public interpretation, a valuable avenue to educate, inform, and entertain the public is lost. Further, as development of the Sabino Canyon Recreation Area accelerates, mitigation of potential impacts to archaeological sites within the area will be necessary, providing another avenue for public interpretation.

Interpretation in Sabino Canyon Recreation Area provides an ideal opportunity to put people back into the landscape. Its exceptional natural setting was a magnet drawing humans throughout the past. By emphasizing the human element equally with the natural environment, we can create a picture of interaction between people and their environment that is presently unavailable elsewhere, filling an interpretive gap.

Goal 2: A Regional View

Interpreting the cultural resources of Sabino Canyon requires placing them in a broader context of human history within the larger Tucson area, southern Arizona, and the Southwest. The activities that took place in the canyon in the past were only a small portion of the daily lives of the people. For both the Archaic people and the Hohokam, the canyon was primarily a resource zone. It provided plant and animal foods and materials that were unavailable beyond the riparian corridor. It was also a source of water for Hohokam farm sites. Their larger and more permanent homes were located elsewhere, along the edges of larger watercourses where the most extensive farming took place. If we focused only on those archaeological sites within the canyon, interpretation would provide an unbalanced picture of the past. Providing a wider perspective by placing Sabino within the context of the local area and the larger region can enhance appreciation of how people have adapted in various ways to the unique conditions of the Sonoran Desert. It also is one way to interpret the past when there is no single important, highly visible archaeological site on which to focus.

Goal 3: Protect the Past

Since the turn of the 20th century, Sabino Canyon has been the most popular outdoor recreation area in the vicinity of Tucson. The high volume of visitors creates potentially damaging impacts to cultural resources through casual artifact collecting, foot traffic, and occasional vandalism. The Forest Service considers interpretation a key to reducing such management problems. Protection of resources through education and awareness is a primary goal of the Interpretive Plan. It is especially important for Sabino Canyon because its resources are inherently fragile and susceptible to even minor impacts.

Interpretive Themes

The integrating theme for Sabino Canyon Recreation Area is Living with the Land, one of the themes developed by the Forest Service in partnership with the Bureau of Land Management and the Corps of Engineers (USDA Forest Service et al. 1989). The overarching message is that people adapted to their environments in ways that molded their lives and influenced their surroundings, a process that continues today. Interpretive subthemes focus on Native American prehistory and history and on Anglo-American history. The subthemes seek to interpret the cultural history and environment of Sabino Canyon in terms that are consistent with the interpretive goals.

An Oasis for the Desert Hohokam

The major Native American subtheme links the unique natural environment of Sabino Canyon with its cultural environment. The visitor learns of the exceptional economic value of the riparian habitat, whose plants and animals were intensively utilized by the Hohokam and the Archaic people before them. Interpreting the riparian plants and animals in human terms provides a new perspective. The subtheme also places Sabino Canyon within the regional system, as a resource zone that was intensively but temporarily used by farmers and collectors who lived elsewhere.

Farming the Desert

A second Native American subtheme focuses on farming techniques and how prehistoric Hohokam and historic Pimans made the desert flourish. It emphasizes the unusual character of desert rivers and streams, the water harvesting and control features that are advantageous, and the crops that were grown. Canal irrigation and agave dry farming of the prehistoric Hohokam are contrasted with Tohono O'odham floodwater or catchin farming. Comparing the different ways in which desert farming can be accomplished underscores continuity between past and present uses of the landscape.

Cattle Ranching in Territorial Days

This subtheme explores the precarious life of Anglo and Mexican ranchers during this turbulent period of Arizona history. Although focusing on a different use of the desert landscape, relationships between people and the environment are stressed. This subtheme also underscores the effects of overgrazing and other impacts in altering the desert environment over the past century.

Building Sabino in the Great Depression

Sabino Canyon exists and is largely accessible because of Depression-era federal works projects. This subtheme highlights the facilities the WPA and CCC built in the canyon. It provides an opportunity to examine the history of the Forest Service in relation to conservation management and federal funding.

Implementing the Goals:
Creating Levels of Discourse and Layers of Interpretation

The diverse mixture of visitors to Sabino Canyon Recreation Area requires that interpretation take place on different levels to meet different needs. Archaeologist and professor I. Jefferson Reid suggested that an effective plan would span simple to complex levels of interpretation. Based on this suggestion, we developed two strategies for implementing the goals of the Interpretive Plan. First, we proposed hierarchical levels of discourse to communicate with the diverse audience. Second, we developed different layers of interpretation.

Three levels of discourse in interpretation recognize the different characteristics of the audience we are addressing. Framing interpretive programs within these levels ensures that we reach as many visitors as possible, that segments of our audience are not ignored, and that the visitor who wants the most information possible will receive it.

Level 1: Functional Interpretations and Materials Identification

Level 1 is the foundation for other levels of discourse. It answers the general question, "what is it?" Visitors are likely to ask first how artifacts and archaeological sites were used, what are the names and uses of plants, and what types of animals and birds live in the canyon. This simplest level of discourse is appropriate for all visitors and for those who often have not been exposed to other types of questions, or do not know what other kinds of questions are answerable.

Level 2: Interpretation of Past Lifestyles

Many visitors will be unsatisfied with functional interpretations of artifacts and ecofacts, and will want to understand how past people wrested a living from the desert. Level 2 uses information from Level 1 in a comprehensive fashion to reconstruct past lifestyles. It is the answer to the "how" questions—how did people live? how did they feed their families? how did they build houses and ceremonial structures? This interpretive level focuses on the activities of daily life, re-creating the challenges that were faced, and reconstructing homes and villages.

Level 3: Explanation

At the highest level of discourse, Level 3 provides answers to the "why" questions. It requires interaction with the visitor who seeks answers to far-ranging questions. What was the nature of Hohokam culture and ideology? Why did their culture collapse? Are the Pimans the descendants of the Hohokam?

These levels of discourse provide solutions to how we communicate with our audience. Accomplishing interpretive goals, however, is best managed through a variety of opportunities and experiences for visitor enjoyment and appreciation (USDA Forest Service 1989). The means by which this is accomplished are potentially almost as diverse as the needs and requirements of the audience. Our Interpretive Plan specified several layers or modes of interpretation. We called them "layers" because they are overlapping and can be combined with levels of discourse in various ways to make interpretive subthemes come alive for the diverse audience.

Layer 1: Visitor Center

The hub of interpretive activities, the Visitor Center performs a number of outreach functions. It can house exhibits, provide a place for videos to be shown and lectures given, and supply brochures, books, maps, and other information. Interpretation is likely to focus on the higher levels of discourse, those of reconstructing past lifestyles and explanation. Adults, especially nonresidents, are most likely to take most advantage of the interpretive potential of the Visitor Center.

Interactive exhibits, such as signed trails, reconstructed dwellings the visitor can enter, and similar displays, are appropriately located at or begin near the Visitor Center. Such exhibits can provide information at any level of discourse but are best suited to functional identifications. They appeal to and are appreciated by school-age children. An emphasis on visual media of all types is important because the impact of Hohokam sites often is disappointingly low to the untrained eye of visitors.

Layer 2: On-Location Interpretation

Outdoor displays, interpretive trails, and similar exhibits that interpret cultural resources at the site provide a direct means of enhancing what the visitor may have difficulty in comprehending alone. For example, we suggested a signed trail to interpret some of the agricultural features of the canyon within the subtheme of Fanning the Desert. Trail interpretation would help visitors recognize the low-visibility piles and lines of rocks as traces of fields where agave and corn were grown. Lower-level discourse is especially appropriate for this type of interpretive facility. Such displays are an especially appropriate means of providing information on site preservation and protection.

Layer 3: Shuttle Tram Guides

We suggest additional training to supply the tram driver/guides with the information necessary to add the human element to the natural environment they now interpret for the public. Because so many different visitors use the trams, interpretation at the lower levels of discourse is appropriate in driver commentaries. We recommend that drivers receive training from professionals to accomplish this goal and that professionals be involved in creating new dialogue.

Layer 4: Sabino Canyon Volunteer Naturalists

The popular guided walks led by the Volunteer Naturalists can be retooled to incorporate prehistory, history, and archaeology to supplement the current emphasis on plant and animal life. We recommend a series of "Guided Walks into the Past" that can emphasize any number of interpretive subthemes and be tailored to suit different age groups. At present, these events are focused on school-age children. As with the shuttle driver/guides, retooling this concept can be accomplished with limited additional training and incorporation of additional dialogue into the existing formats.

Layer 5: Visitor Participation and Public Outreach

Handson outreach and visitor participation programs appeal to many ages and interest groups, providing educational opportunities and involving skilled professionals in the interpretation process. Within this layer, we envision: participatory exhibits in which visitors learn by doing, such as processing mesquite beans with mortar and pestle; demonstrations by experts in crafts, such as flaking stone tools or making pottery; and informal classes and workshops that serve as teaching tools while offering new skills. Public lectures, scheduled to coincide with other events such as Arizona Archaeology Month, provide an opportunity to reach a larger audience with information about prehistory, history, and historic preservation.

For the Future

The fascinating environment of Sabino Canyon cannot be interpreted effectively by itself. Our Interpretive Plan has defined audiences, identified needs, selected goals, and developed strategies for implementation, all geared toward putting people back into the Sabino landscape. The challenge now is to carry out this plan and include visitors in the experience, for they too are part of the human story of Sabino Canyon. As Tucson grows and develops its tourism potential, and as the city continues to expand and draw newcomers, the demands on Sabino Canyon as a recreational center will increase. Archaeologists, conservationists, and federal agencies can forge a cooperative approach to interpretation that will involve the public, the private sector, and the agencies in fulfilling its recreational, educational, and interpretive potential.

Chapter Fourteen

Archaeology and Interpretation at Monticello and Poplar Forest

Introduction

Archaeologists are active participants in ongoing research and interpretation at Monticello and Poplar Forest, Thomas Jefferson's central Virginia plantation homes. Each museum site presents archaeological findings to visitors to enhance their understanding of the process and principles of primary research, Jefferson and the material worlds he created, and 18th and early-19th century life in rural Virginia. Rather than attempt the impossible task of summarizing the cumulative results of more than 20 years of excavations and analysis at these sites, I will outline the ways in which archaeology has contributed to the ongoing interpretation of each property and discuss its strengths and limitations in these museum settings.

In 1769, Thomas Jefferson began construction of his first house at Monticello on land inherited from the estate of his father. The centerpiece of his contiguous 4,700-acre holdings in Albemarle County, Monticello became the site of a unique Palladian home and elaborately landscaped gardens that developed over the course of his lifetime.

Following the death of his father-in-law in 1773, Jefferson inherited the nearly 5,000-acre Poplar Forest tract. For the next 30 years, a series of overseers and a growing community of slaves occupied the Bedford County property, engaging in the annual production of tobacco and wheat. In 1806, on a knoll located between the branches of the Tomahawk Creek, Jefferson began construction of an octagonal dwelling house that served as a retreat for his retirement years. After 1810, the former president visited the property several times each year to escape from the hubbub of life at Monticello and to oversee the management of his plantation affairs (Chambers 1993:4–6, 31–38).

Following Jefferson's death, both properties passed through a period of private ownership before being purchased by organizations devoted to their preservation and public interpretation (Nichols and Bear 1982:69–71, Chambers 1993:208). Monticello, acquired by the Thomas Jefferson Memorial Foundation in 1923, has supported an archaeology department since 1979. Poplar Forest, on the other hand, is a relative newcomer to the museum world. Acquired by the Corporation for Jefferson's Poplar Forest in 1983, the property was opened to the public for the first time three years later. A long-term research program in archaeology began in 1989. Poplar Forest provides a useful case study of how archaeology can benefit a fledgling museum, while Monticello serves as a model for assessing the long-term impact of archaeological research on the interpretation of a well-established historic site.

Through a continuing program of excavations undertaken at each property, archaeologists demonstrate both the depths and the limitations of current knowledge of Jefferson's private worlds—his homes, the landscapes he designed, and the plantation communities that supported his lifestyle. Field and laboratory analyses provide a continuous stream of new evidence to form, support, or refute historic interpretations and to expand interpretive horizons by exploring previously neglected issues (Figure 14.1).

Even at Monticello and Poplar Forest—the beneficiaries of a rich source of documents accumulated over the lifetime of a monumental recordkeeper—archaeology has a strong contribution to make. Jefferson, like many of his contemporaries, found some aspects of life too commonplace to record. He recorded other aspects, particularly those within the realm of architecture and landscape gardening, in such great detail that it is no longer clear which, if any, of his plans and schemes were executed. Physical evidence of foundations or tree plantings can resolve the confusion generated by both conflicting and incomplete documentation. While biases are reflected in the surviving correspondence and commentaries of Jefferson, his family, and his colleagues, archaeology permits such topics as slavery and tenancy to be viewed with a fresh eye (Kelso 1986a; Heath 1991b:10–16; Heath 1994:16–18; Heath 1996b).

At museums actively engaged in archaeological research, excavation sites themselves become useful exhibits that both teach and challenge the public. What better way to demonstrate research in action? Working in a gridded excavation unit, surrounded by the tools of the trade—mapping equipment, cameras, notebooks, labeled artifact bags—the archaeologist can easily inform visitors why he or she is investigating a particular area, how information is systematically gathered, and how understanding of the site changes daily as work progresses. Visitors enter into the research process while it is under way and before interpretations have been codified. They learn that our understanding of the past, like the site itself, is comprised of fragments of information that must be pieced together to form a coherent whole. Often the key pieces are unrecoverable and must be replaced by informed guesswork. Through observing this process visitors gain a clearer understanding of the debt that historical interpretation owes to primary research.

Beyond demonstrating the process of primary research, the archaeological site also provides the opportunity for museum-goers to encounter firsthand an historical structure or feature with related artifacts in context. When looking at the excavated remains of a 20-by-12-foot slave quarter, visitors experience the physical size of a

Figure 14.1. Excavators at Monticello uncover the remains of a walkway connecting the All-Weather-Passageway to the vegetable garden (photograph courtesy of the Thomas Jefferson Memorial Foundation).

slave's home, the workmanship of its construction, and the range of belongings it once contained (Figure 14.2). The impact of such an encounter with the past, when experienced in such a tangible, immediate form, is difficult to achieve through oral or written descriptions alone. It is, in fact, a major factor in the appeal of historic house museums. Through archaeology, lost features of a historic property can be recovered and reexperienced, whether they are relatively minor elements, such as dismantled steps or vanished hedgerows, or major features, such as lost buildings and gardens.

In answering seemingly basic questions, field archaeology addresses the broader issues of research design and methodology— key elements in all types of inquiry into the past. Exhibiting the research process is a valuable interpretive tool. Yet from a practical perspective, it is a limited one. Often sites are quickly backfilled to ensure their preservation. What may be seen in the summer as an open cellar will appear the following spring as a level, grassy plot devoid of activity or interest. Because of the temporary nature of field research, archaeological exhibits must be based on more than site visits alone. Museum staff must find creative ways to integrate both the process and the results of archaeological inquiry into long-term interpretive strategies suited to the goals of their individual historic sites. At the Jefferson properties discussed below, staff have incorporated archaeology into interpretive media ranging from exhibits to museum shop merchandise.

Interpretive Media

At Poplar Forest, information recovered archaeologically is disseminated through a variety of media: temporary exhibits; oral communications such as guided tours, lectures, and classes; and written communications, including brochures and articles. Monticello uses all these interpretive media, to which are added permanent exhibits, restored buildings and gardens, and finally modern reproductions of archaeologically recovered objects produced for sale in the museum shops.

Exhibits and Collections

Individual artifacts and clusters of associated artifacts provide researchers with a significant source of information concerning the material world of Jefferson, his slaves, and his free workers. Excavations at Jefferson's "Wing of Offices," a dependency wing attached to the east side of the Poplar Forest house, have yielded a large assemblage of everyday objects related to domestic life on the property between 1814, when the Wing was completed, and circa 1840, when it was destroyed (Kelso, Patten, and Strutt 1991:41–42; Brooks 1994:7–8) (Figure 14.3). This evidence, combined with findings from Monticello, allows comparisons to be drawn between Jefferson's standard of living at each of his properties. Domestic objects from Poplar

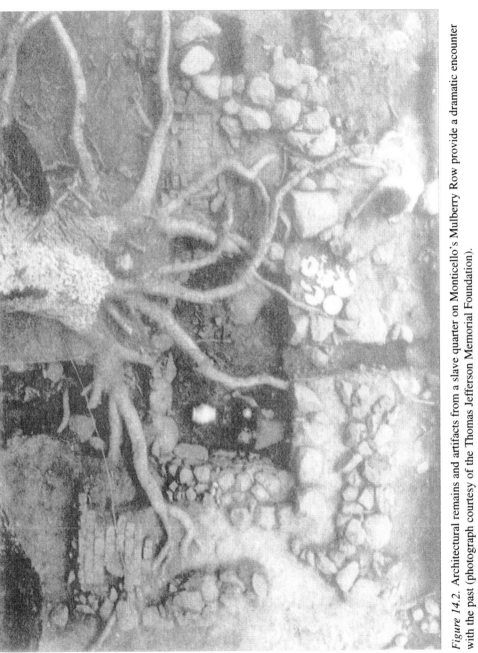

Figure 14.2. Architectural remains and artifacts from a slave quarter on Monticello's Mulberry Row provide a dramatic encounter with the past (photograph courtesy of the Thomas Jefferson Memorial Foundation).

Figure 14.3. The results of excavations at Jefferson's "Wing of Offices" at Poplar Forest are incorpo-rated in house tours and a temporary exhibit housed within the standing structures (photograph courtesy of the Corporation for Jefferson's Poplar Forest).

Forest, primarily tablewares and items related to the preparation and storage of food, appear to be less varied and correspondingly less costly than those found in deposits at Monticello. This difference may be a reflection of the private nature of his life in Bedford and the corresponding degree of informality or simplicity that such privacy allowed (Heath 1994:14–16).

A collection of more than 40,000 excavated objects from Monticello's slave quarters and service buildings, along with the field records of how the objects are related in space and time within each site, provides a valuable database for the study and interpretation of slave life in the American South. One exciting insight suggested by archaeological evidence is the presence of an economic hierarchy even within the skilled slave artisans and servants on the plantation (Kelso 1986a:12). A collection from the domestic site of two white artisans has permitted comparisons of economic status—represented by house size and materials as well as by discarded belongings—between skilled slaves and skilled white workers. Research currently underway at a Poplar Forest slave quarter has further expanded our understanding of the material world of Jefferson's laboring community. Inhabited at a time when Jefferson was an infrequent visitor to the property, the quarter site exemplifies the material conditions common to field hands and others removed from regular contact with plantation owners (Heath 1996b).

Exhibits combine artifacts, site photographs, and reproductions of documents to convey what is currently known about plantation life at each property. The glass window of the Poplar Forest archaeology laboratory allows visitors to view both synthesized data, in the form of changing exhibits mounted behind the window, and the ongoing process of laboratory analysis carried out in the space beyond. Visitors can watch archaeologists catalogue, sort, crossmend, and research objects through a "behind the scenes" window into an active laboratory. Archaeologists have used the site of Jefferson's "Wing of Offices" as the setting of another temporary exhibit at Poplar Forest. Incorporating the original floor levels, wall lines, and hearth foundations of the 1814 dependencies within the framework of later-19th century structures built on top of the site, the exhibit focuses on the process of excavation and interpretation of archaeological sites.

Monticello has developed two permanent exhibits that incorporate archaeological data. The first, located in the basement of the mansion, highlights Jefferson's garden pavilion, the house of a family of skilled slaves, several of the craft buildings on the mountaintop, and recent excavations at Shadwell, the plantation farm where Jefferson was born and spent his boyhood years. The exhibit also incorporates a display of an idealized excavation unit, illustrating for visitors some basic archaeological principles.

The second exhibit, located at an off-site visitors' center, focuses on the private life of Thomas Jefferson and on his plantation home in Albemarle County. Excavated artifacts, combined with surviving objects, illustrate the range of Jefferson's interests, from gardening to reading to fine dining. Artifacts from numerous quarters and craft buildings are combined to explore the range in housing, diet, leisure activities, and occupations experienced by the enslaved families who lived and worked on the mountaintop.

On a particularistic level, excavated artifacts recovered from contexts associated with the Jefferson family are valuable sources of information for Monticello's staff of curators, who use the archaeological collections when investigating questions of provenance. In some cases, decorative arts objects in the curatorial collections are associated with the Jefferson family through oral tradition, but cannot be verified through the surviving documents. Artifacts are consulted as one test for these associations on the assumption that if matching fragments are in our collections, the provenance may be correct.

Artifacts can also confirm documentary information concerning Jeffersonian objects that have not survived to the present, or provide evidence of objects that were never documented. For example, restoration specialists at both museums consult the archaeological collections for appropriate hardware to replicate when undertaking restoration projects. Archaeologically recovered flooring nails were reproduced to fasten a replacement deck to the north terrace at Monticello. The archaeological collections at Poplar Forest contain fragments of a servant's bell system, door hardware, and other objects originally used in Jefferson's octagonal dwelling. These will serve as models for reproduction hardware installed during the future restoration of the building's interior.

Oral and Written Interpretations

At both Poplar Forest and Monticello, the results of ongoing archaeological research are communicated orally and in writing. Research results are passed along to the staff and volunteers through training sessions, in-house newsletters, and in-house reports. Archaeologists can also share their recent findings and answer questions about past projects through seminars for docents, guides and visitor support services staff—those in most frequent contact with visitors.

Including a discussion of slavery and plantation life in each house tour has been one result of the intensive documentary and archaeological research at both historic sites. Each site has also incorporated the results of archaeological research in brochures that accompany self-guided tours of the grounds.

At Poplar Forest, volunteer docents are encouraged to include recent archaeological data as they update and refine their interpretations of the house and related landscape for presentation to the visiting public. Indeed, a discussion of archaeology has become a standard part of each tour, as docents review with visitors the findings from Jefferson's "Wing of Offices" and share recent discoveries from sites currently under investigation. Information imparted through organized tours is supplemented by lectures, open houses, and specialized tours conducted regularly by the archaeology staff.

An ongoing series of informal seminars focusing on current research has been hosted by Poplar Forest archaeological and architectural restoration staff since 1989. In 1996, staff added "Historic Garden Week" tours to the list of public offerings. These tours focused on the archaeological evidence of Jefferson's vanished ornamental landscape at his Bedford County property.

Lectures to school groups, community organizations, and professional associations, as well as articles in popular publications and scholarly journals, expand opportunities for archaeologists at both properties to share information away from each site.

Both the Thomas Jefferson Memorial Foundation and the Corporation for Jefferson's Poplar Forest co-sponsor field schools in historical archaeology through the University of Virginia. The sessions range in length from four to five weeks and run from mid-June through July. Staff archaeologists introduce students to archaeological method and theory while focusing on Jefferson, slave life, and Virginia plantations at the turn of the 19th century. The field schools provide periods of intensive field and laboratory work that result in new findings. Typically 10 to 20 adult students enroll in each session.

Since 1993, Poplar Forest has hosted a one-week summer field school that grants recertification credits to primary and secondary school teachers. Class participants divide their time between hands-on field and laboratory work and workshops designed to explore methods of bringing the multidisciplinary approach of archaeology into the classroom (Figure 14.4). Teachers are encouraged to develop thematic units focusing on archaeology and Thomas Jefferson. Classwork often culminates in site visits by participants and their students during the school year. In this way, Poplar Forest's interpretation is customized to reach school children of all ages as part of their curricula.

Restoration

While landscape restoration awaits further research at Poplar Forest, it has already become an important, though selective, tool for interpreting Monticello during Jefferson's lifetime. There, recent projects have focused primarily on the recreation of Jefferson's mature landscape design, drawing heavily on both documentary and archaeological evidence.

Documents such as plan maps and surveys provide, on the one hand, glimpses into Jefferson's changing concept of the ideal farm, and, on the other hand, his realization of those plans through time. Used alone, plan maps are often ambiguous markers of what might have been. The fragmentary references of compass bearings and distances to fixed points that are preserved in surveys cannot easily convey to the visiting public the magnitude of the changes that Jefferson wrought on the land. Yet physical evidence of original tree-planting holes, walkways, terraces, and fencelines can be combined with documents to produce an accurate blueprint for restoration.

Figure 14.4. Participants in the annual Poplar Forest–University of Virginia seminar "Digging, Learning, and Teaching: Archaeology for Teachers at Poplar Forest" take a multidisciplinary approach to education (photograph courtesy of the Corporation for Jefferson's Poplar Forest).

Figure 14.5. A combination of documentary and archaeological evidence has guided the restoration of the south slope at Monticello. From top to bottom: the vegetable garden, retaining wall and garden pavilion, a berry patch, and the southeast vineyard (photograph courtesy of the Thomas Jefferson Memorial Foundation).

During his lifetime, Jefferson manipulated his environment to integrate balance, symmetry, and order with the functional demands of a farm (Kelso 1990:20–21, Heath 1996a). This manipulation resulted in both long-lasting and temporary transformations of the landscape. In the first of two major earth-moving projects at Monticello, slaves regraded the mountaintop to form a flat platform on which to site Jefferson's house and its associated gardens. In a second project of only slightly lesser magnitude, slaves led by overseer Edmund Bacon created a terraced vegetable garden. Supported by a massive stone retaining wall, the garden stretched 1,000 feet in length. Evidence of these episodes of intensive landscaping, the first completed in 1768 and the second in 1808, is still apparent above ground. These disturbances can be traced in the soil as well, through a comparative study of stratigraphy around the top of the mountain. Interrupted or missing layers indicate areas where grading occurred, while a deeply buried topsoil layer attests to the original grade before filling.

At Monticello, most of the changes to the natural landscape proved to be impermanent. Enclosures, paths, roadways, orchards, vineyards, planting beds, shops, and houses disappeared above ground. Yet each left subtle alterations to the natural stratigraphy of the mountaintop. For example, when laborers dug holes to place fence posts, they disturbed the soil; in refilling around the posts, they mixed many natural layers together. Evidence of these disturbances survives as stains in the soil. Different activities resulted in slightly different stains, varying in depth or dimension or even soil coloring. By recognizing subtle distinctions, archaeologists are able to distinguish a tree-planting hole from a post hole. By recognizing patterned repetitions of these stains, excavators can discover the planting pattern for an orchard or the orientation of a fenced enclosure.

Based on this ability to read the soil, on the preservation of archaeological features, and on the survival of many of the original plan drawings and surveys, Monticello staff have implemented an ambitious landscape restoration that has transformed the mountaintop into an admittedly selective, but historically accurate, approximation of Jefferson's ornamental farm. Today's visitor can wander through two restored orchards, survey the property from a chair inside the garden pavilion, or examine a section of Jefferson's garden paling, all replaced on the landscape through the marriage of archaeological and documentary research (Figure 14.5).

While archaeological data have provided significant evidence used in landscape restoration at Monticello, only a limited number of sites have been restored. Perhaps the best example of how Monticello staff have chosen not to use archaeology as an aid to restoration can be found among the sites bordering the restored garden paling.

Modern steps pass through the paling, leading visitors from the kitchen garden to Mulberry Row—the heart of the plantation's skilled slave community. From 1980 until 1986, archaeologists conducted extensive excavations at a complex of buildings that served as slave quarters, free artisans' houses, and craft shops. There, footprints of houses—ranging from stone-lined cellars and extant stone footings, to post holes

Figure 14.6. Architectural evidence from recent excavations at a ca. 1790–1812 slave quarter at Poplar Forest are interpreted by an exhibit building that represents the siting and dimensions of a two-family cabin discovered on the site (photograph courtesy of Tom Graves).

outlining post-in-ground structures, to the more ephemeral floor levels and root cellars associated with log cabins—were uncovered, documented, dated, and interpreted (Kelso 1986a:6–12).

However, once the sites were backfilled, their stories were not integrated into the overall interpretive plan for the mountaintop until 1991, a full five years after excavations had concluded. In that year, building foundations were outlined at or near ground level. Staff installed signs identifying the functions, dimensions, and dates of use of buildings uncovered by archaeologists. Two years later, "plantation community" tours began to focus on slave life at Monticello. These tours incorporate archaeological evidence, using the re-created building foundations of dwellings and workshops as a backdrop for discussing issues of plantation management and daily life within the slave community. No plans currently exist to reconstruct the Row, or to make visible this aspect of the mountaintop landscape in the same way that the restored orchards, vineyards, paths, or roads have recreated the ornamental farm.

While the buildings that made such a powerful statement about Jefferson's views toward slavery, economic self-sufficiency, and plantation aesthetics remain largely invisible, recent excavations pinpointed the location of mulberry trees that once lined the Row. These elements of the plantation landscape have been restored.

In 1993, archaeologists at Poplar Forest began excavating the site of a slave quarter dating from ca.1790–1812 (Heath 1994:16–18, Heath 1996b). By the spring of 1996, excavators had uncovered the remains of three buildings, including a duplex cabin. Physical evidence of post holes and root cellars provided important information about the orientation, size, and layout of this cabin. Soil chemical residues have suggested the locations for chimneys, while architectural artifacts (daub, wrought nails, and hardware) have confirmed the materials used in construction (Fischer 1996). The archaeological and documentary evidence together suggest that slaves built the cabin of log and supported it by a combination of wooden posts and stone piers.

To augment the current levels of interpretation concerning the Poplar Forest slave community, staff members have constructed a "ghost" building above the archaeological remains of the cabin (Figure 14.6). This structure, built entirely of modern materials, is not intended to replicate the historic building, but rather to represent its dimensions, siting, and plan. By translating the archaeological data into a three-dimensional exhibit, Poplar Forest interpretation staff are endeavoring to communicate essential findings of the excavations while at the same time acknowledging that limitations of the evidence preclude a full-scale reconstruction. The exhibit provides visitors with enough information to visualize the essential structure. More importantly, it provides a physical context within which the stories of individuals who lived and worked at Poplar Forest can be better understood.

Product Line

At Monticello, archaeology has played a role in the development of new product lines for the Foundation's mail order catalogue and on-site shops (Figure 14.7). Currently the shops offer for sale a variety of reproduction ceramic vessels—all adapted from porcelain, pearlware, creamware, and coarse earthenware vessels unearthed at Monticello. Other reproductions or adaptations include: a crystal decanter based on a Madeira decanter recovered from Jefferson's dry well; a padlock; pairs of cuff links and earrings adapted from artifacts excavated along Mulberry Row; and plates, notepaper, napkins, and pot holders bearing the pineapple motif that was discovered on a Federal-period pearlware saucer. New products are introduced annually as a result of ongoing research and market changes.

Primarily an important source of revenue to support preservation at Monticello, museum shop goods also fulfill an educational role. Reproductions of Jeffersonian objects directly link the past to the present by reintroducing popular-18th and early-19th century designs, colors, and forms in a range of everyday items.

Conclusion

Archaeology has contributed greatly to historic interpretation at both Monticello and Poplar Forest in the foothills region of western Virginia, called the Piedmont. Visitors continue to experience firsthand the process of discovering the physical remains of lost buildings, orchards, fencelines, and other historic features. Archaeological exhibits, guided and self-guided tours, lectures, classes, articles and books, restored landscape features, and even gifts reflect the influence of archaeology on the continuing historic interpretation of these properties.

Even after more than 20 years of continuous research at Jefferson sites, archaeologists must continue to seek ways to integrate our results into the "big picture" interpretation of each site. Information must be up-to-date, understandable, and, most of all, accessible. Archaeologists must work hard to ensure that their data continue to contribute to the story, or to suggest ways in which the story can be expanded.

In the future, many more discoveries await those who choose to study Jeffersonian sites. Additional slave quarters, overseers' dwellings, support buildings (including mills, barns, and stables), roads, paths, fencelines, and planting beds remain hidden on the landscapes of Jefferson's former homes. Like pieces of a puzzle, the information recovered from each of these sites will come together to provide a more complete picture of the plantation worlds Jefferson created in the Virginia Piedmont.

Figure 14.7. Wine glass stems, a nearly complete Madeira bottle, mended and whole wine bottles, and a wine bottle seal all contribute to the interpretation of Jefferson's table and his wine cellar. The Madeira bottle has been reproduced for sale in the Monticello museum shops (photograph courtesy of the Thomas Jefferson Memorial Foundation).

Chapter Fifteen

The Interpretation of Slavery:
Mount Vernon, Monticello, and Colonial Williamsburg

In an article entitled *Social Responsibility and the American History Museum,* Edward Chappell, Director of the Architectural Research Department at Colonial Williamsburg, argued that "museums have a responsibility for the broad social implications of what they present, as well as for the accuracy and clarity of the particular subject with which they are dealing" (1989:247). Chappell called for a reanalysis of the way we interpret history and for the interpretation of those aspects of the past—the life of the working class, of women, and of minorities, for example—that museums have largely ignored.

Presenting a more accurate past has long been a concern of museums. Just about every historic house, period restoration, or living history museum constantly searches for new information, be it through directed historical research, the discovery of new documents, the purchase of new objects, paint analysis, or archaeology. Directly or indirectly, this often leads to different-looking rooms, new tours, or reconstructed buildings.

The search for new facts is only part of the battle. Chappell's call for more socially responsible interpretation has often not been heeded. Museums are fairly conservative institutions. Changes in them tend to be more evolutionary than revolutionary. Moreover, museums tend to follow rather than initiate changes in social attitudes. The scholarship on which museum exhibits are based is often out-of-date by the time the exhibit opens. Regardless, social responsibility is a calling to which all museums should aspire.

The authors were greatly assisted by conversations with staff members from Mount Vernon, Monticello, and Colonial Williamsburg. Our thanks to Rosemarie Byrd, Ed Chappell, Peggy Howells, Arthur Johnson, Sandra Johnson, Sylvia Lee, and Robert Watson at Colonial Williamsburg; Rex Ellis, formerly at Colonial Williamsburg and now at the Smithsonian Institution; Dennis Pogue and Esther White at Mount Vernon; and Robin Gabriel, Barbara Heath, Linda Lisanti, and Cinder Stanton at Monticello. The views expressed are those of the authors. Research for this project was supported by a Research Opportunities Fund Grant from the National Museum of Natural History, Smithsonian Institution.

This article considers how the historical fact of slavery is presented and interpreted at Mount Vernon, Monticello, and Colonial Williamsburg. These sites were chosen because they are the most popular historic sites in Virginia and among the most well-attended in the country. Mount Vernon and Williamsburg each attract around a million visitors a year, while Monticello hosts more than 500,000. Further, they are important loci for the development of both an American identity and an understanding of the colonial past. Mount Vernon and Monticello are monuments to Washington and Jefferson, while Williamsburg brings 18th century revolutionary America alive. The inspirational component of these sites is easily seen in the literature of the organizations that operate them (Ellis 1989; Schell 1985; Wallace 1986).

Mount Vernon, Monticello, and Williamsburg were also chosen because they are models for the museum community in developing programs and exhibits. All three sites also have active archaeological programs and incorporate archaeological findings to varying degrees in the interpretation of slave life. Thus, we can see how archaeology factors into their historical interpretation.

Finally, these sites offer some of the best interpretation our country has to offer. Countless plantation homes never address slaves or slavery. Some like Ashlawn-Highland, home of James Monroe, use their reconstructed slave cabin for public programs or to demonstrate colonial crafts. Others like Woodlawn, Nelly Custis's home (now owned by the National Trust for Historic Preservation), continue to sell in the museum shop reproductions of old racist advertisements, dolls of slave families, and other stereotypical images of blacks.

Why Look at Slavery?

Museums *never* present "objective" pasts. No matter the extent of research, the real past will always elude us. What we get instead are re-creations of the past—historic landscapes that reflect the biases and interests of the creators. Although the inherent subjectivity of historical representation is generally acknowledged by the museum community, the visiting public is not always aware of it. Rightly or wrongly, people expect the truth when they go to a museum. "Subjective" interpretations presented in exhibits and restorations, because they are associated with museums, gain status as accurate and true portrayals of the past. But to what extent are they really true and accurate?

Both George Washington at Mount Vernon and Thomas Jefferson at Monticello depended on slaves to work their fields, staff their mansions, and run the plantation craft industries; indeed, half the population in Williamsburg in the 18th century was black, both slave and free. Given the significant black presence at these sites, how is African-American life and labor portrayed today?

Mount Vernon

One of the oldest historic house museums in the United States is Mount Vernon. Following Washington's death in 1799, the plantation was passed down through the Washington family until purchased by the Mount Vernon Ladies' Association (MVLA) in 1858 for $200,000 (Marling 1988). The MVLA continues to own and operate the estate.

Mount Vernon currently sits on 500 acres, a fraction of the 8,000 acres that Washington owned when he died. The property is approximately the size of Washington's Mansion House Farm. One of five farms, the Mansion House Farm was Washington's administrative center and showpiece. The plantation's major crops, first tobacco and then wheat, were grown mainly at the outlying farms. Nevertheless, Washington required approximately 90 slaves to maintain the Mansion House Farm.

Since the beginning of the MVLA's ownership, the decision was made to preserve the estate as Washington left it in 1799. Early suggestions to take down all structures except for the mansion and Washington's tomb were disregarded. The landscape the MVLA purchased, however, was not that which was left by Washington. Many of the buildings on the property were in a sad state of disrepair or had fallen down. Since the mid-19th century, then, the Mount Vernon landscape has been in a constant state of flux as various buildings have been restored, re-created, and filled with objects.

Beginning in the 1930s, the MVLA sponsored archaeological research as part of the restoration process. The vast majority of the excavations were geared toward locating the foundations of outbuildings that no longer existed, tracing fencelines, and identifying landscape and garden features. In the 1980s, an archaeological survey of the property was undertaken by the Virginia Research Center for Archaeology (VRCA). In 1985, the MVLA established its own Archaeology Department (Pogue 1988).

Some archaeological research has focused on the Mount Vernon slaves. Excavations were undertaken in the 1950s to uncover the foundation of the Greenhouse Quarter (Figure 15.1). Unfortunately, the excavation goals were oriented more toward discovering foundations than traces of slave life. This building was reconstructed later in the 1950s and interpreted with objects in the early 1960s. More promising were excavations at the House for Families conducted in the 1980s, first by the VRCA and later by Mount Vernon's Archaeology Department. The House for Families was the major slave quarter on the Mansion House Farm till it was razed sometime in the early-1790s. Excavation of the quarter's cellar yielded a rich deposit of faunal material and artifacts.

Interpretation at Mount Vernon consists of a guided tour of the mansion and kitchen and text on signs at the various outbuildings. A museum and a museum annex display Washington family relics along with architectural and archaeological artifacts. Slavery is primarily interpreted with signs at the quarters. Some artifacts from the House for Families excavations are on display at the museum annex. Near the slave burial ground, the MVLA used to distribute a pamphlet on slavery at Mount Vernon; it has since gone out of print. Slaves are occasionally mentioned on the house tour, generally in response to a question from one of the tourists.

Slavery is benignly portrayed at Mount Vernon. Slaves are faceless and nameless. Aside from the passive presentation of information through signs, visiting the slave quarters is entirely discretionary and easily missed. Only one-quarter of the living space at the Greenhouse is interpreted as a slave residence; the remaining space houses the museum shop, museum annex, and storage space. Thus, slavery is deemphasized at the site. The Spinning House Quarter is a fanciful presentation of slave living conditions. The room is filled with objects, such as furniture, a spinning wheel, nice ceramics, and a pretty coverlet for the bed. The effect is more akin to a quaint country-inn bedchamber than a slave quarter. A visitor could easily gain the impression that slave living conditions were not so bad after all.

Although the museum annex does contain some artifacts from the House for Families excavations, these are simply identified. Little attempt is made to provide some context for them. It is ironic that one learns more about slavery at Mount Vernon and sees more objects from the archaeological investigations at the House for Families in the Smithsonian's Museum of American History exhibit *After the Revolution* than at Mount Vernon itself.

Monticello

Jefferson's Monticello sits on a hill overlooking Charlottesville, Virginia. Monticello, like Mount Vernon, was a showcase farm, a centerpiece for Jefferson's plantation operations. Also like Mount Vernon, Monticello is owned and operated by a private organization, the Thomas Jefferson Memorial Foundation.

Monticello, however, has had a much shorter life as a historic house museum, having been purchased by the Foundation in the 1920s. Furthermore, although the house and grounds are well maintained, there is little pretense that Monticello's landscape is an authentic one, preserved in the manner of Mount Vernon's.

Interpretation at Monticello, like at Mount Vernon, focuses on a guided house tour. We are told that Monticello reflects the personality of its owner perhaps more than any other home (Nichols and Bear 1982:7). Each room is in some way a celebration of Jefferson's intellect, as exemplified by his famous clock, library, automatic doors, octagon room, and dumbwaiters. Aside from the main part of the mansion, most of the estate is interpreted with simple signs. Only the kitchen and the wine cellar in the mansion's service wings have objects in them. The servants' (slave) quarter near the kitchen is not identified.

Aside from period room displays, the Foundation has undertaken two museum exhibits. The first, a small exhibit under the mansion, displays some of the artifacts found during excavations at Monticello. The second and much more extensive exhibit is located in an information center outside the historic area. Mounted in 1986, this

Figure 15.1. The Greenhouse Quarter at Mount Vernon houses a living space interpreted as a slave quarter (courtesy Monticello, Thomas Jefferson Memorial Foundation).

exhibit shows how the house was designed and addresses agricultural production, the life and labor of slaves, and a day in Jefferson's life at Monticello. Interestingly, archaeological objects appear throughout the exhibit. (Figure 15.2).

Archaeology has had a visible presence at Monticello, and much of it has concentrated on the archaeology of slave life. Mulberry Row was a series of cabins and workspaces for both slaves and white servants located off the eastern side of the mansion. Although there were some early archaeological investigations of Mulberry Row in 1957, the bulk of research has been undertaken since 1981 (Gruber 1990; Kelso 1986a, b). These excavations, complemented by Jefferson's extensive farm records, provide excellent documentary and material evidence concerning the organization of slave household space, food practices, and the material conditions of slavery

Given these findings, it is interesting to see how slavery figures into interpretation at Monticello. Until recently, it was not uncommon for interpreters in the house to refer to the slaves as servants. This practice was justified because "servant" was Jefferson's term for his slaves. The problem was that the word "servant" suggested to tourists that someone was paid for his or her services, rather than was owned outright, body if not soul. This is an example of the past serving the present; interpreters were provided a euphemism that allowed them to avoid talking about an uncomfortable subject. Vestiges of this practice continue. The archaeological exhibit beneath the mansion still refers to the slave cabins on Mulberry Row as "servants' houses."

The presentation of artifacts from cabin excavations with no explanatory text can also lead visitors to the wrong conclusions about what they are seeing. The presence of Chinese-export porcelain dishes and teawares in the slave cabins leads to the misperception that slaves ate with better tableware than many of us do today. The truth is that these items were likely mansion hand-me-downs or, in the case of the dishes, mass-produced, inexpensive porcelain pieces.

Unlike at Mount Vernon, there are no reconstructed slave cabins at Monticello, and Mulberry Row was uninterpreted until as recently as 1990—an omission perhaps related to the Foundation's reluctance to confront Jefferson's slaveholding past. In that year, the Foundation first published a pamphlet about Mulberry Row that includes personal information about some of the better-known slaves at Monticello— members of the Hemings family, and Isaac Jefferson. Significantly, it is the opinion of some of the staff at Monticello that archaeological research was a catalyst for these positive changes.

Colonial Williamsburg

Of the sites we visited, Colonial Williamsburg is the most different, and the most difficult to discuss. In contrast to Mount Vernon and Monticello, which are historic house sites of the rich and famous, Williamsburg is a re-created colonial townscape, whose permanent residents were people unknown to most visitors. Reborn in the

Figure 15.2. Exhibit case depicting slave life and labor at Monticello Visitor's Center (photograph courtesy Thomas Jefferson Memorial Foundation).

patriotic fervor of the Colonial Revival and with the wealth of the Rockefellers, Williamsburg is a celebration of 18th century revolutionary America.

Part museum, part playground, part shopping arcade, at Williamsburg one can study decorative arts, learn some history, see colonial craftspeople, eat a colonial-style meal, and buy ample souvenirs to take back home. Williamsburg employs hundreds of people and is an active participant in the planning and development of surrounding tidewater Virginia. Given its size, visibility, resources, and visitation, Williamsburg may be America's most important historic site.

Interpretation takes many forms here. Visitors mostly see costumed interpreters who discuss colonial trades, life in the 18th century, and the families who lived in town. At many sites there is some first-person interpretation whereby interpreters role-play 18th century characters. Also offered are many tours and special programs, such as plays, lectures, and concerts. Finally, the Colonial Williamsburg Foundation operates a decorative arts museum, a folk art center, and an archaeological exhibit.

Black history has made inroads at Colonial Williamsburg, though this was not always the case. For years, one could easily go to the restoration yet hear little about African-Americans and see few black interpreters. Certainly one would have little idea that half the 18th century population of Williamsburg was black (Ellis 1989, 1990; Martin 1973).

The absence of a black presence at Colonial Williamsburg was not due to a lack of information. The Foundation commissioned historian Thad Tate to write a book about Williamsburg's colonial black community. Written in the late 1950s, *The Negro in Eighteenth-Century Williamsburg* was published in 1965. It remains the only published book-length manuscript on the subject. Another source of information was the archaeological research undertaken at a number of slave-related sites in the region—most notably Kingsmill and Carter's Grove—in the early-1970s.

More active interpretation of black history began in 1979 when the Foundation sought the participation of blacks for its new programs in living history. Significantly, in 1988, the Foundation established a Department of African-American Interpretation and Presentations under the direction of Rex Ellis (Ellis 1989:282).

Currently, the interpretation of African-American life at Colonial Williamsburg is restricted to a few venues. Slavery is discussed at Wetherburn Tavern and interpreted for school groups at the Benjamin Powell house (Figure 15.3). Free black and slave life and labor are incorporated into interpretation at the cooper shop. A special tour called *The Other Half* introduces the public to West African history, the slave trade, and slave life in Williamsburg and colonial Virginia. Perhaps most impressive, the Colonial Williamsburg Foundation erected three 18th century slave cabins at Carter's Grove plantation in 1988 and began interpreting them to the public in 1989.

Where slave life has been interpreted, it has been well done. At Carter's Grove and Wetherburn Tavern, visitors begin their tour of the plantation and tavern by visiting areas where the slaves lived and worked. The effect is powerful. Beginning in this way, slavery and slave society frame the rest of the tour for the visitor. Proceeding on

Figure 15.3. A visit to Wetherburn's Tavern at Colonial Williamsburg includes a tour of the tavern and the work and living areas of Henry Wetherburn's slaves (photograph courtesy Colonial Williamsburg Foundation, Williamsburg, Virginia).

to Wetherburn Tavern after visiting the slave quarter and kitchen, we noticed that *most* of the questions from tourists thereafter *revolved around slavery.*

The reconstructed quarter at Carter's Grove is located on the actual site where approximately 24 slaves from the Nathanial Burwell Plantation were housed in the late-18th century. The reconstruction is based on archaeological data recovered from the site and similar sites studied in the Chesapeake Bay area. No foundations or wall trenches were uncovered, yet a series of rectangular soil stains mark the location of storage pits, suggesting that the site was once slave quarters. Similar pits, apparently used for food storage and the safekeeping of valuable objects, have been found at other slave sites in Virginia. The selection of objects for the re-creation of the interior living spaces was based on archaeological findings.

At the cooper shop, we saw interpretation at its best. Felix Simmons, an interpreter/artisan working in the shop, engagingly brought social history into practice. Simmons introduced the audience to both the craft of coopering and the concept of social history. He talked about the lives of blacks, women, and poor whites in Williamsburg in the 18th century. He also discussed how to look at Williamsburg's "historic" landscape, pointing out that it is the Colonial Williamsburg Foundation's re-creation of the past—a vision of what the past was like for a very small portion of the population.

Dressing docents in costumes and role-playing are important to the presentations at Carter's Grove, Wetherburn Tavern, and the cooper shop. But it is interpreting the lives of the poor and historically ignored that makes these sites admirable models for all museums. Unfortunately, since Williamsburg is a big place, the interpretation at these three sites is clearly not representative of what is offered overall. At present, these sites are interpretive islands of black history surrounded by a sea of interpretation that neglects the contributions of women, minorities, and the poor. What we saw at Carter's Grove, the cooper shop, and Wetherburn Tavern should be extended to the rest of Colonial Williamsburg.

The adoption of a social history approach may be hindered by the commercial interests of the Foundation—interests that may predominate at the expense of good history. At Williamsburg, the line between the interpretation of history and the commercialization of history are occasionally very blurred. This is evident both in the restoration area, where shops and interpretive areas front one another, and in the pages of the *Official Guide to Colonial Williamsburg,* where ads for shops and services are mixed in with the text of the guide (Olmert 1985). There is always the fear that, if tour guides or docents depict and discuss slavery or present a mussed-up version of history, they may offend visitors, who may then not want to return to visit (thus threatening the survival of the historic site). Underlying this fear is a presumption that the public does not want to be challenged, that it comes simply for entertainment or to have its preconceived beliefs affirmed.

Looking Back, Looking Forward

Although positive inroads have been made, the presentation of slavery at Mount Vernon and Monticello is best characterized as mostly benign and, occasionally, willfully neglectful. One detects an underlying concern: that to interpret slavery tarnishes the memory of the heroes Washington and Jefferson. Mount Vernon and Monticello are, after all, shrines to these two men. We have to ask ourselves whether their significant accomplishments are diminished by their roles as slave owners. Perhaps we should accept our heroes as they are—rather than construct them as we would *like* them to be.

Colonial Williamsburg has gone further than these other sites in interpreting slavery, but it still has the most to do. The restoration area is very large, and much of the interpretation sorely lacks any inkling of a social-history perspective.

Staff at all three of these historic areas are clearly interested in better interpreting slavery. At Mount Vernon, more of the Greenhouse Quarter is being considered as the setting for a more active interpretation of slavery. Experts have conducted archaeological excavations of field slave cabins to gain a better understanding of the range of slave life and living conditions. As part of a larger effort to interpret Mount Vernon as a working plantation, Monticello staff members have developed a guided tour of Mulberry Row which examines slave life, and installed an exhibiton that depicts the living area of a plantation cook in the basement of the mansion. The goal at Colonial Williamsburg is to mainstream a social-history perspective into all the interpretation.

Conclusion

The outbuildings that serve the plantation mansions at Mount Vernon and Monticello and those that stand behind the stores, taverns, and houses on Duke of Gloucester Street in Williamsburg are sometimes known as dependencies. The term is both ironic and a misnomer, since it is used to indicate less-important structures—places whose existence depended on the will of the property's owner. As Martin (1973) suggests, we need to reconsider "who was dependent on whom." Look at the term *dependency* in a different way and you get a better sense of what its meaning should be—structures peopled by individuals on whom the plantation owners and their way of life depended. Remove the slaves from a plantation and you no longer have a plantation.

Charles Wall, former superintendent at Mount Vernon, writing some 20 years ago about how accurately and fully outbuildings should be restored, asked, "Do we achieve anything of consequence by diverting the attention of the visitor from the significant to the incidental?" (1974:28). What historians, archaeologists, and museum professionals deem significant is a subjective decision. There is no objective standard of significance. The mission of social history is to render significant what has been thought incidental—to make central the important contribution that the common person has made to America's past.

The ultimate goal of social history and good interpretation is not simply to add voices to mainstream history, but rather to mainstream those voices into history. History museums are representations of America and, as such, have an obligation to present a history that includes all of us.

Chapter Sixteen

Museum in the Making:
The Morven Project

The house called Morven (Figure 16.1) in Princeton, New Jersey, served as the state's gubernatorial mansion from 1956 to 1982. More recently (1987 to 1990), it was the subject of intensive archaeological, architectural, and historical research as the New Jersey State Museum prepared to restore the house and grounds for use as a satellite museum of cultural history and decorative arts. While changing uses through time have added to the site's significance, the "Morven mystique" derives from an earlier association with the Stockton family. Richard Stockton, son of the original owner, was one of New Jersey's five signers of the Declaration of Independence. His wife, Annis Boudinot, was the sister of Elias Boudinot, president of the first Continental Congress. Thus, although basically a 19th century structure because of major modifications made by Richard's son and grandson, Morven has become a symbol of the founding of our country.

As David Kertzer points out in his study *Ritual, Politics, and Power*, symbols in a modern political context are complicated. They are characterized by three important properties: condensation of meaning, multivocality, and ambiguity (Kertzer 1988:11). In other words, they combine diverse ideas, are understood by different people in different ways, and cannot be reduced to any single precise meaning. Morven is a perfect example. While representing principles of democracy won through revolutionary struggle, it became known as a gathering place for the socially elite. The site that George Washington visited was also the residence of 20th century governors Meyner, Cahill, Hughes, and Byrne. Some know Morven as the house of Robert Field Stockton, the mid-19th century naval hero who, as every cadet learns, revolutionized warships with the single-screw propeller. Others remember feisty Mrs. Hughes's refusal to house her "extra" children in an outbuilding; she converted the attic to a dormitory and installed an unsightly fire escape as a safety measure.

Although Morven means many things to many people, the tangible tie between New Jersey and the Declaration of Independence is most often cited as the basis for Morven's significance. However, the emotional ties (characteristic of attachment to symbols) are more complex. According to Al Felzenberg (whose doctoral dissertation in political science dealt with the four governors who lived there), Morven is not just the house of a signer; it is New Jersey's most historic house—historic because of what happened there, not necessarily because of what has been physically preserved. In this context, the New Jersey State Museum began restoration and developed an archaeological interpretation program. The symbolic dimension—Morven's ritual role—was often ignored in the process of scientifically investigating the site, but, in retrospect, it is the symbolic dimension that made the project so interesting.

In discussing the New Jersey State Museum's approach and its archaeological interpretation program, we can examine the public's involvement and also assess what has happened since the project was terminated. All this sheds light on the public's response to the interpretation of historic sites. In the case of Morven, the problem of who owns the past is more than an abstraction. Morven has a symbolic meaning for many, and manipulating its future continues to be a sensitive issue.

A Museum in the Making

Morven was given to the state by former governor Walter Edge in the early-1950s on condition that it serve as either a gubernatorial residence or a museum. The structure had exhausted its usefulness as the former when, in 1986, the New Jersey State Museum, a division of the Department of State, assumed administrative responsibility and began developing Morven into a museum of cultural history and decorative arts. Al Felzenberg, Governor Thomas Kean's under-secretary of state; Leah Sloshberg, the museum's dynamic director; and Sue Crilley, curator of cultural history, approached the restoration in a way that set new precedents for historic preservation in New Jersey.

Fundamental to the approach was a commitment to authenticity. The house and grounds would be restored only when enough information on its past was gathered. Recognizing that Morven's mystique was in no small degree the product of myth as well as fact, the State Museum turned to experts in documentary research, architectural history, and archaeology for "the truth." Connie Greiff of Heritage Studies in Hopewell, New Jersey, directed the documentary study; the National Park Service (North Atlantic Historic Preservation Center, Boston) analyzed the standing structure; and Anne Yentsch, formerly the codirector of the *Archaeology in Annapolis* project, headed the landscape archaeology program.

Also fundamental was a commitment to keep Morven open to the public during the research process. The State Museum publicized the project as a "museum in the making." The public was invited to observe historic preservation in action—to come backstage, so to speak. The approach seemed quite natural in the late-1980s when movements in art and literature emphasized process and deconstructing texts rather than analyzing final forms (Norris 1988; Jencks 1989). It also seemed natural to those

Figure 16.1. Morven before archaeological work began. Photograph by Marty O'Grady.

of us archaeologists who are used to being on display. However, at Morven, we did more than dig and answer questions about technique. We talked about how we arrived at interpretations of the archaeological remains. Emphasizing how each generation at Morven, including our own, understood the site in terms of a particular "present" (Yamin and Yentsch 1989a, 1989b), we attempted to explain the process of reconstructing the past. The subsequent dialogue with the public led in an unexpected way to an understanding of the site's significance.

House tours of Morven were generally led by a staff of docents (volunteers from the local Junior League). As the architectural historians from the National Park Service punched holes in walls, x-rayed moldings, and took thousands of paint samples, guides explained the exacting process of figuring out the alterations to a house over time—in this case, over a 230-year period. Each new revelation from the exhaustive documentary study was incorporated into the narrative. Details drawn from primary documents—including letters, journals, deeds, and maps—enriched the guides' description of Morven's first five households, all headed by members of the Stockton family. The Stockton portraits, hanging in otherwise empty rooms, came alive for visitors; a tour of a faded house in disrepair was transformed into a dramatic journey through time. But judging from visitors' reactions, it was the ongoing archaeological work that most thoroughly captured the public imagination.

Archaeology on Display

Hundreds of people swarmed onto the Morven property during the first season of archaeological investigations (summer 1987). Although prepared to give regularly scheduled tours, the archaeological team was overwhelmed by the numbers. Anne Yentsch, the program's director, recognized the need to develop a more formal interpretive program. I was hired in fall 1987 to design an exhibit that would explain the archaeological process and the aims of the work at Morven. By the time the excavations resumed in the spring, we had developed educational activities and an approach to interpretation that reflected the philosophy of the project.

The archaeological research was to recover information on Morven's earlier landscapes that might be used to restore the gardens. Of particular interest was the original 18th century garden created by Richard Stockton and Annis Boudinot. Richard's letters, written while traveling in England in the 1760s, attest to the couple's collaboration on this project. From these letters and a map drawn by French cartographer Louis-Alexandre Berthier during the campaign to Yorktown (1781), we suspect that Morven's first garden was terraced (Figure 16.2). A primary aim of the first season's archaeological program was to determine whether or not the remains of the terraced garden lay beneath the level brick terraces and lawns of the governors' gardens.

Yentsch used backhoe trenches to look for the terraces. The trenches dug in the front yard showed no evidence of terracing, but Trench 3, about 200 feet behind

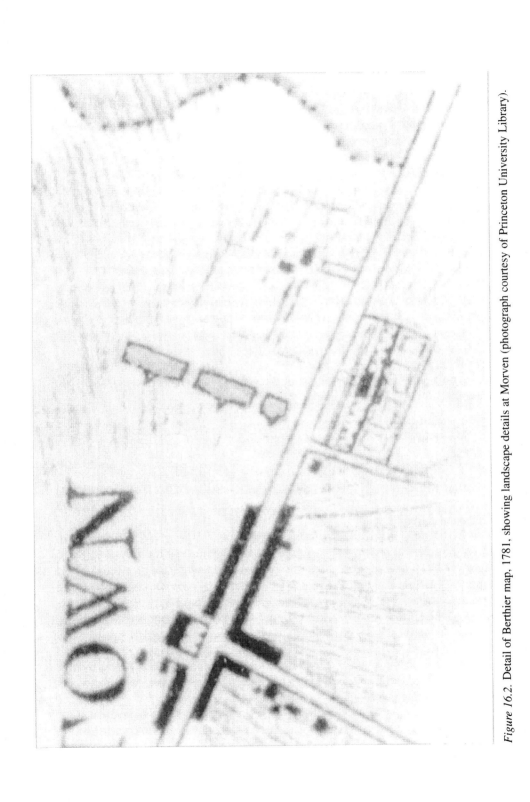

Figure 16.2. Detail of Berthier map, 1781, showing landscape details at Morven (photograph courtesy of Princeton University Library).

the house, revealed a fall of stone buried under about two feet of fill. This apparently represented the underpinning (or possibly a set of "steps") for a terrace that dated to the middle of the 19th century (Figure 16.3).

As we began to develop a route for archaeological tours during the second season (1988), we focused on the steps—the first season's major find. To reach them, visitors followed a brick path. While this path was probably laid during the governors' period, it traced an earlier grass path that was part of Helen Hamilton Shields Stockton's colonial revival garden (Figure 16.4). Helen, wife of Bayard Stockton, was the fifth and last Stockton to live at Morven (1891–1928). Her father, Dr. Charles W. Shields, bought the property from the trustees of Samuel Stockton—a retired army officer and farmer, who had let the house deteriorate and the formal gardens go to seed. Helen guided the restoration of the house and grounds. A proponent of the colonial revival movement, she made every effort to return Morven to its colonial grandeur.

Based on a 1766 letter in which Richard Stockton wrote of a planned trip to Alexander Pope's garden at Twickenham, Helen re-created the garden at Morven using Twickenham as a model. A map of the Morven landscape from Helen's time (Figure 16.5) shows a horse chestnut walk, kitchen garden, terrace, orchards, and lawns—all positioned comparably to similar features in Pope's garden (Stockton 1914).

In addition to the path, the extant remnants of Helen's colonial revival garden include tall spruce trees in the middle of the yard, stone lions flanking a small stair, and a sundial bearing the inscription:

Two hundred years of Morven I record,
Of Morven's house protected by the Lord:
And now I stand among old-fashioned flowers
To mark Morven's many sunlit hours.

The sundial, dated 1901, incorrectly celebrates Morven's 200th anniversary. Helen thought the house was built in 1701, which is actually the date the first Richard Stockton acquired the land.

As we led tours to the steps in the back of the yard, we described Helen's garden, always carefully emphasizing that each generation uses the past for its own purposes (Figure 16.6). While we took a scientific approach seeking objective proof in the ground of Richard and Annis's terraced garden, Helen, by contrast, was satisfied with a reference in a letter. While her garden presumably duplicated the original, she had no actual proof of what the original had been. We, on the other hand, believed the physical remains of the steps was our proof. As visitors stood around the steps, we emphasized their authenticity and, with dramatic effect, talked about how the poetic Annis Boudinot Stockton may have stood at the terrace edge gazing out at a pastoral landscape long since hidden by new property boundaries and residential developments.

The authenticity of the steps was enhanced by contrasting them with remnants of Helen's garden on one side and an even more recent feature on the other: a swimming

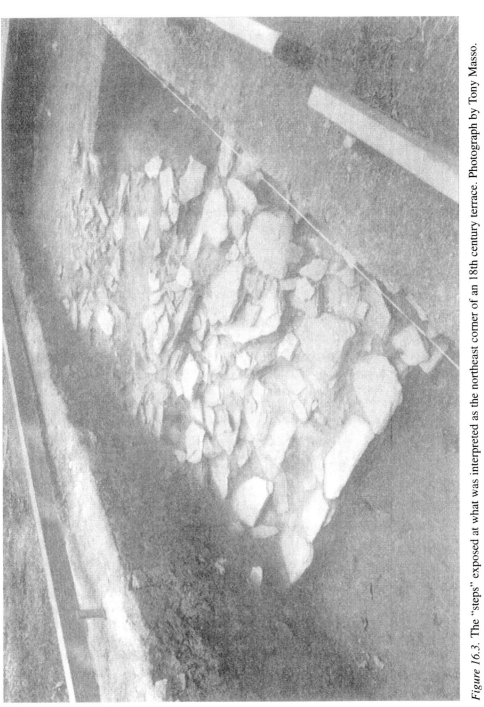

Figure 16.3. The "steps" exposed at what was interpreted as the northeast corner of an 18th century terrace. Photograph by Tony Masso.

pool/cabana/tennis court complex built in the 1930s by Morven's only renter, Robert Wood Johnson (Figure 16.7). The State Museum never intended to include the 1930s complex in its restoration. Associated with a resident who was neither a Stockton nor a governor, the complex didn't seem to fit anyone's idea of what was important about the Morven property. With some encouragement from the archaeological guides, however, visitors understood that the modern features were as much a material expression of landscape use in the 20th century as the steps were in the 18th. These disparate features juxtaposed made both pasts come to life.

The immediacy of experiencing physical remains from different periods excited even the staunchest proponents of an 18th century garden restoration. Attentive groups of otherwise quiet onlookers would often burst into animated argument over which landscape should be restored. Should Helen's trees be cut down to re-create the open terraces of Morven's first garden, or should the terraces be left buried? Should the poolhouse be removed, or should it be adaptively reused in the context of a late-20th century museum exhibit? What about the garden wall addition? Should it be taken down, or should the mid-19th century landscape, of which it was a part, be replanted?

The public's willingness to contemplate landscape restoration decisions was remarkable. On a philosophical level, people appeared to be confronting the reality of the past—of many pasts. Without discussing what those pasts might mean—a complex task—we helped visitors drop, for a moment at least, their romantic vision of how things should have been and begin to appreciate and accept the changes that had taken place through time. The message to the State Museum—and this was unexpected—was that the grounds should not be restored to one moment in time. While such a static approach might produce a beautiful garden (comparable to the William Paca garden in Annapolis, for instance), it would deny the dynamic potential of the site to let people experience the passage of time. That potential, noted by James Deetz during a short visit in March 1988, is what made Morven unusual. It became the theme of the archaeological interpretation program and fed into the museum's plans for the site.

To Restore or Not to Restore

The Morven project ended before final decisions were made about the garden restoration. Soon after entering office in January 1990, New Jersey's governor, James Florio, terminated the research. With a deficit of $600 million the state had other financial priorities. Coincidentally, termination followed a series of controversial articles in the local press. These dwelled on both the nature of the research and its physical effects, attacking the project for, among other things, creating an "unsightly mess" (McClure and Rinaldi 1989) (Figure 16.8). The articles won the critics a considerable amount of public support, including that of three of the four governors

Figure 16.4. Helen Hamilton Shields Stockton's colonial revival garden, 1920s (photograph courtesy of the New Jersey State Museum).

who had lived at Morven. "Cut off the dig," wrote a particularly strident columnist. "It [Morven] is world-renown[ed] as the 18th century home of Richard Stockton. I say use the carriage house out back for displays of other eras, but let's get back to Morven's rootstake the remaining money and reconstruct an 18th century kitchen" (Rinaldi, August 14, 1989).

In spite of her proclaimed commitment to American history, reporter Ann Rinaldi quite clearly stated that she did not think further archaeological research on the garden was necessary since similar research had already been done at Williamsburg and Monticello. "Annis Stockton got garden information out of books," she wrote in her article entitled "The Morven Mess" (September 11, 1989). "Why can't they get theirs out of others' studies?" At least six contradictory themes run through this columnist's series of articles. She laments the loss of "our best historians" while condemning the Morven project as a "laboratory for people who want to use their degrees in fine arts and archaeology"; she wants Morven returned to its "roots," restored "with authenticity," but thinks the research necessary to do just that is costing the taxpayers too much; she wants the ravages done to the property repaired, but doesn't want the Friends of Morven (a group of well-placed, civic-minded citizens) to raise the money to do it ("Why not regular people?" says Rinaldi); and she definitely doesn't want different eras in Morven's history represented no matter what the research results are. Rinaldi's articles bristled with emotion as did her followers' letters to the editor. What came through was not only the perception that Morven as a symbol had been defiled but also an angry resentment of the specialists who had been entrusted with the site's future.

Neither perception should have been surprising. As previously mentioned, Morven's symbolic significance, though attributed to its association with a "signer," depends on a multiplicity of ideas. The very fact that Rinaldi enlisted the support of three of the four governors who lived at Morven in her attack on the project suggests that symbolically the house is as much a 20th century political symbol as an 18th century one. Interestingly, the former governors and their wives seemed more concerned that Morven would no longer be anyone's "home" than with the direction or even expense of the research. "I suppose when the state invests in a museum," wrote Hughes, "it will invest in period furniture. That won't ring a bell with me, and it won't be too impressive with the citizens of New Jersey who remember it as a warm, home-like place" (quoted in an article by Dan Weissman, August 27, 1989). The New York Times reported that Cahill was "shocked" by what he saw and distressed that "they think history stopped in the 1800s and they are obliterating what happened in the last 30 years" (Sullivan 1989).

In actuality, the governors' period was discussed on an archaeological tour. Portions of a major 19th century feature—the chestnut walk—underlay a brick pathway probably dating to the 1950s, and overlay a much more modest fieldstone walk dating to the mid-18th century. The stratigraphic contrast between the three walkways representing three time periods was a highlight of the tour, epitomizing archaeologically

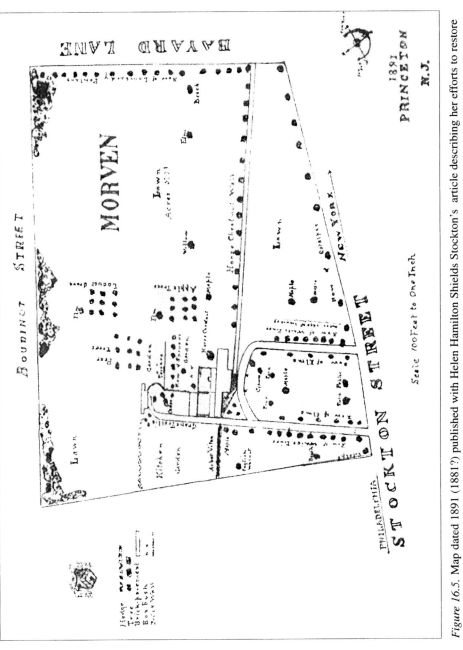

Figure 16.5. Map dated 1891 (1881?) published with Helen Hamilton Shields Stockton's article describing her efforts to restore the Morven garden at Twickenham after Alexander Pope's garden at Twickenham (photograph courtesy of the Garden Club of America)

the juxtapositions seen elsewhere on the site. However, the site was in a sense dese-crated. The destructive nature of the archaeological process, coupled with the State Museum's decision to not expend resources on landscape maintenance during the research, indeed did create a mess. Morven's normally serene, gracefully treed land-scape was dotted with dirt piles and black plastic; brick paths were upturned and hedgerows uprooted. To the uninitiated, especially those emotionally attached to the site as a symbol, no excuse was adequate.

Paradoxically, making sense from the mess was one of the things that excited visitors as they listened to an archaeologist's explanation. That which bothered Rinaldi most—the condition of the site and the proposed interpretation of many eras in Morven's past—was what open-minded visitors responded to most positively. Finding meaning in the dirt became a process of discovery—of learning to see in a new way. Seeing juxtaposed fragments of many pasts made restoration to a single period seem dull and even wrong.

One could argue that more and better tours, in addition to more than minimal maintenance of the grounds, might have prevented the outcry against the Morven project; but there was another problem. Notwithstanding its liberating intentions, the archaeological interpretive program was the creation of a scholarly elite of profes-sionally trained archaeologists. Inspired by Mark Leone, his colleagues in Annapolis, and other members of that elite (Leone, Potter, and Shackel 1987; Handsman and Leone 1989; Potter 1989a), we attempted to develop a program that would not only actively involve visitors in the process of reconstructing the past, but also communi-cate on the deepest level that people "do make their own history and can change it by their actions in the present" (Tilley 1989:114). We did not deliver the past as a "self-sufficient body of facts." Nor did we approach it as a commodity, thus treating the public as "passive consumers" (Tilley 1989:113). Rather, we engaged people's minds and imaginations in the process of trying to understand the archaeologically recovered material fragments and their meaning. There is no question that it worked. Visitors, who by their own admission expected to be bored at Morven, were instead thrilled.

However, *we* chose which fragments would be discussed. As Joan Gero so force-fully points out, archaeologists tend to appropriate the past on their own terms. She writes, "Insisting on the objectification of observation, and accepting as evidence all but only material objects (however mundane), archaeology has focused on the partic-ular questions that it can effectively address while dismissing other possible questions about the past as irrelevant or inappropriate" (1989:96). On the Morven project, this was not true in the extreme, for we went well beyond material objects in our inter-pretations, considering a sequence of ideological contexts and their connections to national cultural trends. Nevertheless and with characteristic arrogance, we dismissed various time-honored myths about the property and managed to insult any number of nonprofessionals in the process. Former governor Hughes's insistence on the 1701 construction date, for instance, was considered stubbornly ignorant; and the public's

Figure 16.6. Rebecca Yamin beginning an archaeological tour in the garden. Photograph by John Hennessy.

attachment to the "signer" as Morven's most important resident rather than his more colorful grandson, Robert Field Stockton, was considered woefully misguided. To a degree, the very acts of deconstructing Morven's myths and using scientific techniques (for example, stratigraphic excavation and phytolith analysis) to investigate its landscape were offensive. Symbols are not to be dissected, especially by scientists who fail to treat them with appropriate reverence.

Conclusions

Taking the path of least resistance or perhaps bowing to the interests that really count politically, the Florio administration chose to return Morven to its role as a "home" rather than a subject of scientific study. The excavation units have been backfilled, the grounds have been groomed, and blooming flowers again surround the stately mansion. Inside, the holes in the walls have been filled and covered with a fresh coat of paint, and efforts are under way to raise $175,000 for reproductions of 18th century mahogany furniture. The house is once again open to the public. A newspaper article published in spring 1991 quoted Mrs. Florio as saying, "A house is a house, but you have to have somebody who loves it.You have to have someone who loves Morven. This is a project that will help get over the hurdle. It will be nice to be able to tell people they should stop by Morven" (Sullivan 1991).

Morven as the "home" of New Jersey's governors and symbol of the founding of the country has clearly won out. The excitement of peeling back the layers of the past and seeing fragments of different periods in contrast to one another has been lost in the controversy, and all analysis has ceased, at least for a time. (A commission including National Park Service professionals, local experts, and interested citizens has been formed to determine Morven's ultimate future. Under the commission's direction, the portion of the ground that was excavated was returned to lawn during the summer of 1991.)

How, then, do we assess the success of the Morven project? Can we recommend the "museum in the making" approach of putting the research process on display? There are clearly dangers, especially when dealing with a site that has symbolic significance for the public. However, the response to archaeological tours was very exciting and suggests a public readiness for involvement in the process of reconstructing the past. The public's ability to appreciate authentic material remains from the past, no matter how fragmentary, also suggests that ongoing archaeology has great potential as an educational tool in a world that is replete with artificiality. The authenticity of remains in stratigraphic context and in contrast to above-ground features from different periods created a remarkable and, at the same time, indescribable drama. Only those who experienced it (through a guided tour) really understood how different it was from the usual museum experience. The problem, then, is to use other opportunities of ongoing archaeology to involve people in the reconstruction of the

Figure 16.7. The poolhouse and swimming pool installed by Robert Wood Johnson who rented the Morven property from 1928 to about 1950. Photograph by Tony Masso.

past, to devote enough human resources to make that possible, and to make every effort to get the skeptical as well as the enthusiastic to share in the experience.

While dismantling the Morven symbol as traditionally perceived, we also saw something else happen. The archaeological tour became a kind of political ritual, a blending of past, present, and future (Kertzer 1988:10). "Pointing out the eighteenth-century walkway, guides suggest the possibility that Richard Stockton trod upon its very stones while pondering whether or not to sign. The depth of the walkway, buried beneath the grandson's more elaborate walk, denotes the passage of time; the visibility of the walk and the visitor's very presence simultaneously bridge time, projecting the event forward until it partakes of the present" (Yamin and Yentsch 1989b:8). Carried to its conclusion, the Morven project would not have just taken a symbol away from the people; it would have created a new and very complex one.

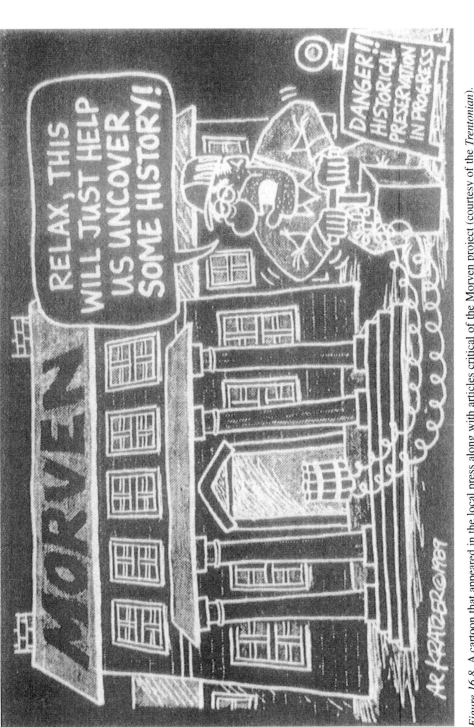

Figure 16.8. A cartoon that appeared in the local press along with articles critical of the Morven project (courtesy of the *Trentonian*).

Chapter Seventeen

Archaeological Preservation:
Drayton Hall

Imagine the challenge in conveying more than 250 years of history with an unrestored and unfurnished house, unidentified outbuildings, hundreds of acres of overgrown landscape, and limited primary documentation. Drayton Hall (Figure 17.1) presented such a challenge when it was acquired from the Drayton family by the National Trust for Historic Preservation in 1974. Since the initial archaeological investigation in 1975, the interpretation of the site today reflects the tremendous impact of two decades of ongoing historical research that has consistently relied on the insight of archaeology.

Drayton Hall, built circa 1738–42, was acquired by the National Trust because of its architectural significance and unique state of preservation. Located on the banks of the Ashley River outside Charleston, South Carolina, the house was held by seven generations of the Drayton Family and has survived a tumultuous history of war, natural disasters, and "progress" to remain one of the finest examples of Georgian-Palladian architecture in the country. The interiors have only been painted once each century, and there are areas where the original paint is still intact. Rooms boast exceptional hand-carved wood moldings and paneled walls. A family growth chart on a door casement records the family and its dogs in pencil since 1886. The building has never had electricity or plumbing added and sits on its original 350-acre tract along with several outbuildings and ruins from the 18th and 19th centuries. Its unparalleled authenticity traces more than two and a half centuries of use and change in a remarkable setting.

Initial plans for the preservation and stabilization of the main house and environs relied on architectural, historical, and archaeological studies that would eventually inform the interpretation. By the time the property was open to the public in 1976, research teams were working to compile a historic structures report documenting a historical overview and the architectural history of the building, including paint analysis. Archaeological testing provided identification of several original landscape features and structures, such as the original drive configuration, a late-18th century

Figure 17.1. Drayton Hall, landfront view (courtesy Drayton Hall).

lightning ground rod, and the kitchen building to one side of the house. Test pits in a ground floor room of the main house helped determine the original flooring material and told the story of several generations of floors that had been undermined by rodents and settling. The range and number of recovered artifacts were outstanding and demonstrated the potential for understanding the material culture of the plantation's occupants. The results of the archaeological work were published as *Drayton Hall: Preliminary Archaeological Investigation at a Low Country Plantation* by Lynne G. Lewis (1978) and provided a documented reference, along with the historic structures report, for the evolving interpretation.

Not surprisingly, the early tours focused on the architectural significance of the building, the state of preservation, and the unprecedented decision to leave the house unrestored and unfurnished. Visitors learned about the materials and craftsmanship of the building as they followed the "great planter, great wealth" storyline, images of which were easily evoked by the dramatic and aesthetic environment. Interpreters were often tempted by the abundance of undocumented stories and local legends that would make delightfully irresponsible and memorable impressions on guests. Meanwhile, documentary, genealogical, oral history, and archaeological research projects continued to flesh out the "stuff and guts" of everyday living in order to provide a "whole" picture of the site over time—proving real life much more interesting than fiction.

The lack of important documents—such as early maps that could provide some clue to the layout of the property—has made archaeology a vital resource for understanding the context of the main house and surviving outbuildings. Tantalizing diary references to a brick kiln, Dovecot[e], magazine, loom house, or tabby corn barn, among others, suggest that there is a significant community of buildings to be discovered that would reveal critical information about the activity and economy of the site. A circa-1850 sketchbook by the great-grandson of Drayton Hall's builder provided visual records of two buildings still on the property, one standing and one in ruin, that could not be positively identified and understood until they were excavated.

The extant building, referred to as the "office" by the Drayton family, dates to the same period as the main house. Constructed of brick with stone steps, the "office" exhibited later additions and some puzzling architectural details, such as an arch in the foundation at ground level. Subsequent study and excavation in 1981 confirmed that the "office" had originally been a seven-seat privy as depicted in the sketchbook. Not visible to the artist was a 30-foot brick drainage pipe extending from the arch below ground and a collection of significant household and personal artifacts, such as chamber pots, plates, bottle glass, broken china dolls, and playing marbles.

The other building, a pile of rubble by the river, was excavated in 1989 on the hypothesis that it was the remains of the "orangery," or greenhouse, depicted in the sketchbook (Figure 17.2). The findings correlated well with the proportions and details of the drawing, down to the placement of the door and a course of decorative curved brick along the foundation. In both cases, archaeology substantiated the

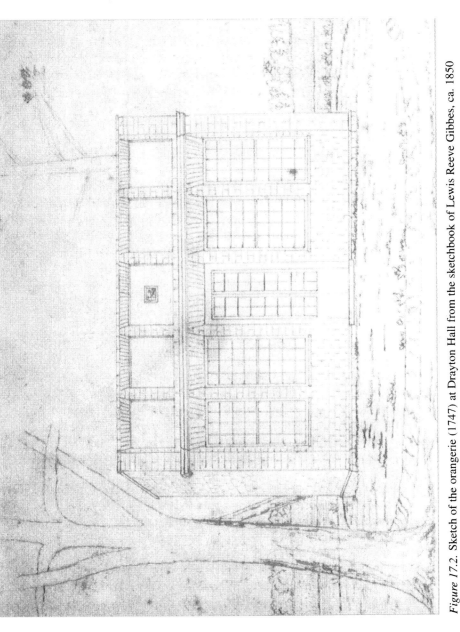

Figure 17.2. Sketch of the orangerie (1747) at Drayton Hall from the sketchbook of Lewis Reeve Gibbes, ca. 1850 (courtesy Drayton Hall).

sketchbook as a reliable resource for two circa-1742 structures, while going beyond the artistic record to explain how the buildings functioned. The use of the buildings, their locations, and artifacts translated into a rich description and comparison of everyday conveniences (or inconveniences), childhood pastimes, and gardening practices that interpreters could use to help visitors relate their own experiences with the lives of people in the past.

After ten excavation projects—ranging from short-term mitigation during the installation of drainage pipes to extensive research in a three-year residency by National Trust archaeologists—the chronology, plan, and evolution of the property is much clearer. Notably, a pattern of continuous use of the site has emerged. It begins with Native American campsites, traces colonial settlement merging into the antebellum period, and continues through the upheavals of the Civil War to current times.

Initiated by the need to install a new drain field, one project recovered clear evidence of the Native American occupation, dating largely from the Early to Middle Woodland periods. Another monitoring project located the site of what is probably the earlier "indifferent dwelling" advertised as part of the property when it was purchased by John Drayton in 1738. Excavations in and around the basement of Drayton Hall have informed us of early building materials that are no longer evident, such as slate for the roof. An abundance of Chinese export porcelain and fine glassware reveals the resources and trade available to an upper-class 18th century family in the South Carolina Low Country.

As the plantation continued to develop, two buildings flanking either side of the main house were built. Archaeological excavations of their remains have dated their construction to approximately 10 to 20 years after Drayton Hall was begun, and identified their use as a kitchen and possibly a laundry. Their state of ruin tells the story of earthquakes, hurricanes, and a garden planted over them. Both were connected to the main house by a low brick and picket fence. The "front" and "back" orientations of the main house were determined by artifact concentrations and landscape features.

Excavation at a Victorian period barn revealed evidence of the industrial use of the property for phosphate mining after the Civil War (Figure 17.3). The strip mining and processing of rock for fertilizer contributed directly to the property's financial recovery, but scarred the land and most likely obliterated important archaeological remains.

All other buildings have been identified along with the probable house sites of slaves, 19th century African-American families, and phosphate mining workers. The total collection of artifacts—some 240,000—include a range of ceramics from prehistoric to 20th century Fiestaware. Not surprisingly, the marked decline in number and variety from the post–Civil War period illustrates a significant shift in property use and family fortunes.

Archaeology's most critical contribution to Drayton Hall has been to provide a model for examining the site as a whole and broadening interpretive thinking beyond the "great planter, great wealth" approach that is so easy to fall into if one highlights

Figure 17.3. Archaeology of the barn site, fall 1990. Archaeologists pictured: Larry Dermody (left) and Lynne Lewis, National Trust for Historic Preservation (courtesy Drayton Hall).

only outstanding architecture and cultural achievement. The presence of artifacts, such as children's toys, buttons, sewing equipment, and kitchen wares, reminds us that the site was also used by women and children, family and slaves. Hoe heads, tool fragments, harness brasses, and dock pilings hint at daily work and transportation. Export porcelains, tea wares, and wine bottles reveal the personal tastes and finances of the owners and the extent of trade beyond Charleston. At the same time, the presence of large amounts of colonoware indicates that slaves, as well as Native Americans, were manufacturing pottery in the area. Seed pits, animal bone, boar tusks, and fish scales are a fraction of the variety of artifacts that inform us of the diet available through hunting and harvesting in the area. The topics of health and hygiene, technology, and craftsmanship become specific and personalized by the artifacts and their context on the property. We see that objects represent people and their way of life.

The house is a powerful artifact in its own right. The bricks and mortar, moldings and floor plans tell the story of the people who constructed, traded, worked around, lived in, visited, and preserved them. Just as with artifacts, the meaning of the house is tied to its context with the land and surrounding community, as well as with the region and the country. The goal of the present interpretation is to have visitors understand how the architecture of the building, combined with archaeological and historical evidence, documents the changes in culture and daily life over the past three centuries. One of the most obvious but effective ways to reinforce this goal beyond the tour, or an exhibit, is to present archaeologists at work. With this "inside" look, visitors share the research and interpretation process, thus validating the integrity of our mission to understand the past.

A natural extension of the general interpretation of the property for visitors is an education program (Figure 17.4) for school children. "How do we know what we know?" is the question that influences the design of and gives purpose to all our curriculum coordinated programs for grades K–12. It is no secret that students learn best when engaged in inquiry, hands-on learning, and decision making. Geared for all

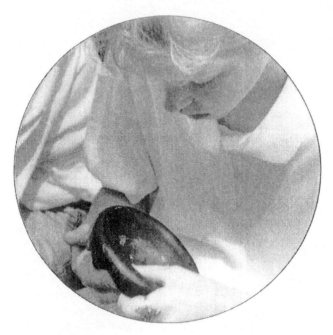

Figure 17.4. Drayton Hall educational program (courtesy Drayton Hall).

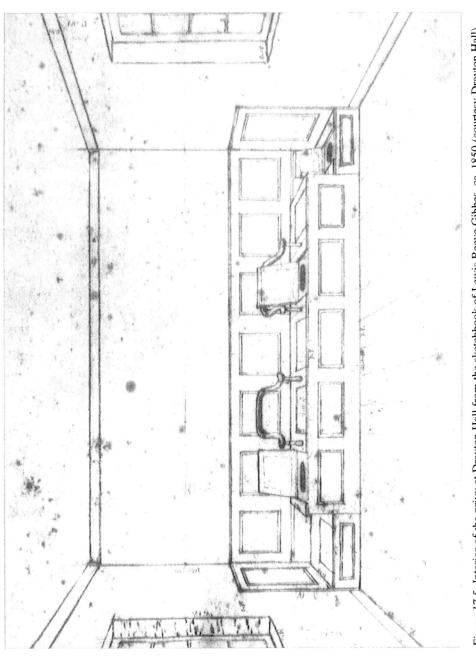

Figure 17.5. Interior of the privy at Drayton Hall from the sketchbook of Lewis Reeve Gibbes, ca. 1850 (courtesy Drayton Hall).

grades and paralleling the interpretation, the student house tour investigates "how to read a building." The Preservation Workshop for grades 4–6 uses hands-on activities with tools and materials to explore "How did they build like that?" *Games Day* helps grades K–3 find the answer to "What was it like to be a child long ago?" Archaeology programs for grades 4–12 specifically address: "How is archaeology important as a research tool? How does an archaeologist work? What is the research process? How is this process a form of preservation? Why should archaeological resources be protected?"

Diaries in the Dirt is a 45-minute program that puts students in the role of archaeologists as they uncover the history of the "office" building. Using oral history accounts, architectural clues, documents, artifacts, and photographs of the actual excavation, students piece together the time line of events that help them interpret the site from its original use as the "privy" (Figure 17.5). The process underscores the limitations of oral history and the necessity of considering a variety of primary sources in research.

Plantation Excavation goes a step further by allowing students to participate in a three-hour model excavation. Some archaeologists, in fear of creating a generation of pothunting amateurs, hyperventilate at the thought of students experiencing the process of an excavation. The purpose of our site is not to teach students and teachers to be archaeologists, but rather to develop their respect for the complexity of the process and the need for professionals to conduct excavations. Students work in teams to map, excavate, sift, wash, label, and analyze our study collection of artifacts as they are unearthed from a layered, seeded pit. Half the program is devoted to learning to analyze an object for material, type, date, and use, and half to interpreting its significance based on the context in which it was found. Indiana Jones is used as a model for what today's archaeologists are *not*, and careful attention is given to emphasizing the value of preserving archaeological resources from vandals and collectors.

It is a concern to us that, though archaeology is part of the school curriculum, every group that comes to Drayton Hall arrives wanting "to dig!" and has stories of all the wonderful things some of them have found in their area. More disturbing are the parents and chaperones who proudly describe all the artifact collections they have and the "great stuff" they have found with metal detectors. While young people are a captive audience, how do we educate and influence adults without alienating them? Our approach is to demonstrate how history would have been lost without archaeology. But how can we be sure that visitors leave understanding that preservation of the past begins with them? It is a public relations challenge that should be a major mission for all historic sites.

The future of archaeology at Drayton Hall was decided on September 21, 1989, when Hurricane Hugo smashed through the South Carolina Low Country. The storm left a wake of mangled buildings and shattered landscape. While disaster preparedness, in part, helped the main house survive with minimal damage, all that remained of the Victorian period barn was the roof sitting sideways on its foundation like a shingled tent. As for the landscape, trees were stripped and snapped off like twigs or uprooted. Over 60 percent of the trees were down, leaving gaping holes in the ground and skyline. The need to reopen the property, along with the threat of fire and blue mold, created a rush for logging and debris removal. Archaeological sites, known and unknown, were in imminent danger from the weight and treads of the logging and clearing equipment.

Drayton Hall conducted an emergency survey project under the direction of archaeologists from the state and National Trust. Using compasses, 50-foot ropes, sighting poles, and neon marker flags, staff and local volunteers navigated in a grid pattern over the impossible terrain of the devastated forest areas, marking all visible surface artifacts uncovered by the storm and uprooted trees. The purpose was to identify artifact concentrations and map potential archaeological sites that required protection from the current logging project, while formulating a site record for future disasters and a research plan for future excavations.

A grant from the South Carolina Committee for the Humanities subsidized *Learning from Hugo: Archaeology and Disaster Recovery at Historic Drayton Hall*—a project to expand the emergency survey. Archaeologists made a grid survey of the whole property that included shovel tests and test pits. Public programs on the importance of preserving archaeological sites before and after disasters were offered locally and at the State Museum, and a technical guide was developed delineating procedures for disaster preparedness and recovery of archaeological resources at historic sites.

While no one would wish for a hurricane, Hugo provided an excellent opportunity to get below the heavy overgrowth and dense forest floor that had previously been inaccessible. The surveys identified future sites for excavation and important areas that will assist in our interpretation of African-American life at Drayton Hall. General and specific locations of slave cabins and post-war tenants' and phosphate miners' homes were found, along with the remains of an 18th century rice pond trunk and significant 19th century artifacts. The loss of the barn revealed the footprint of an industrial machine base and several earlier work sites.

In the spring of 1992, Drayton Hall conducted an unusual project to correlate oral history and archaeology for a documentary video. *I'd Like to See What's Down There* follows the excavation of the childhood homesite of Richmond Bowens, whose remembrances of life at Drayton Hall have been a tremendous resource for research and interpretation. Born at Drayton Hall in 1908, the grandson of freed slaves, Bowens (Figure 17.6) grew up on the property and worked for the Draytons as a young man. At age 84, he assisted National Trust archaeologists, historians, and educators in demonstrating how a variety of primary resources are used to document and interpret the past. The video has since been selected for national television broadcast on the History Channel, a division of the Arts and Entertainment network. A cassette walking tour of the homesite and other archaeological areas and landscape features will be developed next, using the oral history accounts of Bowens, the Drayton family, and others associated with the property.

Figure 17.6. Richmond Bowens (courtesy Drayton Hall).

The surveys after Hurricane Hugo have provided a road map for archaeology and research that we expect will constantly challenge our interpretation into the next decades. Plans for the years to come include further investigation of the "indifferent dwelling" that pre-dates Drayton Hall, along with excavation of the slave quarters, tenant homes, blacksmith's shop, and other work areas. The "orangery" and garden areas have much to offer historic landscape scholarship, and there are still sections in and around the main house that need to be explored for clues to its construction. Archaeology has made the voice of the past strong at Drayton Hall. We look forward to helping visitors hear it.

Chapter Eighteen

Interpreting Archaeology at Little Bighorn

The Battle of the Little Bighorn, or Custer's Last Stand, has been an enduring American legend since that fateful day of June 25, 1876. The near-mythological proportions the story has assumed, recently combined with the public popularity of archaeology, has resulted in widespread public attention to the Custer Battlefield Archeological Project. This attention was focused by an international media blitz that overshadowed the press coverage of the original fight. The overwhelming public interest and how the project attempted to deal with the immediate need for interpretive feedback to the public is the subject of this article.

Battlefields as a whole are really ceremonial sites where the public can see, touch, and experience an interpreted version of the past. Often battlefields are perceived in very romantic terms. This is especially true at Little Bighorn Battlefield National Monument where nearly every visitor arrives with a preconceived notion of the story of the Battle of the Little Bighorn. These notions range from those of the truly literate scholar, to those of the visitor whose misconceptions are generated from having seen one of the many motion pictures or TV productions on the subject.

Visitors' attitudes can be classified into one of several very general and overly simplified categories. First are the Custer detractors who believe that he got what he deserved for whatever reason. Second are the Custer apologists who are convinced that Custer's command was wiped out because of the failure of someone. Often this is the basis for the great cover-up theory. The third category is the "lo, the poor Indian" group who believe Native Americans were mistreated and this victory was their single greatest triumph, even if it signaled the end of a lifeway.

Obviously, no category is exclusively correct or necessarily wrong. The park's interpreters face a real challenge; their oral presentations must be objective and factual, and, at the same time, they must be ready to politely dispel myths generated from often uninformed but widely held beliefs. Furthermore, the interpretive story of the Battle of the Little Bighorn and the interpretation of the archaeological data are not exclusive stories. They must be told together, in context, and based on a firm foundation of the documentary resources.

A Brief History

The Little Bighorn story begins in the spring of 1876 with the enforcement of the United States government policy to return Sioux and Cheyenne Indians to their reservations. By late June, the army had a good idea of the whereabouts of the Indians, but no specific information. Gen. Alfred Terry sent Lt. Col. George Custer and his Seventh Cavalry ahead of two converging columns of soldiers to find the Indians. On the morning of June 25, as they were crossing the divide into the Little Bighorn River valley, Custer let his men rest briefly at a place now known as the Crow's Nest. From here they spotted the Indian camp in the valley below. Custer moved his command into the valley and, in the afternoon, divided his men into three groups. Capt. Thomas McDougall and his company guarded the pack train; Capt. Frederick Benteen led three companies in a southern arc to cut off a southerly escape route; and Custer took the rest of the men toward the Indian encampment.

Before entering the village, Custer further split his own contingent. Three companies, now assigned to Maj. Marcus Reno, were to follow the river on the south bank and attack the village, which was situated southwest of the river. Custer, with the remaining five companies, would follow the north bank, cross the river, and attack at the north end of the village. They would thus encircle the Indians while Benteen's men to the south and west would capture those who attempted to escape. Reno and Custer paralleled each other on the opposite sides of the river until Reno reached the village and initiated the attack. As Reno's men began fighting, they saw Custer and his men riding northwest on the bluffs on the opposite side of the river, toward the lower end of the Indian encampment.

After initial confusion in the village, the Indians confronted Reno's men with heavy opposition. The soldiers were forced back, retreating to the woods near the river and then northeast across the river and up the bluffs. The retreat was confused and disorderly at best. With no skirmishers positioned to defend them, the soldiers crossing the river were easy targets. Many others, who did not hear the retreat call or were not able to move from their positions, were left behind in the woods in the valley. They straggled in over the next 48 hours to rejoin the command.

The men who made it to the top of the bluffs quickly assumed a defensive position and returned the warriors' fire. Custer, meanwhile, had gone north to a ravine now known as Medicine Tail Coulee. From here, he sent Trumpeter John Martin back to Benteen with the message, "Benteen come on Big Village. Be Quick. Bring packs. P.S. Bring packs." Custer was referring to the ammunition carried by the pack train under McDougall's care.

Martin reached Benteen with the message. Benteen followed Custer's trail and came upon Reno's forces in position on the bluff top. The pack train and McDougall's company trailed Benteen and joined the command a short time later. Reno's men wondered what had happened to Custer. They speculated that, like themselves, Custer and his men had assumed a defensive position and were pinned down somewhere to the north. At one point, Capt. Thomas Weir led his company to the north in the hopes of finding Custer's men. The rest of the command followed for about a mile to an area known today as Weir's Point, before being driven back by Indian fire. Some said that from Weir's Point they could see dust and smoke to the north, where they assumed Custer and his men were fighting.

The Indian fire let up during the night of June 25, and some of the men who had been left in the valley used the cover of darkness to rejoin the command. The attack resumed the next morning. Reno's men were pinned down the entire day, but could see a line of Indians leaving the village below them. Twice, when the Indians got too close, Benteen formed his men and charged; the Indians were driven back. Benteen walked the line, encouraging the men and keeping their flagging spirits aloft.

Another blistering Montana June day dawned and, in the intense heat, water became critical for survival, particularly for the wounded. Enlisted men made several trips to the river to fetch water for the injured. Sharpshooters were positioned to draw Indian fire during these forays. When fire again slackened the night of June 26, another foray to the river was made to recover the body of Lt. Benjamin Hodgson, killed while crossing the ford. Individual stories of heroism abound. Some of the sharpshooters and men who went for water were later awarded the Medal of Honor for their gallantry in action.

By the morning of June 27, the Indians were gone. Reno's men saw dust in the distance and then could slowly make out cavalry troops. Several of Reno's officers met Gen. Alfred Terry's and Col. John Gibbon's commands in the Indian village. All wondered where Custer was. Soon the scouting party brought back the news. Custer and his men lay dead on the slopes beside the Little Bighorn River.

The heat that made water such a critical factor during the battle had not treated the bodies kindly. Reno's men were detailed to quickly bury the dead. The deceased were difficult to identify, even for those who had known them well. The regiment did not have much in the way of tools; spoons and cups from mess kits were used to dig. Meanwhile the dead at Reno's position were also buried, their equipment gathered into a pile and burned so as not to fall into the hands of the Indians. The survivors retreated to the mouth of the Little Bighorn where the steamer *Far West* was waiting. The steamer made record time to Bismarck, North Dakota, bearing the wounded and the news.

In all, 210 men died on Little Bighorn Battlefield, including Custer and four members of his family. What happened to Custer? How did it happen? And why did it happen? are the three primary questions that have been asked since the battle. None of the questions, even today, are adequately answered to the satisfaction of all.

Methods of Interpreting Archaeology to the Public

In 1879, roughly one square mile of the battlefield located near Hardin, Montana, was set aside by the army. At the time, the site reflected the societal values of the era and was a suitable memorial for fallen heroes. Interpretation was primarily based on the available documentary resources—the remembrances of those who fought with Reno, those who buried the dead, and a few Indians who participated in the battle. Interestingly, the accounts of the white survivors and those of the Indians were often at odds. For decades, interpretation of the battle remained virtually unchanged, even when in 1941 the battlefield came under the jurisdiction of the National Park Service as the Custer Battlefield National Monument. In 1992 the name was changed by congressional action to Little Bighorn Battlefield National Monument.

It took a potentially tragic wildfire in August 1983 to bring interpretation for the public in line with ever-changing societal values. With vegetation virtually destroyed in the fire, the superintendent of Custer Battlefield National Monument recognized a unique opportunity to commence an archaeological inventory of the battle site. Richard Fox, then a graduate student at the University of Calgary, initially assessed the field for its archaeological potential. His 1983 reconnaissance report was reviewed by the National Park Service, which decided to expand the project to a full-scale inventory with limited excavations. Fox's work had already generated a great deal of interest; undoubtedly there would continue to be widespread public and press attention focused on the project (Scott 1987).

Almost all archaeological investigations begin with a research design. The Custer Battlefield Archeological Project was no different with respect to traditional components—research, logistics, and analytical procedures. However, from its inception, the plan also included a specific element that addressed the need to effectively deal with the public's unflagging interest.

The original plan called for a spokesperson to coordinate activities. Also acting as contact with members of the press, this individual would handle their telephone inquiries and meet with them to brief them on the project's status. When field operations began in 1984, the park superintendent assumed the duties of coordinator. In response to overwhelming public interest, a virtual media blitz descended on the park. Because nearly 40 percent of the superintendent's time was devoted to this special project—time taken away from his normal press of business—a professor of journalism who was also a project volunteer took over as full-time coordinator during the 1985 fieldwork.

Daily early-morning briefings were proposed and proved to be very valuable. Each evening, archaeologists reviewed the results of the day's findings; planned the next day's assignments and work areas; and determined what interpretations would be given to the coordinator the next morning. The coordinator thus received the latest details on important discoveries, current project status, and the location of fieldwork. The coordinator, in turn, prepared press releases; posted information at the entrance of the Visitors Center; and furnished the park's interpreters and staff with copies of all information for public use. This kept the information fresh and uniform, and helped avoid the dangers of off-the-cuff comments and interpretations.

Questions from the public directed to park interpreters and accessible field archaeologists set the tone for the interpretation. The public was most interested in what types of artifacts were being found and how—not if, but *how*—the archaeological study was changing history. In response to the public's demands, we implemented several approaches to what was termed field interpretation. First and foremost was the daily briefing posted at the Visitors Center entrance and distributed to the interpreters. The briefing statements contained information on the types and quantities of artifacts found. We also attempted to ensure that these statements placed the finds in context. If the archaeological work was focusing on the so-called Last Stand Hill, then we included the historical information relevant to that element of the battle. If the archaeological data appeared at odds with the traditional interpretation, we pointed this out. No conclusions were made, but the briefings stressed that future planned, detailed analysis of all the project data would help resolve discrepancies.

A temporary display was also established in the Visitors Center. The display contained a few traditional archaeology tools, a variety of artifacts found during the investigations, a few photographs of fieldwork in progress, and text to briefly explain the process. This display drew a significant amount of attention and generated numerous questions. The staff interpreters used the display as a means not only to tell the archaeological story, but also to generate questions about the varying historical theories on the battle. They could then point out that archaeology could help prove or disprove one or more of those opinions.

A third level of interpretation scheduled during the project was small group tours for in-field interpretation by the archaeologists (Figure 18.1). At the location, usually the site of an excavation for human remains, the archaeologist would present an overview of the project and a summary of findings. The primary focus of the 15- to 20-minute presentation would be the work going on before the group. Every effort was made to stress the roles of both historical archaeology and analytical laboratory techniques in the study of historic sites. In essence, the presentation was an attempt to inform the public about the process of archaeology.

When the archaeologists were working in accessible areas, visitors tended to congregate to watch the excavations. An archaeologist was assigned to provide impromptu interpretations about the locations and answer the torrents of questions (Figure 18.2). In numerous cases, the interest was so great that a single interpretive event often ran to nearly an hour.

The staff interpreters were well versed in the event's history and most had some interest in the material culture of the battle. Thus, a natural feedback system developed between the archaeologists and interpreters, which kept the information flowing in a positive, two-way loop. Archaeological interpretations of specific elements of the

Figure 18.1. Semiformal presentations were given by project archaeologists to enthusiastic audiences (courtesy of the Midwest Archaeological Center, National Park Service).

battle were literally changing daily, and the interpreters were able to share these changes with the public within 24 hours.

Early in the project a means was devised to help the public understand the archaeological process. The approach, which met with great success, involved comparing the archaeological investigation to a crime scene investigation. Most people could easily relate to the analogy of historians as detectives interviewing victims, suspects, and witnesses; and archaeologists as the forensic personnel gathering the physical evidence for a more detailed analysis. Visitors readily accepted the concept that oral accounts could be suspect—for example, someone did not remember correctly, did not see part of the action, or was opinionated. Archaeological data, or the forensic analyses, provided a more complete picture of the situation than oral accounts could

Figure 18.2. During much of the fieldwork, crowds gathered to hear impromptu discussions on the archaeological work (courtesy of the Midwest Archaeological Center, National Park Service).

alone. As physical evidence it does not lie. The artifacts were the actual remnants of the battle, although their position and context (provenience) had to be interpreted. It was stressed that the archaeological artifacts, as they were found, were deposited as a result of a decision made in the past. Perhaps neither that decision nor the process of making it could be reconstructed with the artifacts and their provenience, but the result of that decision could be interpreted.

From the archaeologist's point of view, the opportunity to conduct public interpretation was invaluable. On the one hand, it was enlightening to witness firsthand the public's perception of what archaeology is and how it contributes to understanding the past. On the other hand, it gave archaeologists the opportunity to explain field and laboratory techniques to the visitors. Most archaeologist-to-visitor interpretation took place at one of the many marker sites that dot the field and purport to identify where soldiers died in battle. The visitors' fascination with the recovery of human remains at these excavations provided an ideal opportunity to explain why the study of the bones is important and what a variety of detailed scientific and forensic examinations can tell the archaeologist about the people who died in the battle. (In no case did a visitor voice an opinion that the excavation of marker sites was improper. In fact, descendants of the soldiers killed at the battle visited the excavations and expressed their approval of the investigations.)

Follow-up since the completion of the fieldwork has helped maintain a high public profile for the project. Two books (Scott and Fox 1987; Scott et al. 1989), one monograph (Scott 1991), and several articles (Fox and Scott 1991; Glenner, Willey, and Scott 1994; Scott 1992; Scott and Owsley 1991) have been published on the archaeological investigations. The books and some of the articles (Scott 1991; Scott and Connor 1986; Scott and Harmon 1988; Scott, Connor, and Snow 1988) are sold at the park's Visitors Center. In addition, the results of different aspects of the work are briefly discussed in the Custer Battlefield Historical and Museum Association quarterly newsletter and in the annual slick-format publication *Greasy Grass*. The park's handbook or guidebook was even revised to add results from the archaeological project. Perhaps the most interest has been generated by four positive identifications of human remains.

There were pitfalls to the interpretive effort, as is the case with any project. First, the amount of time project archaeologists devoted to interpretation was not adequately planned for in the project schedule. Field adjustments had to be made and a great deal of planning went into maximizing the archaeologists' exposure to the public without jeopardizing the project mission. Second, the public demanded that immediate conclusions be made in the field. It took a great deal of thought and constraint to answer questions when the data required detailed analysis before arriving at conclusions. We also recognized that not all the questions were possible to answer. It was important to help the public realize that much more behind-the-scenes work was required to formulate conclusions.

Just as there were pitfalls, there were benefits. The positive personal interactions between the archaeological team, the staff interpreters, and the visitors, as well as the project's public visibility, are credited with a 20 percent increase in park visitation. A bonus of the increased visitation and project publicity was a 150 percent increase in sales at the Association bookstore. Association membership also trebled in the same time period. Since the Association funded the majority of the archaeological investigations, the archaeology was, in a sense, paying for itself. The Custer Battlefield Historical and Museum Association ceased to be a National Park Service cooperating association in 1993. The new cooperating association, Southwestern Parks and Monuments, has continued the tradition of support for park archaeological investigations with the study of adjacent private lands in 1994 (Scott 1994), and they continue to offer the various archaeological publications in their on-site sales outlet.

Conclusions

While the project is less in the public eye over a decade after its inception, communication with the public continues. Publicly oriented articles and other publications are still well received. These publications, while geared to a general audience, do not exclude analytical data nor scholarly interpretations. They are written for the informed, but not necessarily scholarly, person. These popular publications are perhaps the most important aspect of the work. They have forced us to write in a clear and concise manner, and taught us to avoid large and impressive words that often daunt the general reader and obscure the true meaning of the prose. Archaeological interpretation, either for tour groups or through printed matter, is not difficult. It is like any other aspect of a project; it must be planned and organized to be worthwhile and effective.

Chapter Nineteen

The Archaeology of Billy the Kid

Introduction

For over 100 years, Billy the Kid and the Lincoln County War (1878–1879) have fascinated historians and the public alike and have provided material for western novels and movies. The Lincoln County War in New Mexico Territory was a violent struggle between two rival factions of businesspeople, ranchers, and lawyers for political and economic control of the largest county in the United States (Wilson 1987). The Alexander McSween house in Lincoln was the scene of one of the events of the war—the famous five-day battle that ended with the burning of the structure, the death of McSween and four others, and Billy the Kid's daring escape amid gunfire (Bell 1992; Nolan 1992; Utley 1989). Archaeological excavations of the McSween House ruins during three seasons from 1986 to 1988 led to the development of a public education and interpretation program. The program focused on the reality versus the myth of Billy the Kid; the causes of the Lincoln County War; and the revision of the public's perception of archaeology, archaeologists, and historic preservation.

Myth Versus Fact

"Quien es? Quien es? Quien es?"
"That's him."
"Quien es? Quien es?"

"I jerked my gun and fired," said Pat Garrett. "Don't shoot, don't shoot, don't shoot Maxwell," Garrett said, knocking down Poe's gun. "That was the Kid that came in there onto me, and I think I have got him," gasped Garrett.

"Pat, the Kid would not come to this place; you have shot the wrong man," stated John Poe.

Garrett replied, "I am sure that was him, for I know his voice too well to be mistaken."
(Utley 1989:193)

Shortly after the shooting, John Poe and others returned to the room in Pete Maxwell's house in Fort Sumner with a lighted candle. "We saw a man lying stretched upon his back dead, in the middle of the room with a six-shooter lying at his right hand and a butcher knife at his left, said Poe" (Utley 1989:194). Thus, at midnight on July 14, 1881, Billy's life ended.

The New Mexican we now know as Billy the Kid was born Henry McCarty. He received the name Henry Antrim when his mother married William Henry Harrison Antrim on March 1, 1873. A few years later, in October 1877, Henry introduced himself as William Bonney to the Heiskell Jones family at their ranch on the Pecos River. The name "Billy the Kid" was first mentioned in the *National Police Gazette* on May 21, 1881, in an article that announced to the nation Billy's dramatic escape from the Lincoln County Courthouse (Dykes 1952:11). Just a few months later, Pat Garrett shot the "Kid" to death.

But, who was Billy the Kid? According to Dr. Robert Utley, the Kid's most recent and even-handed biographer, Billy was like many of the young men of his time:

> The real Billy the Kid was a drifter, saddle tramp, master gunman, and a more than ordinarily successful outlaw. He was a likable youth with many friends. He led an adventurous life on both sides of the law and might have become a respectable citizen had not Pat Garrett's bullet cut him down at twenty-one. (Utley 1987:11)

Not every author was as objective as Utley. Within a month of Billy's death, the nation knew about the life of Billy the Kid through a series of dime novels, all of which were full of errors, if not outright fabrications (Dykes 1952; Fable 1881; Lewis 1881; Morrison 1881). One author's account, Pat Garrett's, was definitely slanted by self-interest. The Code of the West, the unwritten set of rules that most Western men (and women) lived by, did not allow killing an opponent with a shot in the dark (Brown 1991). To explain his actions, Garrett, with the help of Ash Upson, the Roswell postmaster and ghostwriter, wrote *The Authentic Life of Billy the Kid, the Noted Desperado of the Southwest, Whose Deeds of Daring and Blood Have Made His Name a Terror in New Mexico, Arizona and Northern Mexico* (Garrett 1954). The account proved to be as highly biased as its title.

Numerous writers and historians have scrutinized the life of Billy the Kid (Tuska 1983; Utley 1989); others have focused on specific incidents in his life (e.g., Adams 1960; Earle 1988; Mullin 1967; Poe 1933). Tuska, for example, has compared the verifiable historical facts about Billy the Kid's life with those presented in Garrett's book. He identified 75 major errors including Billy's mother marrying Antrim in Colorado. Actually, there is a record of her marrying William Antrim in Santa Fe, New Mexico Territory, at the First Presbyterian Church on March 1, 1873 (Tuska 1983:114–119).

Another error is to say that Billy killed his first man by stabbing him, after the man insulted Billy's mother. This can be traced in part to an August 13, 1881, article in the *Police Gazette* that stated, "Michael McCarty (the Kid) killed one Moore with a butcher knife" (Dykes 1952:12). Garrett (1954:10–11) later expanded on this detail. In truth, Billy's first of 4, not 21, verified killings took place on August 17, 1877, at Camp Grant, Arizona, where he got into a barroom brawl with Windy Cahill. Cahill often slapped the 17-year-old Billy around, tousling his hair and humiliating him in front of the other men. On this night, Cahill started again, calling Billy a pimp. Billy called him a son-of-a-bitch, and the fight was on. Billy pulled his pistol, shot Cahill in the stomach, and fled. Cahill died the next day. The coroner's jury decided that the shooting was criminal, and "Henry Antrim alias the Kid is guilty thereof" (Utley 1989:13). Had Billy not fled, he very probably would have been acquitted on a plea of self-defense.

According to legend, Billy killed 21 men—one for each year of his life. This myth had its origins in his obituary, which was published in the *Santa Fe Weekly Democrat*, July 21, 1881. "Billy Bonny [Bonney], alias Billy the Kid, the twenty-one year old desperado, who is known to have killed sixteen men, and who boasted that he killed a man for every year of his life, will no longer take deliberate aim at his fellow man and kill him, just to keep in practice" (Tuska 1983:124). This myth is also repeated in the *Ballad of Billy the Kid*. It can be verified that Billy killed four men on his own and participated in killing at least five others, although it is unknown whether his bullets actually caused the deaths.

PEOPLE KILLED BY BILLY THE KID

As an individual . . .

August 17, 1877	Frank "Windy" Cahill	At Camp Grant, Arizona, for bullying the Kid
January 10, 1880	Joe Grant	Challenged the Kid, saying he would "kill a man today before you do," and then tried to shoot the Kid
April 28, 1881	James Bell Robert Olinger	At the Lincoln Courthouse during his escape

As a group member . . .

March 1, 1878	Billy Morton Frank Baker William McClosky	Members of the sheriff's posse that killed John H. Tunstall on February 18, 1878
April 1, 1878	Sheriff William Brady Deputy George Hindman	Ambush assassination to remove Brady from the Dolan faction

---

Another favorite myth is the reason for the ambush killing of Sheriff Brady, whose posse murdered John H. Tunstall, an Englishman rancher. Movie producers insist on depicting Tunstall as a "father" figure to Billy the Kid, who supposedly lent the boy books and gave him advice. This image has been perpetuated in such films as the classic *Chisum* with John Wayne and, more recently, in the 1990 film *Young Guns*. In fact, Tunstall, who was killed on February 18, 1878, would have been 25 years old on March 6, 1878; Billy turned 18 that year.

The Lincoln County War is another target for legend. The war has been explained in late-1800s dime novels, 20th century western novels, and movies over the past 60 years as a conflict between different groups. Popular themes are cattlemen versus farmers and homesteaders; cattlemen versus sheepmen; and large ranch owners versus small land owners. The war is more accurately described as a bitter conflict between two factions seeking economic and political control of Lincoln County. At the time, Lincoln County, in southeast New Mexico Territory, was the largest county in the United States—approximately 30,000 square miles, or slightly larger than the states of Connecticut, Delaware, Maryland, Massachusetts, and Rhode Island combined.

There is much verifiable information to support the economic/political explanation. For instance, we know that Lawrence G. Murphy and Emil Fritz, retired commanding officers of Fort Stanton, operated a sutler's (civilian provisioner's) store and served as Indian agents from 1866 until 1873. War Department investigations revealed that Murphy and Fritz did not hold an appointment from the Indian Bureau to act as Indian agents. Simultaneous investigations by the Indian Bureau found that they also did not hold an appointment as post traders from the War Department. On September 2, 1873, the partners were given 24 hours' notice to vacate their building or be removed because of their undesirable business practices, especially as Indian agents (Wilson 1987:39). We also know they established a store in nearby Lincoln, later adding James J. Dolan (1874) and John H. Riley (1876) as partners. The Murphy-Fritz partnership lasted until June 1874 when Fritz died while on vacation in his native Germany (Nolan 1965:449–450). In 1877, Murphy sold his share of the store to Dolan and Riley, who formed J. J. Dolan and Co. (Keleher 1982:54, 56).

In the meantime, on March 3, 1875, Alexander and Susan McSween arrived in Lincoln, where Alex set up a law practice. In the fall of 1877, John H. Tunstall came to Lincoln and eventually formed a business partnership with McSween. By establishing a store and bank, they began to compete with Dolan and Riley for local business and government contracts, including one to supply beef to the nearby Mescalero Indians. McSween and Tunstall were thus directly challenging the economic and political monopoly of Dolan and Riley.

Ethnic and religious differences also contributed to the eventual violence. Murphy, Dolan, and Sheriff Brady were Irish immigrants and Catholic. On the other side, McSween was Canadian and a member of the Presbyterian Church, while Tunstall was an English citizen and Protestant. The distrust and dislike between the two groups were very real. For example, Brady's immigrant family had been forced off their land in Ireland by English-Protestant landlords. The conflict was heightened when McSween and Tunstall planned to establish a school, church, and cemetery near the Tunstall store. Tunstall and McSween were eventually buried in unmarked graves in the cemetery—a final testimony of their defeat.

Even the physical location of the two groups' establishments helped set the stage for an eventual standoff, with the Murphy/Dolan (Irish-Catholic) faction located on the south side of the only street in Lincoln and the Tunstall/McSween (English-Protestant) opposition on the north side.

The inevitable confrontation was not long in coming. Prior to Tunstall's arrival in Lincoln, Murphy had become one of McSween's clients. As Murphy's lawyer, McSween was involved in procuring a settlement on a $10,000 life insurance policy that the deceased Fritz had with a company that had gone bankrupt. Dolan convinced the Fritz heirs that McSween had embezzled the life insurance money. A writ of attachment was obtained for McSween's property. The McSween House was inventoried, and, because of his business partnership with Tunstall, the sheriff's posse also went to attach Tunstall's horse herd. In the process, the posse killed Tunstall, claiming that he resisted the attachment.

Over the next five months, numerous clashes occurred between the McSween and Dolan forces. Both sides had legally deputized posses with warrants to arrest the members of the other faction. It was the burning of the McSween house and the shooting death of McSween that brought an end to the major confrontations.

Legend claims that Susan McSween played her piano to entertain her husband and his supporters, including Billy, as the house burned. One of the songs she played, according to Burns (1926), was "The Star-Spangled Banner." That this took place is most unlikely. The group had been under siege for four and a half days. Around two o'clock on the afternoon of the fifth day, the fire began raging through the house, probably burning out a room every 30 to 45 minutes, destroying the house in less than six hours. In reality, the burning horsehair (in sofas and chairs) and wool from furniture, clothing, rugs, and bedding produced numerous poisonous gases that surely would have affected the defenders physically and mentally.

Also misleading are the various movie portrayals of the house in different styles, including a two-story clapboard frame structure. An artist's reconstruction of the house has been developed based on historical descriptions of the house and architectural styles typical of other 1870s-style buildings in Lincoln and New Mexico (Figure 19.1). Archaeologists and historians believe the structure was a one-story, U-shaped adobe house.

Following the McSween incident, many of the participants of the local war remained in Lincoln County and became productive citizens. Others left Lincoln County either to lead normal lives or to continue their outlaw ways and die young. Billy, however, remained a hunted man. He probably would have been just another unknown individual, footnoted in history books, except for the publication of *The Saga of Billy the Kid* by Walter Noble Burns (1926). This December 1926 Book of the Month Club selection was widely read. Who *knows* how many people received it as a Christmas present! In it Burns described Billy as a persecuted youth who was noble, courageous, and handsome but forced to exist through violence (Tatum 1982:102). The legend, revived from earlier dime novels, continues to this day.

These are but a few of the many errors of "historical fact" that the public accepts as true simply because they have been repeated so often for such a long time—in the case of Billy the Kid, for over a century since his death in 1881. (For further study of the myth and fact concerning Billy the Kid, I recommend Tuska [1983], Tatum [1982], and Utley [1989] as beginning points.) Overcoming such deep-rooted misconceptions was a great challenge for the archaeologists and interpreters who took part in the McSween Project.

The McSween Project:
Interpreting the Lincoln County War and Billy the Kid

Background

Archaeological excavations of the McSween House ruins during three seasons (1986–1988) provided an opportunity to develop a public education and interpretation program that incorporated the goals of archaeology and historic preservation. The program focused on the reality versus the myth of Billy the Kid; the true causes of the Lincoln County War versus those portrayed by television, movies, and paperback western novels; and a revision of the public's perception of archaeology and archaeologists. The McSween Archaeological Project had two major goals:

1. To conduct archaeological research to both locate the remains of the burned house and study the remaining material culture; and

2. To present a public education and volunteer program that focuses on archaeology, history, and historic preservation, using the ongoing archaeological excavations as a case study (Kirkpatrick and Hart 1989).

The project was jointly sponsored by the Lincoln County Heritage Trust, a private nonprofit organization, and the State Monuments Division, Museum of New Mexico. Human Systems Research, Inc., a nonprofit corporation, was the archaeological contractor. Trust personnel organized the publicity program, while Human Systems Research conducted the excavations and organized site tours with assistance from the rangers of the State Monuments Division.

The Setting

Lincoln is a very small settlement in south-central New Mexico, between the larger communities of Roswell and Ruidoso. Houses are spread for about one mile along both sides of U.S. Highway 380, the only street in Lincoln. The population ranges from 60 to 75 people, depending on births and deaths during the year. The McSween House site is located in the center of Lincoln and is easily visible to all who

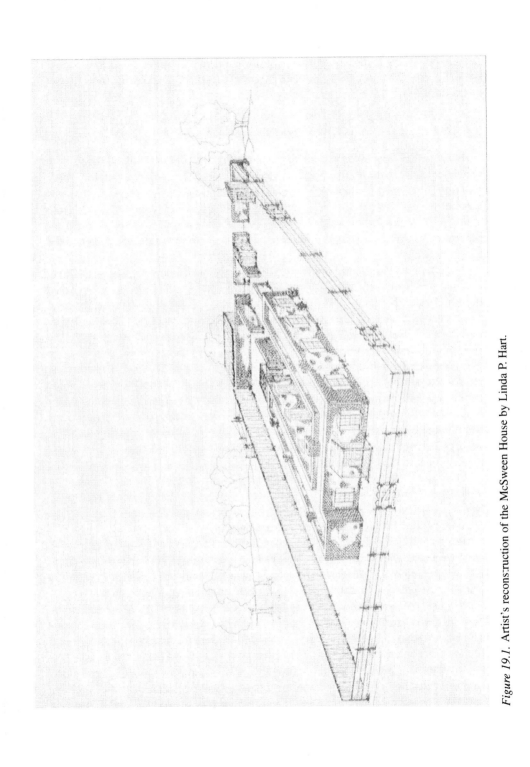

Figure 19.1. Artist's reconstruction of the McSween House by Linda P. Hart.

come to tour the local museums. These museums—often in original structures—contain interpretive displays on the Lincoln County War and other events of local history and western life.

The Program

The program was designed so that visitors could observe and converse with archaeologists at work, follow a self-guided tour, and visit an on-site museum. Visitors were introduced to the site by a colorful interpretative sign (Figure 19.2) that showed the McSween House floor plan and provided a brief history of the Lincoln County War. Visitors then walked over to one of the excavation units to watch the archaeologists work. We usually allowed visitors to come within one meter (three feet) of the units.

The archaeologists greeted the visitors and briefly explained what they were doing and what they had been finding. After this initial conversation, visitors often asked questions about the types of artifacts found and the prehistoric Indians in the area. They frequently asked, who was Billy the Kid? And what was the Lincoln County War all about? The archaeologists gave brief but clear answers and encouraged additional questions and comments; often they pointed out artifacts or exposed features to help answer the questions. Conversations lasted from 5 to 30 minutes, depending on the visitors' interests and the group size. Archaeologists continued to work while visitors watched them unearth new discoveries. The very interested visitor might spend two to three hours watching archaeologists work at the different grids. Some visitors would show up at 8:30 in the morning to see what we were doing and then stop back during the day—between visits to different Lincoln museums—to view our progress. One family from nearby Ruidoso came to watch us every Sunday during the 1986 and 1987 seasons; they also followed our progress through newspaper articles and television news spots. Ultimately, access to the excavations enabled visitors to witness the grid system, excavation techniques, exposed features, the screening procedure, and the recovery of artifacts.

After watching the archaeologists, visitors proceeded to the Fresquez House—a more recent structure on the site. Here they could peer through the windows and doors to view the house excavations. They could also see into the laboratory, which is located in the house, and watch the cleaning and cataloguing of artifacts.

The small, informal museum inside the house displayed artifacts in several cases. These included cartridges, beads, ceramics, cloth, pepper corns, coffee beans, glassware, and marbles, which had been excavated from the site. As archaeologists found exceptional or interesting artifacts, they cataloged and placed them in the cases. We often overheard impressed visitors telling others that they saw this cartridge or that piece of china being uncovered just an hour earlier. In addition to the artifacts, photographic enlargements of some of the participants of the war and of historic

Figure 19.2. Sign introducing the project (courtesy of Lincoln County Heritage Trust).

Lincoln were displayed on the wall of the museum. These provided additional inter-pretive material.

To complement the program, handouts about the site were produced. Available in the museum, these usually had to be restocked daily because of the demand. Also, a walking tour with numbered signs keyed to a one-page handout proved very success-ful for those interested in a brief tour. The archaeological excavation units were included as numbered stops. Groups could request a special tour from the project director, the rangers, or the volunteers. The use of volunteers was another important component of the program. They augmented the crew while learning archaeological methods.

Evaluation

The public education program was very successful from several standpoints. For instance, the media provided excellent and accurate coverage of the project through television and radio news stories and interviews; through articles in New Mexico and Texas newspapers; and in an article in *New Mexico Magazine.* Each year sev-eral thousand visitors come to Lincoln. While we were there, they came not only to visit the community but to see the archaeology "dig" that they had heard about through the media or from neighbors and friends. These visitors came from nearby communities within some 60 miles and from larger and more-distant cities, such as Las Cruces, Albuquerque, and El Paso. Others came from the rest of the United States, England, Germany, France, Mexico, and Australia.

The project was successful in another, more subtle, way. In addition to the public interpretative program, Human Systems Research provided a serious education pro-gram for more than 100 volunteers who actively contributed to the project during the three field seasons. Volunteers were trained in screening, cataloging, mapping, and other nonexcavation tasks. They interacted with visitors, providing their own perspective on working at an archaeological site. Several site visitors later returned to volunteer after talking with archaeologists and volunteers. Some of the more serious volunteers have continued to work on other projects, and one adult volunteer has even gone on to finish an M.A. in anthropology.

Interpretive Concerns

Site interpreters must deal daily with the preconceived notions and common miscon-ceptions that visitors bring with them. The words "Isn't it true that . . . ?" can strike terror in the hearts of most historical interpreters and archaeologists, since 95 percent of the time the rest of the sentence is incorrect. As site interpreters, we must then present the historical facts to the audience, while saving face for the sincerely inter-ested but poorly informed questioner.

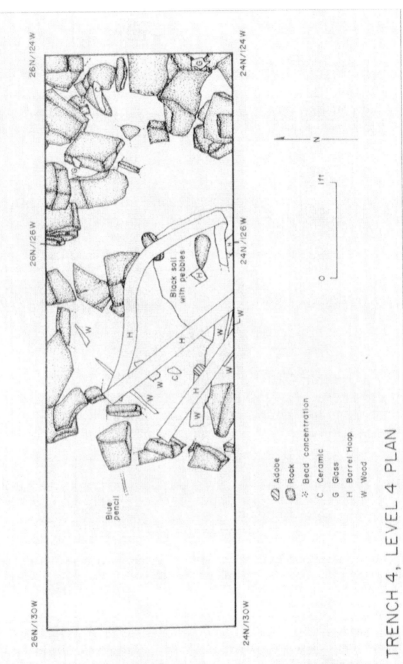

26N/130 W   26N/126 W   26N/124 W

Blue pencil

Black soil with pebbles

24N/130 W   24N/126 W   24N/124 W

⌀ Adobe
⬭ Rock
∴ Bead concentration
C Ceramic
G Glass
H Barrel Hoop
W Wood

N

0   1ft

TRENCH 4, LEVEL 4 PLAN

Figure 19.3. Trench 4, Level 4 plan (courtesy of the Lincoln County Heritage Trust, Lincoln, New Mexico).

Figure 19.4 In-situ water barrel hoops and stave fragments in Trench 4, Level 4 (courtesy of the Lincoln County Heritage Trust, Lincoln, New Mexico).

We were fortunate with many of the Billy the Kid questions. Because there is so much misinformation about him, we could often identify the source of the misinformation—usually one of the popular movies, books, articles from western magazines, or cowboy ballads. Once this was done, we had a point of reference to answer the question.

For example, visitors to Lincoln often thought Billy the Kid was a cold-blooded murderer because he killed 21 men. In responding, we cited Billy's obituary in the *Santa Fe Weekly Democrat* as the source of the alleged "fact." We further explained that the misconception was reinforced by the lyrics of a cowboy ballad that was composed by the Reverend Andrew Jenkins in 1926, after he read a flyer stating that *The Saga of Billy the Kid* was the December 1926 Book of the Month Club selection. The ballad was used to promote the book and was later recorded by Vernon Dalhart in 1929; by Woody Guthrie in the 1930s; by Tex Ritter in the 1940s and again in the 1950s; and by Ry Cooder in the 1970s (Tuska 1983:Appendix A). After discussing how the error became part of the Billy the Kid legend, we talked about the four men he is known to have killed as an individual. We also explained that Billy was not friends with Pat Garrett, the 22nd man he supposedly killed (according to the ballad). Our approach left visitors with a positive and productive learning experience.

Another concern, common to all projects, was limited funding for the excavations and artifact analysis, as well as restricted budgets for site interpretation. Fortunately, the goals of the project were specific. The archaeologists were to locate the remains of the house, obtain a sample of the material culture, and provide a significant interpretative program. Had the goal been to find a great many artifacts and expose large areas of the house, financial constraints would have proved a serious problem. Also, we were able to keep some of the costs down by using volunteers. During the three years of the project, volunteers donated 3,900 hours or over $20,000 worth of labor. Had it not been for the volunteers, the project would probably not have been as successful as it was.

Conclusion

The interpretation of the McSween House site, of the true life story of Billy the Kid, and the Lincoln County War was made easier because of the well-known individuals and historical events associated with the site. The tours, the museum displays, the active excavations, and the volunteer program all provided opportunities for better interpretation. The household items excavated from the remains of the McSween house gave visitors a glimpse of the everyday life of two of the war's participants. Exposure to archaeology and discussions of preservation helped inform the public about the importance of places as well as events in New Mexico history. The fact that someone as infamous as Billy the Kid was involved provided a "hook" to tell a multiplicity of stories about the place and the times, as well as a point of departure. Many visitors who knew little about New Mexico history left with a better understanding of Billy the Kid as a person, the Lincoln County War as a political and economic event, and the role of archaeology as part of our everyday lives.

Bibliography

Adams, Ramon F.
1960 *A Fitting Death for Billy the Kid.* University of Oklahoma Press, Norman.

Addyman, P.
1991 Tourism and the Presentation of Monuments in Zimbabwe. Draft Consultant's Report, UNDP/UNESCO Project (ZI88/028).

Alcock, L.
1975 *The Discipline of Archaeology.* College Courant, Glasgow.

Alderson, William T., and Shirley Payne Low
1985 *Interpretation of Historic Sites.* American Association for State and Local History, Nashville.

Andah, B. W.
1990a Tourism as Cultural Resource: Introductory Comments. In *Cultural Resource Management: An African Dimension*, edited by B. W. Andah, pp. 116–119. Wisdom Publishers, Ibadan.
1990b The Museum and Related Institutions and Cultural Resource Management. In *Cultural Resource Management: An African Dimension*, edited by B. W. Andah, pp. 116–119. Wisdom Publishers, Ibadan.

Arizona Department of Commerce
1989 *A Planning Guide to Tourism Development for Rural Areas.* State of Arizona, Phoenix.

Baker, Frederick, and Julian Thomas (eds.)
1990 *Writing the Past in the Present.* Saint David's University College, Lampeter, England.

Barker, Donnie B.
1990 An Archaeological Reconnaissance Survey of Drayton Hall. South Carolina Department of Parks, Recreation and Tourism Research Manuscript Series 2, Columbia. Unpublished report on file at Drayton Hall.

Barlow, A.
1990 Still Civilizing? Aborigines in Australian Education. In *The Excluded Past: Archaeology in Education,* edited by P. Stone and R. MacKenzie, pp. 68–85. Unwin Hyman, London; Routledge pbk. 1994.

Bartlett, Michael H., Thomas M. Kolaz, and David A. Gregory
1987 *Archaeology in the City.* University of Arizona Press, Tucson.

Belgarde, M. J.
1994 The Transfer of American Indian and Other Minority Community College Students. In *The Presented Past: Heritage, Museums, and Education,* edited by P. G. Stone and B. L. Molyneaux, pp. 460–477. Routledge, London and New York.

Bell, Bob Boze
1992 *The Illustrated Life and Times of Billy the Kid.* Boze Books, Cave Creek, Arizona.

Bender, S., and R. Wilkinson
1992 Public Education and the Academy. *Archaeology and Public Education* 3:1–3.

Betts, Edwin M. (ed.)
1944 *Thomas Jefferson's Garden Book 1766–1824, with relevant extracts from his other writings.* American Philosophical Society, Philadelphia.

Blancke, S., and Cjigkitoonuppa J. P. Slow Turtle
1994 Traditional American Indian Education as a Palliative to Western Education. In *The Presented Past: Heritage, Museums, and Education,* edited by P. G. Stone and B. L. Molyneaux, pp. 438–452. Routledge, London and New York.

Blatti, Jo (ed.)
1987 *Past Meets Present: Essays about Historic Interpretation and Public Audiences.* Smithsonian, Washington, D.C.

Borman, R.
1994 "The Fascinating World of Stonehenge": An Exhibition and Its Aftermath. In *The Presented Past: Heritage, Museums, and Education,* edited by P. G. Stone and B. L. Molyneaux, pp. 179–189. Routledge, London and New York.

Borun, Minda
1991 *Confronting Naive Notions Through Interactive Exhibits.* Paper presented at the First Annual Museum Education Research Colloquium, Washington, D.C.

Boylan, P. J.
1991 Museums and Cultural Identity. *Museum Visitor,* pp. 9–11.

Brockington and Associates, Inc.
1990 *An Archaeological and Historical Overview of the Drayton Hall Tract, Incorporating Data from the 1990 Survey. Phase I Survey.* Atlanta, Georgia. Report on file at Drayton Hall.

Brooks, Alasdair M.
1994 A Summary of Recent Wing Site Cermaic Analysis at Poplar Forest. Manuscript on file, The Corporation for Jefferson's Poplar Forest, Forest, Virginia.

Brown, Richard Maxwell
1991 *No Duty to Retreat: Violence and Values in American History and Society.* Oxford University Press, New York.

Burger, J.
1990 *The Gaia Atlas of First Peoples.* Robertson McCarta, London.

Burns, Walter Noble
1926 *The Saga of Billy the Kid.* Doubleday Page, Garden City, New York.

Carmichael, D., J. Hubert, B. Reeves, and A. Schanche (eds.)
1994 *Sacred Sites, Sacred Places*. Routledge, London.

Carnerio, Robert L.
1991 Destruction of an Unreconstructed Constructionist. *Anthropology Newsletter* 32(6):3.

Chambers, S. Allen, Jr.
1993 *Poplar Forest and Thomas Jefferson*. The Corporation for Jefferson's Poplar Forest, Forest, Virginia.

Chappell, Edward A.
1989 Social Responsibility and the American History Museum. *Winterthur Portfolio* 24(4):247–265.

Cleere, H. F. (ed.)
1984 Approaches to the Archaeological Heritage. Cambridge University Press, Cambridge, U.K.
1989 *Archaeological Heritage Management in the Modern World*. Unwin Hyman, London.

Collett, D. P.
1992 The Archaeological Heritage of Zimbabwe: A Masterplan for Resource Conservation and Development. UNDP and UNESCO Project Report (Zim 88/028).

Concord Monitor
1991 Letters to the Editor. 17 December:B-6.

Conkey, Margaret W., and Janet Spector
1984 Archaeology and the Study of Gender. In *Advances in Archaeological Method and Theory 7*, edited by Michael B. Schiffer, pp. 1–38. Academic Press, New York.

Corbishley, Mike, and Peter G. Stone
1994 The Teaching of the Past in Formal School Curricula in England. In *The Presented Past: Heritage, Museums, and Education*, edited by P. G. Stone and B. L. Molyneaux, pp. 383–397. Routledge, London and New York.

Cotter, John L., and J. Paul Hudson
1957 *New Discoveries at Jamestown*. National Park Service, U.S. Government Printing Office, Washington, D.C.

Dahiya, N.
1994 A Case for Archaeology in Formal School Curricula in India. In *The Presented Past: Heritage, Museums, and Education*, edited by P. G. Stone and B. L. Molyneaux, pp. 299–314. Routledge, London and New York.

Danson, Edward B.
1957 An Archaeological Survey of West-Central New Mexico and East-Central Arizona. *Papers of the Peabody Museum of Archaeology and Ethnology* 1(44). Harvard University, Cambridge.

Danson, Edward B., and Harold E. Molde
1950 Casa Malpais, A Fortified Pueblo Site at Springerville, Arizona. *Plateau* 22(4):61–67.

Davis, H.
1989 Is an Archaeological Site Important to Science or to the Public, and Is There a Difference? In *Heritage Interpretation: The Natural and Built Environment,* edited by D. Uzzell, pp. 96–99. Belhaven, London.

Davis, Karen L., and James G. Gibb
1988 Unpuzzling the Past: Critical Thinking in History Museums. *Museum Studies Journal* 3(2):41–46.

Deetz, James F.
1988 Material Culture and Worldview in Colonial Anglo-America. In *The Recovery of Meaning: Historical Archaeology in the Eastern United States,* edited by Mark P. Leone and Parker B. Potter, Jr., pp. 219–233. Smithsonian Institution Press, Washington, D.C.

Delgado Cerón, I., and C. I. Mz-Recaman
1994 The Museum Comes to School in Colombia: Teaching Packages as a Method of Learning. In *The Presented Past: Heritage, Museums, and Education,* edited by P. G. Stone and B. L. Molyneaux, pp. 148–158. Routledge, London and New York.

Detweiler, Susan Gray
1982 *George Washington's Chinaware.* Harry N. Adams, New York.

Devine, H.
1994 Archaeology, Prehistory and the Native Learning Resources Project: Alberta, Canada. In *The Presented Past: Heritage, Museums, and Education,* edited by P. G. Stone and B. L. Molyneaux, pp. 478–494. Routledge, London and New York.

Dimbleby, G.
1977 Training the Environmental Archaeologist. *Bulletin of the Institute of Archaeology* 14:1–12.

Dykes, J. C.
1952 *Billy the Kid: The Bibliography of a Legend.* University of New Mexico Publications in Language and Literature No. 7. University of New Mexico Press, Albuquerque.

Earle, James H. (ed.)
1988 *The Capture of Billy the Kid.* Creative Publishing, College Station, Texas.

Ekechukwu, L. C.
1990 Encouraging National Development through the Promotion of Tourism: The Place of Archaeology. In *Cultural Resource Management: An African Dimension,* edited by B. W. Andah, pp. 120–125. Wisdom Publishers, Ibadan.

Ellis, Rex Marshall
1989 *Presenting the Past: Education, Interpretation and the Teaching of Black History at Colonial Williamsburg.* Ph.D. diss., School of Education, College of William and Mary, University Microfilms, Ann Arbor.
1990 A Decade of Change: Black History at Colonial Williamsburg. *Colonial Williamsburg* 12(3):14–23.

Ereira, A.
1990 *The Heart of the World.* Jonathan Cape, London.

Ettema, Michael J.
1987 History Museums and the Culture of Materialism. In *Past Meets Present,* edited by J. Blatti, pp. 62–84. Smithsonian, Washington, D.C.

Evans, J.
1975 *Archaeology as Education and Profession.* Institute of Archaeology, London.

Fable, Edmund
1881 *The True Life of Billy the Kid.* Denver Publishing Co., Denver.

Fagan, Brian
1990 Rethinking Prehistory. *Archaeology* 43(4):32–39.

Feder, Kenneth
1990 *Frauds, Myths, and Mysteries.* Mayfield, Mountain View, California.

Fischer, Lisa E.
1996 Report on the Chemical Analysis of Soils at the Poplar Forest Quarter Site. Manuscript on file, The Corporation for Jefferson's Poplar Forest, Forest, Virginia.

Fox, Richard A., Jr.
1983 Archeological Investigations at Custer Battlefield National Monument. Manuscript on file, Little Bighorn Battlefield National Monument, Crow Agency.

Fox, Richard A., Jr., and Douglas D. Scott
1991 The Post–Civil War Battlefield Pattern. *Historical Archaeology* 25(2):92–103.

Frost, J.
1983 Archaeology and the Media. Unpublished B.A. diss., Department of Roman Studies, Institute of Archaeology, London.

Garrett, Pat F.
1954 *The Authentic Life of Billy the Kid.* University of Oklahoma Press, Norman.

Gathercole, P., and D. Lowenthal (eds.)
1990 *The Politics of the Past.* Unwin Hyman, London; Routledge pbk. 1994.

Gero, Joan M.
1989 Producing Prehistory, Controlling the Past: The Case of New England Beehives. In *Critical Traditions in Contemporary Archaeology, Essays in the Philosophy, History and Sociopolitics of Archaeology,* edited by Valerie Pinsky and Alison Wylie, pp. 96–103. Cambridge University Press, New York.

Geuss, Raymond
1981 *The Idea of a Critical Theory.* Cambridge University Press, Cambridge, U.K.

Gibb, James G., and Karen L. Davis
1989 History Exhibits and Theories of Material Culture. *Journal of American Culture* 12:27–35.

Glavin, Terry
1991 Archeologist Rocked by Stó:lo Stone Person. *Vancouver Sun,* 17 June:B-3.

Glenner, R., P. Willey, and Douglas D. Scott
1994 Back to the Little Bighorn: Remains of a 7th Cavalry Trooper Recovered at Little Bighorn Battlefield in 1903 Provide a Glimpse of 19th-Century Dental Practices. *Journal of the American Dental Association* 124(7):835–843.

Greengrass, Mara
1993 State Archaeology Weeks: Interpreting Archaeology for the Public. National Park Service, Technical Brief. No. 9. Washington, D.C.

Gregory, T.
1986 Whose Fault Is Treasure-Hunting? In *Archaeology, Politics and the Public,* edited by C. Dobinson and R. Gilchrist, pp. 25–27. York University Publications, York, U.K.

Groneman, B.
1992 A Response to Blanchard. *Archaeology and Public Education* 3:9–10.

Gruber, Anna
1990 *The Archaeology of Mr. Jefferson's Slaves.* Unpublished master's thesis, Department of Early American Culture, University of Delaware, Newark.

Hall, J.
1991 Museum Education: Adapting to a Changing South Africa. *Journal of Education in Museums* 12:10–14.

Handsman, Russell G., and Mark P. Leone
1989 Living History and Critical Archaeology in the Reconstruction of the Past. In *Critical Traditions in Contemporary Archaeology, Essays in the Philosophy, History and Sociopolitics of Archaeology*, edited by Valerie Pinsky and Alison Wylie, pp. 117–135. Cambridge University Press, New York.

Harrington, J. C.
1940 Partnership at Jamestown. *The Regional Review* 5(2–3):3–6.
1946 Interpreting Jamestown to the Visitor. *The Museum News* 24(11):7–8.
1952 Historic Site Archeology in the United States. In *Archaeology of Eastern United States,* edited by James B. Griffin, pp. 335–344. The University of Chicago Press, Chicago.
1955 Archaeology as an Auxiliary Science to American History. *American Anthropologist* 57(6), Part 1:1121–1130.
1957 *New Light on Washington's Fort Necessity.* The Eastern National Park and Monument Association, Richmond.
1962 *Search for the Cittie of Ralegh.* Archeological Research Series No. 6, National Park Service, Washington, D.C.
1965 *Archeology and the Historical Society.* The American Association for State and Local History, Nashville.
1966 *An Outwork at Fort Raleigh.* Park Resource Studies, Eastern National Park and Monument Association, Richmond.

Heath, Barbara J.
1990 Archaeology and Interpretation at Jefferson's Monticello. Mid-Atlantic Association of Museums Meeting, Session *Archaeology and Museums: Toward a More Perfect Union.* Princeton, New Jersey.
1991a A Report on the Archaeological Excavations at Monticello, Charlottesville, VA, The Stewart/Watkins House 1989–1990. Manuscript on file, The Thomas Jefferson Memorial Foundation, Charlottesville, Virginia.
1991b Artisan Housing at Monticello: The Stewart/Watkins Site. *Quarterly Bulletin of the Archaeological Society of Virginia* 46(1):10–16.
1994 Discovering the Plantation World of Poplar Forest. *Notes on the State of Poplar Forest,* 2:13–18.
1996a Plantations and Small Farms in Nineteenth-Century Virginia. In *The Archaeology of Nineteenth Century Virginia,* edited by Theodore Reinhart and John H. Sprinkle, Jr. Published for the Archaeological Society of Virginia. Dietz Press, Richmond, in press.
1996b *Making a Home: The Archaeology of a Poplar Forest Slave Quarter.* The Corporation for Jefferson's Poplar Forest, Forest, Virginia.

Held, David
1980 *Introduction to Critical Theory: Horkheimer to Habermas.* University of California Press, Berkeley.

Hensel, Karen
1991 Learning Through a Lens. *Journal of Museum Education* 16(1):11–13.
1987 Families in a Museum: Interactions and Conversations at Displays. Ed.D. diss., Columbia University.

Her Majesty's Inspectorate (HMI)
1990 *A Survey of Local Education Authorities' and Schools' Liaison with Museum Services.* Her Majesty's Stationery Office, London.

Hewison, R.
1987 *The Heritage Industry.* Methuen, London.

Hoare, R.
1983 Archaeology, the Public and the Media. Unpublished master's thesis, Department of Archaeology, University of Edinburgh.

Hodder, Ian
1986 *Reading the Past.* Cambridge University Press, Cambridge, U.K.
1991a Interpretive Archaeology and Its Role. *American Antiquity* 56(1):7–18.
1991b Reply to Robert Carnerio. *Anthropology Newsletter* 32(6):3.
1991c *Reading the Past.* 2d ed., Cambridge University Press, Cambridge, U.K.
1994 Material Culture in Time. In *Interpreting Archaeology: Finding Meaning in the Past.* Hodder et al. (eds.), Routledge, London and New York.

Hodder, Ian, Michael Shanks, Alexandra Alexandri, Victor Buchli, John Carman, Jonathan Last, and Gavin Lucas (eds.)
1994 *Interpreting Archaeology: Finding Meaning in the Past.* Routledge, London and New York.

Hoepfner, Christine, Mark P. Leone, and Parker B. Potter, Jr.
1987 The Preserved Is Political: A Critical Theory Agenda for Historical Interpretation of Monuments and Sites. *ICOMOS Information* 3:10–16.

Hoffman, Teresa L.
1988 Arizona Archaeology Week: Expanding Public Awareness Through a Federal and State Partnership. *CRM Bulletin* 11 (July 1988).
1991 Stewards of the Past: Preserving Arizona's Archaeological Resources Through Positive Public Involvement. In *Protecting the Past,* edited by George S. Smith and John E. Ehrenhard, pp. 253–259. CRC Press, Boca Raton, Florida.

Hoffman, Teresa L., and Shereen Lerner
1988 *Arizona Archaeology Week: Promoting the Past to the Public.* Technical Brief No. 2. National Park Service, Archaeological Assistance Program, Washington, D.C.
1989 Arizona Archaeology Week: Promoting the Past to the Public. In *American Society for Conservation Archaeology Proceedings 1988, Papers from the Symposium Held at the 53rd Annual Meeting of the Society for American Archaeology, Phoenix,* edited by A.E. Rogge and John Montgomery, pp. 31–37. Portales, New Mexico.

Hohmann, John W.
1989 Responding to the Indiana Jones Syndrome: The Besh-Ba-Gowah Archaeological Program. In *American Society for Conservation Archaeology Proceedings 1988, Papers from the Symposium Held at the 53rd Annual Meeting of the Society for American Archaeology, Phoenix,* edited by A.E. Rogge and John Montgomery, pp. 17–24. Portales, New Mexico.
1990 *A Management Plan for the Besh-Ba-Gowah Archaeological Park, Globe, Arizona.* Studies in Western Archaeology No. 1. Louis Berger and Associates, Phoenix.
1991 A Master Stabilization, Development, and Interpretive Plan for the Proposed Casa Malpais Interpretive Archaeological Recreation Area. Ms. on file, Town of Springerville and Arizona State Historic Preservation Office.

Honerkamp, Nicholas, and R. Bruce Council
1984 Individual Versus Corporate Adaptations in Urban Contexts. *Tennessee Anthropologist* 9(1):22–31.

Honerkamp, Nicholas, and Martha Zierden
1989 *Charleston Place: The Archaeology of Urban Life.* The Charleston Museum Leaflet No. 31.

Honerkamp, Nicholas, R. Bruce Council, and M. Elizabeth Will
1982 An Archaeological Investigation of the Charleston Convention Center Site, Charleston, South Carolina. Ms. on file, National Park Service, Interagency Archeological Services Division, Atlanta.

Hooper-Greenhill, E.
1989 *Initiatives in Museum Education.* Department of Museum Studies, Leicester.
1991a *Museum and Gallery Education.* Leicester University Press, Leicester.
1991b *Writing a Museum Education Policy.* Department of Museum Studies, Leicester.

Hoornbeek, Billie
1978 Archaeological Survey of the Lakes Region of New Hampshire, 1977–1978. Manuscript on file, New Hampshire Division of Historical Resources/State Historic Preservation Office, Concord.

Hubert, J.
1989 A Proper Place for the Dead: A Critical Review of the "Reburial" Issue. In *Conflict in the Archaeology of Living Traditions,* edited by R. Layton, pp. 131–164. Unwin Hyman, London; Routledge pbk. 1994.
1991 After the Vermilion Accord: Developments in the "Reburial Issue." *World Archaeological Bulletin* 5:113–118.

Hume, Gary W.
1982 Lochmere Archaeological District National Register Nomination. Manuscript on file, New Hampshire Division of Historical Resources/State Historic Preservation Office, Concord.

Hume, Gary W., and Parker B. Potter, Jr.
1991 Archaeological Education as a Tool for Historic Preservation. Paper presented at the annual meeting of the Society for Historical Archaeology, Richmond, Virginia.

Jameson, John H., Jr.
1994a The NPS Public Interpretation Initiative Program. In *Public Archaeology Review* 2 (3): 2–5. Center for Archaeology in the Public Interest, Indiana University–Purdue University, Indianapolis.
1994b The Importance of Public Outreach in Archaeology. *SAA Bulletin* 12 (3): 16–17. Society for American Archaeology, Washington, D.C.
1995 Review of *Looking at History: Indiana's Hoosier National Forest Region, 1600 to 1950.* In *Historical Archaeology* 29 (4): 104–106.

Jameson, John H., Jr., John E. Ehrenhard, and Wilfred M. Husted
1992 Federal Archaeological Contracting: Utilizing the Competitive Procurement Process. *Technical Brief No. 7* (revised 1992), Archaeological Assistance Program, National Park Service, Washington, D.C.

Jamieson, John
1994 One View of Native Education in the Northwest Territories, Canada. In *The Presented Past: Heritage, Museums, and Education,* edited by P. G. Stone and B. L. Molyneaux, pp. 495–510. Routledge, London and New York.

Jencks, Charles
1989 *What Is Post-Modernism?* St. Martin's Press, New York.

Kehoe, A.
1990 "In 1492 Columbus sailed . . . .": The Primacy of the National Myth in American Schools. In *The Excluded Past: Archaeology in Education,* edited by P. Stone and R. MacKenzie, pp. 201–214. Unwin Hyman, London; Routledge pbk. 1994.

Keleher, William
1982 *Violence in Lincoln County, 1869–1881: A New Mexico Item.* University of New Mexico Press, Albuquerque.

Kelso, William M.
1986a The Archaeology of Slave Life at Monticello: A Wolf by the Ears. *Journal of New World Archaeology*, 6(4):5–20.
1986b Mulberry Row: Slave Life at Thomas Jefferson's Monticello. *Archaeology* 39(5):28–35.
1990 Landscape Archaeology at Thomas Jefferson's Monticello. In *Earth Patterns, Essays in Landscape Archaeology*, edited by William Kelso and Rachel Most, pp. 7–22. University Press of Virginia, Charlottesville.

Kelso, William M. and Rachel Most (eds.)
1990 *Earth Patterns, Essays in Landscape Archaeology*. University Press of Virginia, Charlottesville.

Kelso, William M., Drake Patten, and Michael A. Strutt
1991 Poplar Forest Archaeology Research Report for NEH Grant 1990–1991. Manuscript on file, The Corporation for Jefferson's Poplar Forest, Forest, Virginia.

Kenyatta, J.
1938 *Facing Mount Kenya*. Martin Secker and Warburg, Nairobi.

Kertzer, David I.
1988 *Ritual, Politics, and Power.* Yale University Press, New Haven.

Kirkpatrick, David T., and Linda P. Hart
1989 *Archaeological Test Excavations at the Alexander McSween Site, Lincoln State Monument, Lincoln County, New Mexico*. Human Systems Research Report Nos. 8714 and 8825. Tularosa, New Mexico.

Kiyaga-Mulindwa, D., and A. K. Segobye
1994 Archaeology and Education in Botswana. In *The Presented Past: Heritage, Museums, and Education,* edited by P. G. Stone and B. L. Molyneaux, pp. 46–60. Routledge, London and New York.

Klein, Terry H., and Amy Friedlander
1983 *A Public Consumption Report, Archaeological Investigations at Wilmington Blvd., New Castle County, Delaware. Archaeology Series* No. 12. Delaware Department of Transportation, Dover.

Knopf, Richard, and Tom C. Parker
1990 Rethinking About Tourists. *Arizona Hospitality Trends* 4(4):2.

Kraft, Richard, and Mitchell Sakofs (eds.)
n.d. *The Theory of Experiential Education*. 2nd ed. Association for Experiential Education, Boulder, Colorado.

Layton, R. (ed.)
1989 *Who Needs the Past?* Unwin Hyman, London; Routledge pbk. 1994.
1990 *Conflict in the Archaeology of Living Traditions*. Unwin Hyman, London; Routledge pbk. 1994.

Lazaroff, David W.
1993 *Sabino Canyon: The Life of a Southwestern Oasis*. University of Arizona Press, Tucson.

Leone, Mark P.
1983 Method as Message: Interpreting the Past with the Public. *Museum News* 62(1):35–41.
1988 The Georgian Order as the Order of Merchant Capitalism in Annapolis, Maryland. In *The Recovery of Meaning: Historical Archaeology in the Eastern United States,* edited by Mark P. Leone and Parker B. Potter, Jr., pp. 235–261. Smithsonian Institution Press, Washington, D.C.
1989a Establishing the Meaning of Objects in Context. In *Perspectives on Anthropological Collections from the American Southwest* (Anthropological Research Papers, No. 40), edited by Ann L. Hedlund, pp. 141–148. Arizona State University, Tempe.
1989b Keynote Address: Sketch of a Theory for Outdoor History Museums. In *Proceedings of the 1987 Annual Meeting* 10:36–46. The Association for Living Historical Farms and Agricultural Museums, Ann Arbor.

Leone, Mark P., and Parker B. Potter, Jr.
1984 *Archaeological Annapolis: A Guide to Seeing and Understanding Three Centuries of Change.* Historic Annapolis, Inc., and the University of Maryland, Annapolis.
1992 Legitimation and the Classification of Archaeological Sites. *American Antiquity* 57(1):137–145.

Leone, Mark P., Parker B. Potter, Jr., and Paul A. Shackel
1987 Toward a Critical Archaeology. *Current Anthropology* 28(3):251–302.

Lewis, John Woodruff [Don Jenardo, pseud.]
1881 *The True Life of Billy the Kid.* Wide Awake Library, No. 451. Frank Tousey, New York.

Lewis, Lynne G.
1978 *Drayton Hall: Preliminary Archaeological Investigation at a Low Country Plantation.* The Preservation Press, National Trust for Historic Preservation in the United States, Washington, D.C.
1985 The Planter Class: The Archaeological Record at Drayton Hall. In *The Archaeology of Slavery and Plantation Life,* edited by Theresa Singleton, pp. 121–140. Academic Press, Orlando.

Lewis, Lynne G., and Larry D. Dermody
1991 *Barn Storming: Post Hurricane Hugo Excavation at the Drayton Hall Barn Site Fall 1990.* National Trust Archaeological Research Center Monograph Series No. 2. Report on file at Drayton Hall and Montpelier Research Center, Montpelier Station, Virginia.

Louis Berger & Associates, Inc.
1987 *Druggists, Craftsmen, and Merchants of Pearl and Water Streets, New York: The Barclays Bank Site.* Report on file at the New York City Landmarks Preservation Commission, New York.

Lowenthal, D.
1985 *The Past Is a Foreign Country.* Cambridge University Press, Cambridge, U.K.
1993 Remembering to Forget. *Museum Journal* June:20–22.

MacKenzie, R., and P. Stone
1990 Introduction. In *The Excluded Past: Archaeology in Education,* edited by P. Stone and R. MacKenzie, pp. 1–14. Unwin Hyman, London; Routledge pbk. 1994.

Marling, Karal Ann
1988 *George Washington Slept Here: Colonial Revivals and American Culture, 1876–1986.* Harvard University Press, Cambridge.

Martin, Paul S., John B. Rinaldo, and William Longacre
1961 Mineral Creek Site and Hooper Ranch Pueblo, Eastern Arizona. *Fieldiana: Anthropology* 52.

Martin, Zora
1973 Colonial Williamsburg—A Black Perspective. *Journal of Museum Education: Roundtable Reports,* June.

Mason, Andrew
1994 *The Hatzic Rock Site: A Charles Culture Settlement.* Unpublished master's thesis, Department of Anthropology and Sociology, University of British Columbia, Vancouver.

Masson, P., and H. Guillot
1994 Archaeofiction with Upper Primary-School Children 1988–1989. In *The Presented Past: Heritage, Museums, and Education,* edited by P. G. Stone and B. L. Molyneaux, pp. 375–382. Routledge, London and New York.

Mazel, A., and G. Ritchie
1994 Museums and Their Messages: The Display of the Pre- and Early-Colonial Past in the Museums of South Africa, Botswana and Zimbabwe. In *The Presented Past: Heritage, Museums, and Education,* edited by P. G. Stone and B. L. Molyneaux, pp. 225–236. Routledge, London and New York.

Mbunwe-Samba, P., M. L. Niba, and N. I. Akenji
1994 Archaeology in the Schools and Museums of Cameroon. In *The Presented Past: Heritage, Museums, and Education,* edited by P. G. Stone and B. L. Molyneaux, pp. 326–337. Routledge, London and New York.

McClure, Sandy, and Ann Rinaldi
1989 Three Former N.J. Governors Seek Quick End to Morven "Mess." *The Trentonian,* September 6.

McGhee, Robert
1989 Who Owns Prehistory? The Bering Land Bridge Dilemma. *Canadian Journal of Archaeology* 13: 13–20.

McGimsey, C. R., III, and H. A. Davis
1977 *The Management of Archaeological Resources: The Airlie House Report.* Special publication of the Society for American Archaeology.

McManamon, Francis P.
1994 Presenting Archaeology to the Public in the USA. In *The Presented Past: Heritage, Museums, and Education,* edited by P. G. Stone and B. L. Molyneaux, pp. 61–81. Routledge, London and New York.

Messenger, Phyllis M. (ed.)
1989 *The Ethics of Collecting Cultural Property: Whose Culture? Whose Property?* University of New Mexico Press, Albuquerque.

Mohs, Gordon

1987 *Spiritual Sites, Ethnic Significance and Native Spirituality: The Heritage and Heritage Sites of the Stó:lo Indians of British Columbia.* Unpublished master's thesis, Department of Archaeology, Simon Fraser University, Burnaby, British Columbia.

1990 The Upper Stó:lo Indians of British Columbia: An Ethnoarchaeological Review. Master's thesis, Department of Archaeology, Simon Fraser University, Burnaby, British Columbia.

1992 Excavations at Hatzic Rock, DgRn 23. Report on file, Archaeology Branch, Victoria.

1994 Stó:lo Sacred Ground. In *Sacred Sites, Sacred Places*, edited by David L. Carmichael, Jane Hubert, Brian Reeves and Audhild Schanche, pp.184–208. Routledge, New York.

Momin, K. N., and A. Pratap

1994 Indian Museums and the Public. In *The Presented Past: Heritage, Museums, and Education,* edited by P. G. Stone and B. L. Molyneaux, pp. 290–298. Routledge, London and New York.

Morrison, John W.

1881 *The Life of Billy the Kid.* Morrison's Sensational Series, No. 3. John W. Morrison, New York.

Mortimer, T.

1991 Reader Says Natives Should Pay for Hatzic Rock. *Abbotsford Times,* 21 September:7.

Mullin, Robert N.

1967 *The Boyhood Life of Billy the Kid.* Southwestern Studies Monograph No. 17. Texas Western Press, El Paso.

Naisbitt, John and Patricia Aburdene

1990 *Megatrends 2000: Ten New Directions for the 1990s.* William Morrow, New York.

Ned, Darrell

1990 Ancient Stó:lo Past Confirmed. *Stó:lo Nation News,* November–December:2.

New South Associates

1989 *Drayton Hall Archaeological Testing of the Orangerie.* New South Associates Technical Report 11, Stone Mountain, Georgia. Copy on file at Drayton Hall.

New York City Landmarks Preservation Commission (NYCLPC)

1966 71 Pearl Street Designation #LP0041, 71 Pearl Street files at the New York City Landmarks Preservation Commission, New York.

1980 Recision of 71 Pearl Street Designation #LP0041, 71 Pearl Street files at the New York City Landmarks Preservation Commission, New York.

1986a 17 State Street files at the New York City Landmarks Preservation Commission, New York.

1986b *Memorandum of Agreement Regarding the Public Exhibit Space at 17 State Street.* 17 State Street files at the New York City Landmarks Preservation Commission, New York.

Nichols, Frederick D. and James A. Bear, Jr.

1982 *Monticello, A Guidebook.* Thomas Jefferson Memorial Foundation, Charlottesville, Virginia.

Noël Hume, Ivor
1969 *Historical Archaeology.* Alfred A. Knopf, New York.
1994 *The Virginia Adventure.* Alfred A. Knopf, New York.

Nolan, Frederick W.
1965 *The Life and Death of John Henry Tunstall.* University of New Mexico Press, Albuquerque.
1992 *The Lincoln County War: A Documentary History.* University of Oklahoma, Norman.

Norris, Christopher
1988 Deconstruction, Post-Modernism and the Visual Arts. In *What Is Deconstruction?* edited by C. Norris and A. Benjamin, pp. 7–30. St. Martin's Press, New York.

Norris, Walter B.
1925 *Annapolis: Its Colonial and Naval Story.* Thomas Y. Crowell, New York.

Nzewunwa, N.
1994 The Nigerian Teacher and Museum Culture. In *The Presented Past: Heritage, Museums, and Education,* edited by P. G. Stone and B. L. Molyneaux, pp. 283–289. Routledge, London and New York.

Olmert, Michael
1985 *Official Guide to Colonial Williamsburg.* The Colonial Williamsburg Foundation, Williamsburg, Virginia.

Olofsson, U. K. (ed.)
1979 *Museums and Children.* UNESCO, Paris.

Palmer, R. E.
1969 *Hermeneutics: Interpretation Theory in Schliermacher, Dilthey, Heidegger, and Gadamer.* Northwestern University Press, Evanston, Illinois.

Parker, Scott K.
1990 Memorandum to George McDaniel, Director, Drayton Hall. Report with accompanying map of post–Hurricane Hugo archaeological reconnaissance survey, February 17–18, 1990.

Pinsky, Valerie, and Alison Wylie (eds.)
1989 *Critical Traditions in Contemporary Archaeology.* Cambridge University Press, Cambridge, U.K.

Podgorny, I.
1994 Choosing Ancestors: The Primary Education Syllabuses in Buenos Aires, Argentina, Between 1975 and 1990. In *The Presented Past: Heritage, Museums, and Education,* edited by P. G. Stone and B. L. Molyneaux, pp. 408–417. Routledge, London and New York.

Poe, John W.
1933 *The Death of Billy the Kid.* Houghton-Mifflin, New York.

Pogue, Dennis
1988 *Archaeology at George Washington's Mount Vernon: 1931–1987.* File Report No.1, Mount Vernon Ladies' Association, Mount Vernon, Virginia.

Pokotylo, David L.
1991 Archaeological Assessment of the Hatzic Site (DgRn 23). Report of file, Archaeology Branch, Victoria.

Pokotylo, David L., and Andrew Mason
1991 Public Attitudes towards Archaeological Resources and Their Management. In *Protecting the Past,* edited by John E. Ehrenhard and George S. Smith, pp. 9–18. CRC Press, Boca Raton.

Potter, Parker B., Jr.
n.d. Ethnography in Annapolis. For *Annapolis Pasts: Contributions from Archaeology in Annapolis,* edited by Paul A. Shackel, Paul Mullins, and Mark Warner (in press).
1984 From Annapolis to Rockbridge: Approaches to Presenting Archaeology to the Public in the Uplands of Virginia. In *Uplands Archaeology in the East, Symposium 2* (Cultural Resources Report No. 5), edited by Michael B. Barber, pp. 273–283. USDA, Forest Service, Southern Region, Atlanta.
1989a *Archaeology in Public in Annapolis: An Experiment in the Application of Critical Theory to Historical Archaeology.* Ph.D. diss., Department of Anthropology, Brown University. University Microfilms, Ann Arbor.
1989b Why Teach Archaeology? Paper presented at the annual meeting of the Society for Historical Archaeology, Baltimore.
1990 The "What" and "Why" of Public Relations for Archaeology: A Postscript to DeCicco's Public Relations Primer. *American Antiquity* 55(3):608–613.
1991a Self-Reflection in Archaeology. In *Processual and Postprocessual Archaeologies: Multiple Ways of Knowing the Past,* edited by Robert W. Preucel, pp. 225–234. Center for Archaeological Investigations, Carbondale.
1991b What Is the Use of Plantation Archaeology. *Historical Archaeology* 25(3):94–107.
1994 *Public Archaeology in Annapolis: A Critical Approach to History in Maryland's "Ancient City."* Smithsonian Institution Press, Washington, D.C.

Potter, Parker B., Jr., and Mark P. Leone
1986 Liberation Not Replication: "Archaeology in Annapolis" Analyzed. *Journal of the Washington Academy of Sciences* 76(2):97–105.
1987 Archaeology in Public in Annapolis: Four Seasons, Six Sites, Seven Tours, and 32,000 Visitors. *American Archaeology* 6(1):51–61.
1992 Establishing the Roots of Historical Consciousness in Modern Annapolis, Maryland. In *Museums and Communities,* edited by Ivan Karp, Christine Mullen Kreamer and Steven D. Lavine. Smithsonian Institution Press, Washington, D.C.

Pryor, Francis
1989 Look What We've Found—A Case Study in Public Archaeology. *Antiquity* 63:51–61.

Raina, V. K.
1992 Instructional Strategies Used by Indian History Teachers. *Teaching History* April:24–27.

Reeve, J.
1989 Training of All Museum Staff for Educational Awareness. In *Initiatives in Museum Education,* edited by E. Hooper-Greenhill, pp. 30–32, Department of Museum Studies, Leicester.

Reinhard, Karl
1990 Pollen Analysis of the Miles Brewton House, Charleston, South Carolina. Ms. on file, The Charleston Museum.

Reitz, Elizabeth
1986 Rural/Urban Contrasts in Vertebrate Fauna from the Southern Coastal Plain. *Historical Archaeology* 20(2):47–58.

Reitz, Elizabeth, and Martha Zierden
1991 Cattle Bones and Status from Charleston, South Carolina. In *Perspectives in Zooarchaeology: Essays in Honor of P. W. Parmalee,* edited by Bonnie Styles, James Purdue, and Walter Klippel, pp. 395–405. Illinois State Museum Publications, Springfield.

Renfrew, Colin
1982 *Towards an Archaeology of Mind.* Cambridge University Press, Cambridge, U.K.

Renfrew, Colin, and Paul Bahn
1991 *Archaeology: Theory, Method and Practice.* Thames and Hudson, New York.

Richardson, W. (ed.)
1988 Papers from Archaeology Meets Education Conference. *CBA Educational Bulletin 6.*

Riley, Elihu
1887 *"The Ancient City": A History of Annapolis in Maryland, 1649–1887.* Annapolis: Record Printing Office. (Reprinted in 1976 by the Anne Arundel–Annapolis Bicentennial Committee.)

Riley, T. J.
1992 The Roots of Illinois: A Teacher Institute. *Archaeology and Public Education* 3:6–7.

Rinaldi, Ann
1989 History Is Closed. *The Trentonian,* August 9.
    Digging in at Morven. *The Trentonian,* August 14.
    Morven "I Was Horrified." *The Trentonian,* August 18.
    The Morven Mess. *The Trentonian,* September 11.
1990 The Ruining of Morven. *The Trentonian.*
    Morven's Future. *The Trentonian.*

Robbins, Ian
1990 A Battle to Beat the Blade. *Abbotsford Times,* 28 November:8c.

Rockman, Diana diZ., and Nan A. Rothschild
1984 City Tavern, Country Tavern: An Analysis of Four Colonial Sites. *Historical Archaeology* 18(2):112–121.

Rogge, A.E.
1991 Teaching with Archaeology: An Arizona Program. In *Protecting the Past,* edited by George S. Smith and John E. Ehrenhard, pp. 129–134. CRC Press, Boca Raton, Florida.

Rogge, A.E., and Patti Bell
1989 *Archaeology in the Classroom: A Case Study from Arizona.* Technical Brief No. 4, National Park Service, Archeology Assistance Division, Washington, D.C.

Rogge, A.E., and John Montgomery (eds.)
1989 *Fighting Indiana Jones in Arizona*. American Society for Conservation Archaeology
    Proceedings 1988, Papers from the Symposium Held at the 53rd Annual Meeting of the
    Society for American Archaeology, Phoenix. Portales, New Mexico.

Rosengarten, Dale, Martha Zierden, Kimberly Grimes, Ziyadah Owusu, Elizabeth Alston, and
    Will Williams III
1987 *Between the Tracks: Charleston's East Side During the Nineteenth Century*. Archaeolog-
    ical Contributions 17, The Charleston Museum.

Rothschild, Nan A., Eugene Boesch, and Diana Wall
1987 *The Excavation of the Stadt Huys Block*. Report on file at the New York City Landmarks
    Preservation Commission, New York.

Schell, Suzanne B.
1985 On Interpretation and Historic Sites. *Journal of Museum Education: Roundtable Reports*
    10(3):6–10.

Scott, Douglas D.
1987 Surviving the Second Battle of the Little Bighorn: Methods of Effectively Dealing with
    a Media Blitz. In *Captivating the Public Through the Media While Digging the Past*,
    compiled by Kristen Peters, Elizabeth Comer, and Roger Kelly. Technical Series No. 1,
    Baltimore Center for Urban Archaeology.

Scott, Douglas D. (ed.)
1991 Papers on Little Bighorn Battlefield Archeology: The Equipment Dump, Marker 7, and
    the Reno Crossing. *Reprints in Anthropology Volume 42*, J and L Reprint Co., Lincoln.
1992 So as to Render Unserviceable to the Enemy: Archaeology at the Reno-Benteen Equip-
    ment Disposal Site. *5th Annual Symposium*, pp. 84–96. Custer Battlefield Historical and
    Museum Association, Hardin, Montana.
1994 Archeological Investigations on the Dyck Property and Adjacent Properties, Little Big-
    horn Battlefield National Monument: A Preliminary Report. Manuscript on file, National
    Park Service, Midwest Archeological Center, Lincoln.

Scott, Douglas D., and Melissa A. Connor
1986 Post-Mortem at the Little Bighorn. *Natural History* 95(6):46–55.

Scott, Douglas D., and Richard A. Fox, Jr.
1987 *Archaeological Insights into the Custer Battle*. University of Oklahoma Press, Norman.

Scott, Douglas D., and Dick Harmon
1988 A Sharps Rifle from the Battle of the Little Bighorn. *Man at Arms* 10(1):12–15.

Scott, Douglas D., and Douglas Owsley
1991 Oh, what tales bones could tell—and often do! *Greasy Grass* 7:33–39.

Scott, Douglas D., Melissa A. Connor, and Clyde Snow
1988 Nameless Faces of the Little Bighorn. *Greasy Grass* 4:3–5.

Scott, Douglas D., Richard A. Fox, Jr., Melissa A. Connor, and Dick Harmon
1989 *Archaeological Perspectives on the Battle of the Little Bighorn*. University of Oklahoma
    Press, Norman.

Seeden, H.
1994 Archaeology and the Public in Lebanon: Developments Since 1986. In *The Presented Past: Heritage, Museums, and Education,* edited by P. G. Stone and B. L. Molyneaux, pp. 95–108. Routledge, London and New York.

Shanks, M., and C. Tilley
1987 *Re-constructing Archaeology.* Cambridge University Press, Cambridge, U.K.

Shetel, Harris, M. Butcher, T. Cotton, J. Northrup, and D. C. Slough
1968 *Strategies for Determining Exhibit Effectiveness.* American Institute for Research, Pittsburgh.

South, Stanley
1964 Interpreting the Brunswick Town Ruins. *The Florida Anthropologist* 17(2):56–62.
1971 The Historical Archaeologist and Historic Site Development. *The Conference on Historic Site Archaeology Papers* 5:90–102. The University of South Carolina, South Carolina Institute of Archaeology and Anthropology, Columbia.
1977 The Archaeologist's Responsibility in Cultural Resource Management Studies. In *Method and Theory in Historical Archaeology,* edited by Stanley South, pp. 317–330. Academic Press, New York.
1989 From Archaeology to Interpretation at Charles Towne. In *Studies in South Carolina Archaeology: Essays in Honor of Robert L. Stephenson,* edited by Albert C. Goodyear III and Glen T. Hanson, pp. 157–168. Anthropological Studies 9, University of South Carolina, South Carolina Institute of Archaeology and Anthropology, Columbia.
1992 Archaeology and Education at Santa Elena 1992. *Pastwatch* 1(1). Newsletter of the Archaeological Research Trust, University of South Carolina, South Carolina Institute of Archaeology and Anthropology, Columbia.

Stahl, Robert J.
1986 Stahl Perceptual Information Processing and Operations Model—SPInPrOM. Paper presented at the 1986 Rocky Mountain Regional Social Studies Conference, Phoenix.

Steiner, Robert
1991 A Canadian Town Is Less Monolithic Thanks to a Big Rock. *Wall Street Journal,* 30 October:A1, A10.

Stevens, William O.
1937 *Annapolis: Anne Arundel's Town.* Dodd Mead, New York.

Stockton, Helen Hamilton Shields
1914 A Quest for a Garden. Read at the Annual Meeting of the Garden Club of America, Tuesday, May 12.

Stone, Peter G.
1992 The Magnificent Seven: Reasons for Teaching about Prehistory. *Teaching History* October:13–18.
1994 *Report on the Development of the Education Service of the National Museums and Monuments of Zimbabwe.* English Heritage, London.

Stone, Peter G., and R. MacKenzie (eds.)
1990 *The Excluded Past: Archaeology in Education.* Unwin Hyman, London; Routledge pbk. 1994.

Stone, Peter G., and Brian L. Molyneaux (eds.)
1994 *The Presented Past: Heritage, Museums, and Education.* Routledge, London and New York.

Stumpf, Gary
1990 The Site Steward Program. In *Annual Report of the Arizona State Historic Preservation Office* and *Annual Report of the Arizona Archaeology Advisory Commission.* State Historic Preservation Office, Arizona State Parks, Phoenix.

Sullivan, Joseph F.
1989 Epic Home Touches Off a Second Battle of Princeton. *New York Times*, August 31.

Sullivan, Patricia
1991 Haberle Reaches Out for Donations to Restore Homeyness to Morven. *Star Ledger,* May 15.

Tate, Thad W.
1965 *The Negro in Eighteenth-Century Williamsburg.* The Colonial Williamsburg Foundation, Williamsburg, Virginia.

Tatum, Stephen
1982 *Inventing Billy the Kid: Visions of the Outlaw in American, 1881–1981.* University of New Mexico Press, Albuquerque.

Terrell, John
1991 Disneyland and the Future of Museum Anthropology. *American Anthropologist* 93(1):149–153.

Tilley, Christopher
1989 Archaeology as Sociopolitical Action in the Present. In *Critical Traditions in Contemporary Archaeology, Essays in the Philosophy, History and Sociopolitics of Archaeology,* edited by Valerie Pinsky and Alison Wylie, pp. 104–116. Cambridge University Press, New York.
1990 *Reading Material Culture.* Blackwell, Oxford.

Trinkley, Michael
1984 Analysis of Ethnobotanical Samples. In *Meat in Due Season,* by Jeanne Calhoun et al., Archaeological Contributions 9, The Charleston Museum, Charleston.

Tuska, Jon
1983 *Billy the Kid, a Bio-bibliography.* Greenwood Press, Westport, Connecticut.

Ucko, P. J.
1994 Museums and Sites: Cultures of the Past within Education—Zimbabwe, Some Ten Years On. In *The Presented Past: Heritage, Museums, and Education,* edited by P. G. Stone and B. L. Molyneaux, pp. 237–282. Routledge, London and New York.

USDA Forest Service, Southwestern Region
1976 *Final Environmental Statement*. Santa Catalina Planning Unit, Coronado National Forest, Albuquerque.
1989 *Serving People by Opening Doors to the Past*. Cultural Resources Interpretive Action Plan, Albuquerque.
1991 *Sabino Canyon Interpretive Plan*. Draft prepared by Wendy Walker with contributions by David W. Lazaroff and Stephanie M. Whittlesey. Coronado National Forest, Tucson.

USDA Forest Service, Southwestern Region; Bureau of Land Management, New Mexico State Office; and U.S. Army Corps of Engineers, Albuquerque District
1989a *Living with the Land: Peoples and Cultures of the Chama, Interpretive Prospectus*. Albuquerque.
1989b *Heritage Interpretation: The Natural and Built Environment*. Belhaven, London.

Utley, Robert M.
1987 Who Was Billy the Kid? *Montana History* 37(3):2–11.
1989 *Billy the Kid: A Short and Violent Life*. University of Nebraska Press, Lincoln.

Uzzell, D.
1989 Heritage Interpretation: The Natural and Built Environment. Belhaven, London.

Varnado, Brien
1991 The Joseph Manigault House Reopens. *The Charleston Museum Newsletter*, April–June, Charleston.

Versaggi, Nina M.
1986 Hunter to Farmer: 10,000 Years of Susquehanna Valley Prehistory. Roberson Museum, Binghamton, New York.
1994 Blacks, Indians and the State in Colombia. In *The Presented Past: Heritage, Museums, and Education*, edited by P. G. Stone and B. L. Molyneaux, pp. 418–437. Routledge, London and New York.

Vollmer Associates
1986 *Final Environmental Impact Statement for Proposed Project at 17 State Street, New York City*. Report on file at the New York City Planning Commission, New York.

Wade, Peter
1994 Blacks, Indians and the State in Colombia. In *The Presented Past: Heritage, Museums, and Education*, edited by P. G. Stone and B. L. Molyneaux, pp. 418–437. Routledge, London and New York.

Wall, Charles C.
1974 Restoration—A Survey. Ms. on file, Mount Vernon Ladies' Association, Mount Vernon, Virginia.

Wall, Diana
1986 Comment for the Public Hearing on the Draft Impact Statement for the proposed construction of a 41-story office building located on Block 9, Lots 7, 9, 11, and 23, 17 State Street, Manhattan, CEQR no. 85215M, BSA no. 53285BZ, Board of Standards and Appeals Chambers, 9 July 1986. *PANYC Newsletter* 30:8–9.

Wall, Diana diZerega
1987 *At Home in New York: Changing Family Life in the Late Eighteenth and Early Nineteenth Centuries.* Ph.D. diss., Department of Anthropology, New York University, New York.

Wallace, Michael
1986 Visiting the Past: History Museums in the United States. In *Presenting the Past,* edited by Susan Porter Benson, Stephen Brier, and Roy Rosenzweig, pp. 137–161. Temple University Press, Philadelphia.

Wandibba, S.
1994 Archaeology and Education in Kenya: The Present and the Future. In *The Presented Past: Heritage, Museums, and Education,* edited by P. G. Stone and B. L. Molyneaux, pp. 349–358. Routledge, London and New York.

Watson, L.
1990 The Affirmation of Indigenous Values in a Colonial Education System. In *The Excluded Past: Archaeology in Education,* edited by P. Stone and R. MacKenzie, pp. 88–96. Unwin Hyman, London; Routledge pbk. 1994.

Weissman, Dan
1989 Three Former Governors Voice Concern Over Archaeological Digs at Morven. *Sunday Star Ledger,* August 27.

Whittlesey, Stephanie M., and Karen C. Harry
1990 Sabino Canyon Survey. Final report submitted to Coronado National Forest, Sabino Canyon Archaeological Plan, Contract No. 4081970302. Statistical Research, Inc., Tucson.

Wilbanks, Ralph
1980 *Drayton Hall: An Underwater Archeological Survey in the Ashley River.* University of South Carolina Research Manuscript Series 159, South Carolina Institute of Archaeology and Anthropology. Copy on file at Drayton Hall.

Willey, Gordon R., and Philip Phillips
1958 *Method and Theory in American Archaeology.* University of Chicago Press, Chicago.

Wilson, Deborah
1991 The Fight to Save the House at Hatzic Rock. *Globe and Mail,* 24 August:D3.

Wilson, I. R.
1991 Archaeological Assessment of the Sunnyside Drive Subdivision and the Hatzic Rock Site DgRn 23. Report on file, Archaeology Branch, Victoria.

Wilson, John P.
1987 *Merchants, Guns, and Money: The Story of Lincoln County and Its Wars.* Museum of New Mexico Press, Santa Fe.

Witz, L., and C. Hamilton
1994 Reaping the Whirlwind: The *Reader's Digest* Illustrated History of South Africa and Changing Popular Perceptions of History. In *The Presented Past: Heritage, Museums, and Education,* edited by P. G. Stone and B. L. Molyneaux, pp. 29–45. Routledge, London and New York.

Woodoff, Jeremy
1986 Proposed mitigation plan for 17 State Street. Cover letter and plan submitted to the Honorable Sylvia Deutsch, Chair, NYC Board of Standards and Appeal, August 22, 1986. 17 State Street files at the New York City Landmarks Preservation Commission, New York.

Wright, P.
1985 *On Living in an Old Country.* Thetford Press, Thetford, U.K.

Yamin, Rebecca, and Anne E. Yentsch
1989a Interpretation in the Ethnographic Present, Morven, Princeton, New Jersey. Paper presented at the First Archaeological Congress, Baltimore, Maryland.
1989b Symbols in the Garden—Interpretation at Morven. Paper presented at the Council for Northeast Historical Archaeology Annual Meeting, Morristown, New Jersey.

Zierden, Martha
1984 Urban Archaeology in Charleston: A Museum Interpretation. *South Carolina Antiquities* 16:29–40.
1991 The Urban Landscape, the Work Yard, and Archaeological Site Formation Processes in Charleston, South Carolina. Paper presented at the Winterthur Museum Conference "Historical Archaeology and the Study of American Culture," Winterthur, Delaware.

Zierden, Martha, and Jeanne Calhoun
1984 *An Archaeological Preservation Plan for Charleston, South Carolina.* Archaeological Contributions 8, The Charleston Museum.
1986 Urban Adaptation in Charleston, South Carolina, 1730–1820. *Historical Archaeology* 20(1):29–43.
1990 An Archaeological Interpretation of Elite Townhouse Sites in Charleston, South Carolina, 1770–1850. *Southeastern Archaeology* 9(2):79–92.

Zierden, Martha, and Debi Hacker
1987 *Charleston Place: Archaeological Investigations of the Commercial Landscape.* Archaeological Contributions 16, The Charleston Museum.

Zierden, Martha, and Bernard L. Herman
1996 Charleston Townhouses: Archaeology, Architecture and the Urban Landscape, 1750–1850. In *Landscape Archaeology: Studies in Reading and Interpreting the American Historical Landscape,* edited by Rebecca Yamin and Karen Bescherer Metheny, University of Tennessee Press, in press.

Zimmerman, L. J., S. Dasovich, M. Engstrom, and L. E. Bradley
1994 Listening to the Teachers: Warnings about the Use of Archaeological Agendas in Classrooms in the United States. In *The Presented Past: Heritage, Museums, and Education,* edited by P. G. Stone and B. L. Molyneaux, pp. 359–374. Routledge, London and New York.

About the Contributors

MARK BOGRAD is curator at Lowell National Historical Park in Lowell, Massachusetts. His interests include historical interpretation in museums, African-American archaeology, and archaeological theory. Collaborating with Theresa Singleton, he wrote "The Archaeology of the African Diaspora in the Americas", *Guides to the Archaeological Literature of the Immigrant Experience in America, Number 2* (Society for Historical Archaeology, Tucson, Arizona, 1995).

GREGORY BRASS is a graduate student in cultural anthropology at McGill University. He resides on the Mohawk Territory of Kahnawake (Quebec) with his wife, Ojistoh Horn, and their infant daughter, Kanontienentha.

SHERENE BAUGHER is an Assistant Professor of Archaeology in the Department of Landscape Architecture at Cornell University and is a faculty member of Cornell's Archaeology Program and American Indian Program. From 1980 to 1990, she served as the first official archaeologist for the City of New York. Her publications focus on status and class in 18th- and 19th-Century America. She works with planners and Native Americans to excavate and preserve endangered Indian, colonial, and 19th-century sites.

NANCY JO CHABOT is the assistant registrar for the New Hampshire Historical Society's Museum of New Hampshire History. She holds a B.A. degree from the University of the Maryland and an M.A. from Binghamton University. In addition, she spent a semester studying with Ian Hodder at Cambridge, England. Chabot has extensive archaeological field experience with both client-funded and grant-funded research. She has worked on archaeological projects in Virginia, Maryland, New York, and New Hampshire, as well as in Honduras and Israel.

KAREN LEE DAVIS is the Director of the Museum Assessment Program at the American Association of Museums (AAM). Davis started at AAM in 1992 as its first assistant director of education. Her prior positions include administrator of education and

Originally published in 1994 as "Introduction: A Framework for Discussion" in *The Presented Past*, edited by P. G. Stone and B. L. Molyneaux. Routledge: London and New York.

interpretation at the Jefferson Patterson Park and Museum, St. Leonard, Maryland, and director of the Hallockville Museum, Binghamton, Kentucky. Davis holds a Ph.D. in anthropology from the State University of New York, Binghamton. She is the author of several articles on museology and anthropology, including "History Exhibits and Theories of Material Culture" in the *Journal of American Culture* and "Unpuzzling the Past: Critical Thinking in History Museums" in the *Museum Studies Journal,* which she coauthored with James G. Gibb. Davis is active in the museum community, serving on several boards.

JOHN EHRENHARD heads the National Park Service's Southeast Archaeological Center in Tallahassee, Florida. As chief of the Center, he oversees archaeological data recovery and technical assistance programs in the southeastern United States, the Commonwealth of Puerto Rico, and the U.S. Virgin Islands. With over 25 years of experience as a professional archaeologist, Ehrenhard has traveled in 27 foreign countries and has conducted or overseen research in 18 states and territories. He is the author or coauthor of 46 books, monographs, and articles and is recognized as a national leader in the movement for federal archaeological stabilization and preservation.

MARY FARRELL has worked in archaeology in Maryland, West Virginia, and Virginia, as well as in the Sierra Nevada of California. She now has the good fortune of working for the Coronado National Forest (Arizona) as assistant forest archaeologist. She also dabbles in historic building stabilization and preservation, prehistoric and historic archaeology of southeast Arizona, and rock-art recording.

BARBARA HEATH received her Ph.D. in historical archaeology from the University of Pennsylvania. She formerly directed the Department of Archaeology at Monticello and is currently the Director of Archaeology at Thomas Jefferson's Poplar Forest. Heath's research interests include historic landscapes, plantation slavery, and public interpretation.

MARGARET HEATH is Chief Heritage Education Project Manager for the Bureau of Land Management (BLM), based at the Anasazi Heritage Center, Dolores, Colorado. The focus of her work is nationwide implementation of Project Archaeology, a program that trains teachers how to use archaeology in the classroom in such a way that students will learn to preserve and protect their cultural heritage. She is the former Director of Education at the Crow Canyon Archaeological Center in Cortez, Colorado. She taught in the Denver area for seven years before becoming involved in heritage education in the early 1980s. Heath holds a B.A. degree in anthropology and an M.A. in education administration from the University of Colorado–Boulder. She is married, with two children. She recently received an Honorable Mention Award for Excellence in Interpretation from the BLM.

TERESA L. HOFFMAN is the former Deputy State Historic Preservation Officer for Arizona, where she facilitated public involvement in archaeology and historic preservation through a broad range of public programs. She is currently a senior project manager with Archaeological Consulting Services, Ltd. As a member of both the Society for American Archaeology Public Education Committee and the board of directors for the Malpais Foundation (a private, nonprofit organization dedicated to managing Casa Malpais National Historic Landmark as an archaeological park), she continues to promote public involvement in archaeology.

NICHOLAS HONERKAMP is a UTC Foundation Professor at the University of Tennessee–Chattanooga, and since 1980 has served as the Director of UTC's Institute of Archaeology. His interests include urban and industrial archaeology, southeastern prehistoric archaeology, long-distance running, and the Fender percussion bass.

WILLIAM R. ISEMINGER received his B.A. degree in anthropology from the University of Oklahoma, and his M.A. in anthropology from Southern Illinois University–Carbondale. He has worked at Cahokia Mounds for 25 years, conducting archaeological field schools, preparing museum exhibits, writing and editing publications related to the site, and developing and implementing education programs, special events, and other public programming. He currently serves as director of public relations and exhibit coordinator for Cahokia Mounds State Historic Site. He recently received a Lifetime Professional Achievement Award from the Illinois Association of Museums.

JOHN H. JAMESON, JR. is a staff archaeologist with the National Park Service's Southeast Archaeological Center in Tallahassee, Florida. His nearly 18 years of federal service have encompassed a broad range of experience in archaeological field work and cultural resource management in several regions of the United States. He is a recognized leader in the rapidly emerging fields of archaeological education and public interpretation. Jameson is the organizer and coordinator of the National Park Service's Public Interpretation Initiative Program, a long-term public outreach program, international in scope, that has involved numerous government-sponsored symposia, training workshops, seminars, and publications on the topic of public education and interpretation of cultural resources.

DAVID T. KIRKPATRICK is an archaeologist and the Associate Director of Research and Public Education, Human Systems Research, Inc., Las Cruces, New Mexico. He earned his Ph.D. at Washington State University. Since 1972, he has conducted interdisciplinary studies of New Mexico's prehistoric and historic cultures, publishing the results in both technical and popular reports. He is actively involved in local and statewide programs that contribute to the preservation of New Mexico's diverse cultural heritage, from Paleoindians to the end of the Cold War. Annually, he is coeditor for the "Papers in Honor of" series published by the Archaeological Society of New Mexico.

MEGGETT LAVIN is Curator of Education and Research for Drayton Hall, a National Historic Landmark and museum property of the National Trust for Historic Preservation, in Charleston, South Carolina. She is responsible for interpretation, public programs, collections care, and research, and "happily wears all the other hats of a small site, as needed!" Since joining the Drayton Hall staff in 1981, Lavin has developed internationally recognized heritage education programs in architecture and archaeology for students K–12, and provided numerous workshops on the topic for educators, professional meetings, and museum consultations. Her publications include "The Docent Educator," *National Trust Forum*, and "Archaeology and Public Education," *Society for American Archaeology*. She has also been interviewed for videotapes produced by the National Park Service and PBS. Lavin holds a B.A. in writing and literature from Wheaton College in Norton, Massachusetts, and was a 1983 Kellogg Fellow in museum education at the Field Museum of Natural History in Chicago.

DAVID POKOTYLO is Associate Professor of Archaeology in the Department of Anthropology and Sociology, University of British Columbia–Vancouver. His major areas of interest are the archaeology of the Canadian far west (plateau and subarctic regions), lithic analysis, quantitative methods, and public archaeology. He continues to collaborate with the Stó:lo Nation in research and public interpretation at X̱á:ytem.

PARKER B. POTTER, JR. is a student at the Franklin Pierce Law Center in Concord, New Hampshire. Before that, he was employed as a milker at Highway View Farm in Boscawen, New Hampshire. Once upon a time Potter was an archaeologist. He holds a B.A. from Washington and Lee University; his M.A. and Ph.D. degrees are from Brown University. Potter has published articles in *Historical Archaeology*, *American Antiquity*, *Current Anthropology*, and several edited volumes. His most recent book is *Public Archaeology in Annapolis: A Critical Approach to History in Maryland's Ancient City*.

DOUGLAS D. SCOTT received his Ph.D. degree from the University of Colorado–Boulder in 1977. He has worked for the Oklahoma Historical Society and the U.S. Bureau of Land Management. Since 1983 he has been a Division Chief with the National Park Service's Midwest Archaeological Center in Lincoln, Nebraska. He also teaches at the University of Nebraska–Lincoln. His recent research has focused on understanding behavior in conflict situations, with a focus on American Civil War battlefields and Plains Indian Wars battlefields. Scott has also participated in several United Nations–sponsored human rights investigations in various war-torn areas of the world. He has published extensively on his work in regional and national journals, and serves as the senior editor of two books on the archeological investigations at the Little Bighorn Battlefield National Monument.

THERESA A. SINGLETON is curator of historical archaeology in the Department of Anthropology at the Smithsonian Institution's National Museum of Natural History. Her interests include the archaeology of the African diaspora, American slavery, and museum presentation. She edited *The Archaeology of Plantation Life* (Academic Press, 1985), and has published numerous articles on the archaeology of African-American life. She also wrote, with Mark Bograd, "The Archaeology of the African Diaspora in the Americas," *Guides to the Archaeological Literature of the Immigrant Experience in America, Number 2* (Society for Historical Archaeology, Tucson, Arizona, 1995).

KAROLYN SMARDZ initially trained as a classical archaeologist with degrees from Wilfrid Laurier and McMaster universities in Ontario, Canada, but quickly moved into the nascent field of public archaeology in the early 1980s. By 1985, in cooperation with prehistorian Peter Hamalainen, she had established the first archaeology education and research facility in any municipal school board in the world, the Archaeological Resource Centre (A.R.C.) of the Toronto Board of Education. The facility was closed as a result of budget cuts in 1993, after more than 100,000 children and members of the public had participated in hands-on learning at historic urban sites and in the A.R.C. labs. Smardz has published and spoken on an international scale, emphasizing the methods, standards, and ethics that she perceives to be essential for operating effective, engaging public programs while safeguarding the archaeological record. She is currently the Manager of Public Archaeology and Development for the Institute for Minnesota Archaeology, and she is editing two books on educational archaeology.

STANLEY SOUTH, a leading historical archaeologist in the United States, has had a profound influence on the history and theoretical development of the archaeological discipline since the 1950s. His early work on public interpretations and reconstructions at Town Creek Temple Mound and Bethabara in North Carolina, Charles Towne in South Carolina and elsewhere have provided standards for emulation. His latest archaeological endeavor, an ambitious and productive series of archeological studies of the 16th-century Spanish site at Santa Elena in South Carolina, promises to provide new scientific information as background to effective public presentations of this important site.

PETER STONE is qualified and experienced as both a teacher and an archaeologist. He has worked for 16 years in the field of archaeological and heritage education, and has conducted doctoral research on teaching the prehistoric archaeological past to young children. He has published extensively and has coedited two major volumes: *The*

Excluded Past: Archaeology in Education, and *The Presented Past: Heritage Museums and Education.* For the last nine years Stone has worked for English Heritage, formally as a regional education officer and latterly with national responsibility for developing links with adult and higher education. His overseas work has included training the education service of the Museums and Monuments Commission of Zimbabwe and serving with UNESCO in developing an international teaching kit for World Heritage sites and the World Heritage Convention.

DIANA DIZEREGA WALL is an Associate Professor of Anthropology at City College of New York. She has worked extensively in urban archaeology in New York and is the author of *The Archaeology of Gender: Separating the Spheres in Urban America* as well as numerous other articles.

STEPHANIE WHITTLESEY became captivated with archaeology while on a "floating university" sponsored by Chapman College that literally sailed around the world. She went on to pursue graduate studies in anthropology and archaeology at the University of Arizona and was associated for many years with the university's field school at Grasshopper, Arizona. As senior principal investigator for Statistical Research, Inc., a private cultural resources consulting firm in Tucson, she has recently dedicated her work to meshing the requirements of CRM with high standards of research. Whittlesey has developed a particular interest in public outreach, believing that a prime responsibility of archaeologists is to disseminate the results of research to the public that supports it. She is currently exploring a number of creative avenues for public outreach, including drama and living history. With Jefferson Reid, she recently completed a book, *The Archaeology of Ancient Arizona* (University of Arizona Press), on Arizona archaeology and prehistory written, for a general audience.

REBECCA YAMIN is a principal archaeologist and senior project manager with John Milner Associates in Philadelphia. She is currently directing the analysis of material recovered on the site of a new federal courthouse in lower Manhattan, once part of the infamous Five Points neighborhood, which was characterized in the 19th century as New York's worst slum. Yamin received her Ph.D. in anthropology from New York University in 1988 and subsequently joined the Morven Landscape Archaeology Project in Princeton, New Jersey, where she developed an interpretive program for the site. Her dissertation focused on local trade in pre-Revolutionary New Jersey. She is the coeditor of the recently published *Landscape Archaeology: Reading and Interpreting the American Historical Landscape.*

MARTHA ZIERDEN is Curator of Historical Archaeology at The Charleston Museum, where she has been involved in archaeological research and public interpretation. Her studies in the last decade have focused on development of the urban landscape, as well as on the everyday life of 18th and 19th century urban residents.

INDEX